CALIFORNIA IN-DOORS AND OUT

WOMEN ON THE MOVE

*A series of Books on the American West and Midwest
by Women who Traveled and Settled there
between 1835 and 1877*

CALIFORNIA
IN-DOORS AND OUT

(1856)

FACSIMILE

With an Introduction by

MADELEINE B. STERN

528220

NIEUWKOOP   *   B. DE GRAAF

1972

Facsimile of the edition New York, 1856.
ISBN 90 6004 301 4
LC 72-86547

INTRODUCTION

During a comparatively short period in time, the attention and the hope of the world were focused upon the American West. The discovery of gold in California brought fortune-hunters by overland and sea routes — prospectors from the States and from China, from the penal colony of Australia and from Mexico and South America. Armed with pick and shovel they swarmed in to stake their claims, camping on the mountains. California's population mushroomed, its 20,000 inhabitants of 1848 increasing to well over 200,000 four years later. In the wake of the goldseekers came the gambling saloons and the lawlessness that triggered the formation of Vigilante Committees. A quiet community of Spanish-American ranchers was suddenly metamorphosed into a commonwealth of hustlers and a new State of the Union.[1]

The non-mining areas of California reacted to the changes in the State. In Santa Cruz County the decade 1850 to 1860 was labeled with good reason the Squatters' Period. A population of less than 650 centered about the Mission; other inhabitants

1. Allan Nevins and Henry Steele Commager, *The Pocket History of the United States* (New York [1951]), pp. 197 f; Louis B. Wright, *Life on the American Frontier* (New York [1971]), pp. 162, 170, 172, 175.

were scattered in ranch houses around Pescadero. Schooners plied to San Francisco from the port of Santa Cruz. Over mountain and plain cattle ranged in the thousands. The County of grazing pastures, orchards and farms soon attracted emigrants and miners who could exchange their gold dust for land renting at $100 an acre. Having built their houses of shakes and clapboards, the Americans began to imitate the costume and style of the Spanish don while their women, few in number, wore poke bonnets. To visit neighboring ranches they traveled *a caballo,* by horseback, fording the streams, for there were no bridges, taking two days for the journey to San Francisco.

The emigrants stirred up Santa Cruz. The 1850's were years of potato farming, the shipping of lumber from County sawmills, Spanish trade. They were years of fierce political campaigns and duels. Newspapers were established; a County jail was built. To the diversion of an old-fashioned camp meeting was added the attraction of a discussion on new-fashioned reforms fresh out of the East. By the end of the decade the Santa Cruz Turnpike had been completed and the County's population approached 5,000.[2]

2. Rolin G. Watkins, ed., *History of Monterey and Santa Cruz Counties, California* (Chicago, 1925) I, 434, 437-450.

VIII

One American settler in Santa Cruz was a woman who brought to the West a belief in self-development and in universal brotherhood that helped shape the land of her adoption. She brought also a perceptive eye and a fluent pen that would record the progress of the Far West during its most exuberant and flamboyant period. Out of her life in Santa Cruz she would produce a book of extreme significance that mirrored with precision "the wonderful country to which, for the last five years, the eyes of the civilized world have been turned with new hope."[3] Like all of El Dorado, Santa Cruz had many Argonauts. Not the least of them was Eliza Farnham.

By the time she arrived in Santa Cruz she was thirty-four years old, a woman whose attitudes had been formed by the life she had lived. If she believed in self-development, she did so with cause for she had almost literally developed herself. Born Eliza Burhans in 1815 in Rensselaerville, New York State, she had early lost her mother and been separated from brother and sisters. Barely tolerated in the home of unsympathetic relatives and denied schooling, she had somehow found books that filled moments snatched from farming chores in a back-

3. Eliza W. Farnham, *California, In-Doors and Out* (New York, 1856), p. 366. All quotations, throughout, unless otherwise indicated, are from this work.

woods community. After a second marriage her father had died and the orphan was finally entered in a ladies' seminary in Albany.[4] There she studied not only books but herself, and indeed an itinerant phrenologist, Lorenzo Fowler, examined her skull, perceptively analyzing her character as "self-directing" and "disposed to lead and influence others"[5] — qualities that would stand her in good stead when she reached the Golden State.

Before that time the groundwork for pioneering in the Far West was laid in the Middle West. Her character already shaped by the denials of a tragic childhood, Eliza had in 1835 followed her sister Mary to the State of Illinois. There she married a New England attorney, Thomas Jefferson Farnham, who was to become an explorer of note in the American Northwest. There too she made a home and bore and lost her first son. The story of her five-year sojourn in the "Sucker" State provided

4. For Mrs. Farnham's early life, see Samuel Burhans, Jr., *Burhans Genealogy* (New York, 1894), pp. 180, 193; [Eliza Farnham], *Eliza Woodson; or, The Early Days of One of the World's Workers* (New York, 1864), *passim* [This was dedicated to her friend G.B.K. (Georgiana Bruce Kirby)]; "Eliza Woodson Burhans Farnham," *DAB; Notable American Women 1607-1950, A Biographical Dictionary* (Cambridge, Mass., 1971) I, 598 ff; Information from Miss Gladys Tilden, Berkeley, California.

5. *The Phrenological and Physiological Almanac for 1849* (New York, n.d.), p. 31.

X

Eliza Farnham with the material for an important book on the Midwest, *Life in Prairie Land.*[6]

That book was written while its author was leading still another extraordinary life. Having returned East from Illinois, Eliza Farnham was in 1844 appointed matron of the Female Prison at Sing Sing, New York. There she applied to prison life the progressive, forward-looking point of view that had been molded in part by her years as a settler in the Middle West. The phrenological concept that crime was the result of under- or over-developed mental faculties which could be stimulated or checked as necessary; lectures, books, instruction, music, kindness – were all introduced by Mrs. Farnham to the prison overlooking the Hudson River, and for four years she added appreciably to the penitentiary's great movement toward reform. She was joined in her work by an assistant, Georgiana Bruce, a young Englishwoman who had participated in the communal experiment at Brook Farm, Massachusetts, and who would one day share Eliza's life in Santa Cruz. Like most reformers, Eliza was far in advance of her day and by 1848, branded as an infidel, she was forced to abandon her prison post.[7]

6. Eliza W. Farnham, *Life in Prairie Land* (New York, 1855), Reprinted Nieuwkoop, 1972, with an Introduction by Madeleine B. Stern.

7. W. David Lewis, *From Newgate to Dannemora The*

By this time Eliza Farnham had given birth to two more sons and had seen her husband depart for his second journey to California. There he practised law, built a schooner and carried on a freighting business on San Francisco Bay and the Sacramento River — a business that became extremely brisk after the discovery of gold. In addition, as a reward for legal services, he was given a tract of valley land beyond the Santa Cruz Mission. In September of California's eventful year of 1848, Thomas Jefferson Farnham contracted "intermittent fever" and died in San Francisco.[8]

The thirty-two-year-old Eliza Farnham who had long been familiar with death and separation now had two sons to support and an estate to take charge of three thousand miles away. Besides the personal considerations of a widow, she was evolving the more grandiose project of a reformer. She would assemble a company of cultivated eastern women to help civilize and populate the rude and

Rise of the Penitentiary in New York, 1796-1848 (Ithaca, N.Y., [1965]), pp. 177, 236-251.

8. Hubert Howe Bancroft, *The Works* (San Francisco, 1886) XX, 734; *Santa Cruz County, California. Illustrations Descriptive of its Scenery* (San Francisco, 1879), p. 27. Thomas Jefferson Farnham's death notice appeared in the [San Francisco] *Californian* (September 16, 1848), p. 3 — an issue that contained considerable information on the recent discovery of gold.

sparsely settled communities of the West. A short
term as instructor at the Perkins Institution for the
Blind in Boston[9] did not interfere with her purpose
and on February 2, 1849, she issued a circular des-
cribing the plan for western emigration by the dis-
taff side:

> The death of my husband, Thomas J. Farnham,
> Esq., at San Francisco, in September last, renders
> it expedient that I should visit California during
> the coming season. Having a desire to accomplish
> some greater good by my journey thither than to
> give the necessary attention to my private affairs,
> and believing that the presence of women would
> be one of the surest checks upon many of the
> evils that are apprehended there, I desire to ask
> attention to the following sketch of a plan for
> organizing a party of such persons to emigrate to
> that country.

> Among the many privations and deteriorating in-
> fluences to which the thousands who are flocking
> thither will be subjected, one of the greatest is
> the absence of woman, . . .

> It would exceed the limits of this circular to hint
> at the benefits that would flow to the growing
> population of that wonderful region, from the
> introduction among them of intelligent, virtuous
> and efficient women. Of such only it is proposed
> to make up this company. It is believed that
> there are hundreds, if not thousands, of such
> females in our country who are not bound by

9. Maud Howe [Elliott] and Florence Howe Hall, *Laura
    Bridgman* (Boston, 1903), pp. 232 f; Lewis, *op.cit.*,
    pp. 250, 256.

any tie that would hold them here, who might, by going thither, have the satisfaction of employing themselves greatly to the benefit and advantage of those who are there, and at the same time of serving their own interest more effectually than by following any employment that offers to them here.

It is proposed that the company shall consist of persons not under twenty-five years of age, who shall bring from their clergyman, or some authority ... satisfactory testimonials of education, character, capacity, &c., and who can contribute the sum of two hundred and fifty dollars, to defray the expenses of the voyage, make suitable provision for their accommodation after reaching San Francisco, until they shall be able to enter upon some occupation for their support, and create a fund to be held in reserve for the relief of any who may be ill, or otherwise need aid before they are able to provide for themselves.

It is believed that such an arrangement, with one hundred or one hundred and thirty persons, would enable the company to purchase or charter a vessel, ... and that the combination of all for the support of each, would give such security, ... as would remove all reasonable hesitation from the minds of those who may be disposed and able to join such a mission. ...

The New-York built Packet Ship ANGELIQUE has been engaged to take out this Association. She is a spacious vessel, ... ready to sail from New-York about the 12th or 15th of April.[10]

10. The broadside circular was reproduced by The Book Club of California, through the courtesy of which, and

Eliza Farnham's project was recommended by several of the nation's bigwigs, among them the editor Horace Greeley and the poet William Cullen Bryant, the preacher Henry Ward Beecher and the spiritualist judge J.W. Edmonds. But despite such endorsements from high places, the plan did not materialize. Eliza herself fell ill and apparently the unattached women of the East did not share her belief in the advantages of a universal sisterhood in the West. As Eliza would put it, "Only three ladies, of more than two hundred who communicated with me, came out in my company."

It was a voyage that would have tested the stamina of the staunchest of women. One of the sea routes to California at mid century was via Cape Horn, a passage that lasted between four and six months.[11] Eliza's voyage was perhaps more difficult than most for the ship, commanded by a brutal and cruel captain, carried bad water and insufficient fire. The twenty-two passengers aboard included Eliza's two sons, Charles and Edward, and their nurse who

through the good graces of Mr. David Magee, it has again been reproduced. See *Eliza Farnham's Bride-Ship An 1849 Circular Inviting Young Women of the East to go to California* (The Book Club of California, 1952). Eliza's circular was reprinted in her *California,* pp. 25-27; see also p. 380.

11. T.J. Farnham, *Life, Adventures, and Travels in California* (New York and St. Louis, 1849), p. 432.

defected from service by marrying the steward. "The universal topic of conversation on all vessels bound to California," Eliza would write, "is gold. Digging, the size of lumps, the operation of quartz machinery, amalgamators, coarse gold, fine gold, northern mines, southern mines, . . . dry diggings" — these considerations occupied "the weary months." A nine-day stop at Santa Catharina, Brazil, for fresh water — the result·of Eliza's petition — punctuated the long voyage. After they had rounded the Horn a stop at Valparaiso, Chile, proved all but fatal to her plans. There she engaged a Chilean woman as nurse for her boys and upon the captain's refusal to allow the native aboard without a passport, Eliza hastened to the consul's office. In the course of her visit there the ship set sail with her sons aboard. Left with a single shilling, "destitute, in a city of strangers," Eliza Farnham was supplied with money and a wardrobe by a resident clergyman and after a month's wait boarded the "Louis Philippe" out of Baltimore for San Francisco. After the thirty-eight-day voyage she was forced to wait another nine before "getting within the Golden Gate." Finally in fog and rain the ship dropped anchor off North Beach and Eliza's extraordinary peregrinations came to a happy end. Her boys had been cared for by a friend aboard ship; a family reunion terminated the adventurous·

saga and heralded a new life in California.

A two-month interim in San Francisco, occupied principally with litigation, preceded Eliza's arrival in Santa Cruz. Her "annoyances and trials" in the City of the Golden Gate were such as to preclude any immediate relish of its colorful contrasts. She would visit there again however in a mood more receptive to its attractions. Meanwhile, her initial reaction was that a woman in the San Francisco of 1850 was a freak in a sideshow:

> At that period in the history of San Francisco, it was so rare to see a female, that those whose misfortune it was to be obliged to be abroad felt themselves uncomfortably stared at. Doorways filled instantly, and little islands in the streets were thronged with men who seemed to gather in a moment, and who remained immovable till the spectacle passed from their incredulous gazé. Bold-faced unfortunates, . . . were occasionally to be seen in bar-rooms, or, perhaps, hatless and habitless on horseback in the streets, or the great gaming-houses that never were emptied of their throngs.

Santa Cruz seemed kindlier to the woman who was Eliza Farnham. After the voyage from San Francisco topped by a two-mile walk, she arrived on February 22, 1850, with her two small sons, her ship's companion Miss Sampson, and a farmer at the estate bequeathed her by her husband, El Rancho

La Libertad. The valley of Santa Cruz, about seventy miles south of San Francisco and twenty miles north of Monterey, with its old Mission buildings, its coastal stream the San Lorenzo empty-ing into the Bay, its view of the Pacific, its heights and plains, was to be Eliza's home for more than five years.

Against the beauty of its background, El Rancho La Libertad seemed a "forlorn habitation." A casa made of slabs, it boasted "not a foot of floor, nor a pane of glass, nor a brick, nor anything in the shape of a stove." Hearing the sound of the distant surf, seeing the redwoods pierce the sky, Eliza in her "meditations ... inverted the black walls, turned them inside out, laid an ideal floor, erected imaginary closets, ... set apart corners for bed-rooms." Before reconstruction could begin, the barrels and packing-cases which had been landed through the surf on the beach had to be transported to the house — a process that cost $25 for landing every boat-load of goods and another $8 for re-moving each wagon-load the two miles to La Libertad. Eliza's years in Prairie Land had taught her how to keep house in a near wilderness. Now, dining on steak, crackers and milk provided by neighbors, sleeping in a tent, she lived a half-nomadic life while she attacked the problems of creating order out of chaos. The stove she had shipped was unboxed; the wetted linens and clothing were dried; with hired help a door and windows were cut and glazed with cloth. By March 1, the house had been made habitable. It would serve until a new one could be built.

Meanwhile there was farming to be done. Although it was mining that made California a State, there was far more to the State than mining. Similarly there was far more to Eliza Farnham than housekeeping.

She faced the task of farming in Santa Cruz with no team, a two years' sward to be turned, and dilapidated fences. For $75 she bought an "Eagle" plow in San Francisco, borrowed two horses and a mule, and, with her hired hands, began plowing in March 1850. While planting, fencing and even making implements went on, Eliza Farnham was introduced to the problem of labor relations in the California of the mid-century, where $2 a day was the minimum wage and the scarcity of competent help the major difficulty:

> In California, the relation that elsewhere exists between employer and employed is reversed. The man who does not know but he might make a hundred dollars per day at the mines is not likely to engage with you at two or three dollars, without causing you to feel . . . the favor he confers by staying. Most of the floating laborers . . . were

either too infirm in health to be able to go to the mines, or too intemperate to trust themselves there. Invalids, or drunken sailors, were the staple of the laboring community.

With the often dubious help of Spanish or Indian laborers, Eliza confronted the problems of farming in general and of farming in Santa Cruz in particular. One crop was attacked by grasshoppers and half the planting destroyed; herds of cattle searching for food ravaged the potato field; wild mustard grew among the wheat; the trees she had ordered were delayed so long on the Isthmus that they were dead upon arrival; in one season the ground was planted four times without yielding a single crop for harvest.

Yet there were harvests and there were rewards. While wood was sawed at a mill six miles away for Eliza's new house, she took charge of her ranch. Asparagus and potatoes, melons and tomatoes, squash and beets, parsnips, carrots and onions were planted; twenty-five acres of wheat were sown. Fences, ditches and water-courses were repaired; grape and strawberry vines set out; fruit trees ordered from New York and scions from a neighbor's orchard cut.

Eliza herself was the focal point of her ranch. Dressed in a costume antedating the "Bloomer," *"à la monsieur,"* with red top boots — her grave face shaded by a sombrero — she rode off to round up a cow or superintend her fields. The chores continued. The plows moved on while seagulls, blackbirds and buzzards wheeled overhead. Cattle, purchased on foot from a Spaniard who had lassoed them, were slaughtered and the salt meat diet gave way to fresh beef. Cows were milked; a "bee" of neighbors gathered together to help eradicate the mustard weed; wheat was harvested; cabbages might sell for $1.50 apiece. A pig, dubbed Susannah the Second, was imported to become the pet of the rancho. At night Eliza read aloud while the household made sacks for the harvest.

As the months and the years passed, Eliza Farnham saw enough of farming in Santa Cruz to formulate a set of interesting opinions on the State's agricultural operations and one woman's part in them. One day she would write:

> To the struggling advocates of Woman's Rights, it may seem a hopeful sign of the times that one of their sex should put forth a book claiming to be in any degree descriptive of farming, especially when they make the delightful discovery that the writer speaks in a great measure from personal experience in the business. But it must not be forgotten that life in California is altogether anomalous, and that it is no more extraordinary for a woman to plough, dig, and hoe with her own hands, . . . than for men to do all their household labor for months.

She became convinced that there was no other State in which agriculture could be so successfully pursued as here in the land of the vine and the olive:

> If half the stout hearts and strong hands, that every year leave home for the mining regions of California, were as resolutely directed towards her teeming vales and plains and hills, ... there would be an annual saving of wealth, health, life, and virtue.

"I ... have an abiding faith," she concluded, "that there is something in California besides its mines."

Yet mining — the dry or wet diggings — the piles of gold dust — were literally embedded in the State of California and were already part of its history. An observer as keen as Eliza Farnham could scarcely spend years in El Dorado without visiting the mines and voicing her opinions on the miners.

Leaving her boys in charge of Miss Sampson and the hands, she occasionally took off *a caballo* to mining country. Mining methods interested her sufficiently for her to record the techniques used with shovel, pick and pan in dry diggings and their yield of from one cent to ten dollars a pan. Elsewhere she saw banks of earth thrown up, ponderous engines for crushing quartz — "one of the most impressive and significant sights of this age." She observed with intelligence the use of rocker, tom, long tom, sluice, and later on the hydraulic process in river mining. She took notes on what she saw and heard — the rush of the current, the clink of spades among the gravel — and once she herself washed a panful of

XXII

earth for a speck of gold.

Eliza comprehended the far-reaching significance of that June day in 1848 when the first gold nugget had been discovered in California and she interpreted it perceptively:

> News was sent to the Bay. Men roused themselves from their sleepy trading, mounted horses, or took . . . small boats . . . and set out for the mines. The first excited adventurers came down with laden pockets and crazed brains; sailors left their vessels; lazy Spaniards their ranchos; merchants their stores; clerks their desks. The news flew over the country, and went to sea in vessels . . . and thus commenced that gathering which has since revolutionized — physically as well as politically — one of the most beautiful . . . lands . . . and opened an era in history which . . . inspires the progressive mind with more rational hope for man, than any that has preceded it.

The less beneficent effects of the discovery were not lost on the woman who rode through the diggings. The dominating motive of the gold-hunting emigrant was necessarily selfish; the effect of his emigration upon his family often disastrous. "The lamentable consequences of the deterioration which women suffer in the journey across the plains are painfully manifest in all the mining towns," she would write, and she would note in the towns themselves the pervading addiction to drink and profanity, scheming and gaming. By his very nature the gold-hunter was a speculator and "the first tide of gold ... turned every town into a continuous gaming-house." Indeed, the country's entire trade struck her as a game of chance where there was no ordered scale of profits, no regulation of sale based upon cost, where $40 could be demanded for a spring-balance worth $1. The California Yankee was simply the New England Yankee with his sharpness sharpened, the wooden nutmeg genus converted into a manufacturer of gold beads, his sights set upon "some *'spec'* ... some scheme."

The transitory mining population with no deep stake in the social welfare increased the incidence of crime — often abetted by the connivance of unscrupulous officials. As a result the public relied upon Lynch Law and Vigilance Committees, those "people's courts" to which Eliza Farnham would give close attention when she came to record her California experiences:

> Juries have been empanneled on the spot; witnesses examined; and proof made, ... and, if the accused were found guilty, his doom was pronounced, and swiftly executed, in a cool, altogether unique manner; and the people, in an hour or two, fell quietly back upon their picks, pans, and toms, as if nothing had happened out of the daily routine of their lives.

Concepts stimulated Eliza's mind but people captivated her imagination. With broad brush strokes she would paint the dramatis personae of the mining towns — the rude and churlish Pike County people, the chattering Frenchmen and Spaniards, the Sonorians and Chileans, the Missourians, Chinese and Irish, the Kanakas and Yankees who patronized a roadside "hotel" that was bar-room and store, post-office and gambling-saloon in one. "In the course of your hour's rest," she marveled, "you have seen representatives from a dozen different nations, and each of the four quarters of the globe — a succession which the wilds of no country but California can present, and what is even more wonderful, each of your parties is equally at home."

It was not only to visit the mining regions that Eliza donned her riding habit and mounted her horse Sheik. An excursion for strawberries might lure her several miles up the coast while her growing reputation as a homeopathic "medico" might take her on "doctoring" trips to neighboring ranchos. Dons and caballeros, Indian boys and women drudges sat unknowingly for their portraits while Mrs. Farnham treated a case of rheumatism with magnetic passes. The woman who had been matron of Sing Sing visited California's State Prison, exposed its mismanagement and helped effect its reform. Eventually she took to the lecture circuit in the Golden State, appearing in Sacramento or

Oroville, Butte County, to discourse upon "The Organic Laws Applied to Human Conditions."[12]

Eliza's most frequent horseback journeys were those to and from San Francisco, where she saw to her funds. Accompanied by an escort armed with two revolvers, she rode past redwoods and shale cliffs, missions and orchards, spending a night in a Spanish rancho and dining on *tortillas, caldo* and *frijole.* As she had taken notes on the diggings she now took notes on the City of the Golden Gate. The facts she gathered would enrich her book as her vignettes would color it. In 1853, sixteen newspapers were issued in San Francisco, most of them "fearless, in times of public commotion." Between thirty and fifty vessels entered or departed the port each day. At its wharves she could see tall clipper masts and steamers, great store-houses and commission establishments. Malays and Chinese, Swedes, Yankees and Britons swarmed as white-sailed vessels dipped down to the Golden Gate. Though the city had been six times destroyed by fire it had become — in Eliza's view at least — "the fourth if not the third city on the continent." Its schools and churches, its bars and theaters testified to its extraordinary growth. Its only constant attri-

12. *American Phrenological Journal* (April, 1856), pp. 84 f; *Life Illustrated* (April 12, 1856), p. 189.

bute was change. Its architecture changed with its population. In the kaleidoscope that was San Francisco one could view the Spanish or Mexican woman "sitting at monte, with a cigarita in her lips," the bearded miner with his leather sack of gold, Chinese tailors, Parisian artistes and Swiss watchmakers, riders on the Mission Road bound for the bull and bear fights, parvenus and nouveaux-riches, the pretentious and the upright. The social state of San Francisco was "chaotic"[13] and − to one observer at least − San Francisco was "an epitome of the state." Eliza would write:

> California is well represented, in many of its features, by its metropolis. The rapid growth, the incongruous character, the extremes of condition, the inextinguishable energy, the material luxury, and the spiritual coarseness − the pretension and the ignorance . . . in San Francisco, characterize the state.

Of all these, "inextinguishable energy" alone characterized the household of El Rancho La Libertad. By the summer of 1850 the lumber had been sawed for Eliza's new house and on the appropriate date of July 4th, after the first celebration of Independence Day in Santa Cruz, the

13. Compare the remark of Mrs. Frank Leslie after her 1877 journey to the coast: "Let us conclude that the climate, like the society, like the morals, and like the social habits of San Francisco, is a little mixed." See *California A Pleasure Trip from Gotham to the Golden Gate* (New York, 1877, reprinted Nieuwkoop, 1972), pp. 119 f.

lines were stretched to mark its plan and foundation. The woman who was dairy-maid and farmer, housekeeper and "doctor" now became journeyman carpenter. While Miss Sampson cooked and cared for the boys in the shanty, the site was leveled and sills were cut, hewn and drawn. In her Turkish pants Eliza joined in the construction work: "My first participation in the labor of its erection was the tenanting of the joists and studding for the lower story, a work in which I succeeded so well, that during its progress I laughed . . . at the idea of promising to pay a man $14 or $16 per day for doing what I found my own hands so dexterous in." Sometimes she spent the entire day on the roof, shingling. Equipped with hammer and nail-pocket she alternated roofing with discussions of Swedenborg, shingling with reading aloud. Zinc and paints, stores and fixtures were shipped in but often lost when boat-loads capsized in the surf. For zinc lying at the bottom of the Bay, tin cannisters were substituted. At last two rooms were partitioned and floored, calico was stretched on the walls, a carpet laid, and the week before Christmas the household moved from the old shanty to the new house:

> We occupy the smaller of the two apartments into which the house is divided — the outer and larger being a store-room for trunks, boxes, furniture, etc., which the tents cannot receive. We

have a rough floor laid in the apartment we live in, through the middle of which ascends a pillar, which we call Pompey's pillar since it has been covered with white cloth . . . . Pompey's pillar, with the help of a curtain on one side and the foot of a bedstead draped on the other, subdivides this commodious apartment into a bedchamber and room for general purposes. In the former, Miss S. [Sampson], the two boys and myself, have our lodgings. . . . On the other side of this wall, in the outer room, the men have their beds or berths. . . .

Our room . . . was . . . fifteen feet in length on one side, and about ten feet on the other. The width, at one end, was ten feet, at the other fourteen, and the roof sloped down at the narrow end to the height of about five feet from the floor. It would astonish housekeepers at home to know that in this space we kept and used every day . . . two bedsteads of ordinary size, a sofa, a large dressing-table, a breakfast-table, six or eight chairs, a . . . closet, generally from sixty to eighty volumes on shelves about the walls, and four or five large trunks. In the space left after these were stowed, we received visitors, took our meals, made our butter, . . . and did the other household offices of the family.

A mill was rented for flour that would be preferable to "the sour stuff we had been getting from San Francisco at $40 to $60 the barrel." Eliza Farnham had a new backdrop against which to play out her role as Californian.

During days filled with farming and housekeeping in the new Rancho La Libertad she somehow found time to participate in the social activities of the West and to introduce to it the reforms she had imported from the East. Attendance at temperance meetings or church services would yield interesting observations when she came to write her book. The Methodist denomination she would label "the first to take up the outposts of new society," and of Puritanism she would remark with acumen, "Tough and tenacious though it was, [it] would have been shorter lived had the Mayflower landed her inflexibles on this laughing coast."

Reading — often aloud — was Eliza's forte; she carried "some convenient-sized volume (bless the duodecimo)" on all her excursions and from her publishing friends, the phrenologists Fowler and Wells in New York, she ordered books on Swedenborg and spiritualism, Carlyle's *Miscellanies* and Emerson's *Essays,* along with stories for her boys. "Send them as early as you can for I think I want them to night."[14]

It was not only spiritualism that excited Eliza's attention but most of the other fads and fancies, eccentricities and reforms of her day. She was in-

14. Eliza W. Farnham to Fowler and Wells, Santa Cruz, November 15, 1850, reprinted in Madeleine B. Stern, "Two Letters from The Sophisticates of Santa Cruz," *The Book Club of California Quarterly News-Letter* (Summer, 1968), pp. 51-62. The original is in the Fowler-Wells Collections, Collection of Regional History and University Archives, Cornell University.

terested in the various phases of the "newness," from magnetism and mesmerism to health fads and dress reform, from phrenology to hydropathy, from the rights of prisoners to the rights of women. What is more, seeking always to improve society, she sought also to impart her beliefs and interests in "the new philosophy" to any willing ears in Santa Cruz. As another visitor to the area would observe, "The most agreeable people were westernized Yankees, who had forgotten the cramped life of the East, but had not divested themselves of the ... good taste in which they had been trained."[15] Such as these might listen to the disquisitions of Eliza Farnham, but as for the women she herself sadly concluded: "There is little in the condition of California society ... to engage the higher orders of female intelligence, and, among all earnest women of this class whom I have met, there is a universal feeling of being sadly out of place, ... The necessities to be served here are physical .... None but the pure and strong-hearted of my sex should come alone to this land."

During part of her sojourn in Santa Cruz, Eliza was joined by a woman apparently "pure" and assuredly "strong-hearted." Georgiana Bruce, who

15. Georgiana Bruce Kirby, *Years of Experience An Autobiographical Narrative* (New York and London, 1887), p. 231.

as assistant matron at Sing Sing had shared many of Eliza's experiences there, shared also her interests in the many-faceted reforms of the day. Curiously enough, her earlier life too bore many points of comparison with Eliza's. She was the woman who would figure importantly in Mrs. Farnham's *California* under the transparent disguise of "Geordie."

Born in Bristol, England, in 1818, Georgiana Bruce had been a posthumous child and, as she herself would write, "It is a bad beginning to be born of grief. It narrows the chest and makes the blood less buoyant."[16] Georgiana's grief intensified when her mother made an unfortunate second marriage. The family's funds were soon dissipated and, forced to earn her own living, Georgiana ventured to America with a younger brother. At about twenty-two she served as pupil-teacher in the celebrated socialist community of Brook Farm, Massachusetts, where she met the brightest lights on New

16. Kirby, *Years of Experience, op.cit.,* p. 2 and *passim.* For Georgiana Bruce Kirby, see also Georgiana B. Kirby, *Transmission; or, Variation of Character through The Mother* (New York [1889]), *passim; The Phrenological Journal* (April, 1887), p. 224; Stern, "Two Letters from The Sophisticates of Santa Cruz," *loc.cit., passim;* Information from Miss Gladys Tilden, Berkeley, California; *Woodhull & Claflin's Weekly* (August 2, 1873), pp. 5 f. Wallace Stegner caricatures Georgiana Kirby as Mrs. Elliott in his recent novel, *Angle of Repose* (New York [1971]).

England's horizon from Nathaniel Hawthorne to that citizen of the world, Margaret Fuller, with whom she "talked freely on the marriage question." With Eliza Farnham she acted freely on the penal reform question. After her work at Sing Sing she was offered a position in Columbus, Ohio, as teacher of children who were three-fifths white. In order to test the complexion of applicants she was asked to use a card stained the appropriate shade. This requirement was as distasteful to Georgiana Bruce as she was to her superiors. Castigated as a "Garrison Abolitionist" and a colleague of Eliza Farnham, she returned to the East. Georgiana's many talents included "a natural gift for nursing." By the time the California gold fever had spread over the Union she decided that, since "everywhere . . . men congregated there would be more or less sickness,"[17] her healing art might stand her in good stead out West. In May 1850, therefore, she followed her friend Eliza on the road to El Dorado where she would remain for the rest of her long, productive life.

With her she brought not only her teaching and nursing abilities but "endless tidings . . . of coteries; of societies; of individuals; of late books; of reform

17. G.B. Kirby, *Years of Experience, op.cit.,* pp. 268 f, 314 f.

movements; . . . The association people, the anti-slavery folks, the prison reformers, the phrenological set, . . . authors, editors,. . . female medical colleges and practitioners, Homoeopathy, water-cure, spiritual knockings, Swedenborg revelations." In their Turkish or Albanian dress of pants and tunic the two women transplanted onions or rode on horseback, discussed the rights of women and introduced to Santa Cruz the latest fads and isms of a century peppered with fads and isms.

Within the next few years Georgiana would marry, becoming Georgiana Bruce Kirby, and Eliza would remarry. A short and stormy union with an Irishman, William Fitzpatrick, would end in separation and divorce. Eliza would also lose her son Edward. The medical skill of neither Georgiana nor Eliza was sufficient to restore the health of the ten-year-old boy who had never been vigorous and in 1855 he died.[18] Eliza, who had now lost two sons and one husband and was about to part with her second husband, would return East with her remaining son Charles.

Before she did so, however, she would co--ordinate her reactions to California and write her book on the subject. Her conclusions, scattered

18. Burhans, *op.cit.,* p. 226; *Notable American Women* I, 599.

among her pages, are as fresh and provocative today as they were in the mid-nineteenth century. In the West nothing was constant but fluctuations and contradictions. Hand in hand with "brilliant achievements" went "moral turpitude." "If . . . the modern hell of the world is 'not to succeed,' it is the concentrated, intensified hell of California." Yet signs of progress were omnipresent — towns and cities rising up, schools, libraries, churches, hospitals. If mining had led to crime it had also stimulated the "growth of that republican sentiment whose rugged justice threatens the throne and smiles upon the hovel." The heterogeneous elements of California's first generations, representing "every variety of mental condition, of hereditary prejudice, of traditional influence, and every extreme of social and religious bigotry" had here all been brought "upon a common platform."

Much of the evil of California could be expunged, she believed, by the presence of courageous women. She did not hesitate to reveal such evils as she had found — the "frauds, forgeries, and briberies," the "relics of ancient tyranny" witnessed by reactionary laws on the property rights of women and the death penalty for theft. California was indeed the gateway between the old and the new worlds. In Eliza Farnham's thoughtful eyes it was also "the world's nursery of freedom" and "the

nucleus and home of the extreme of democratic tendencies." She wore the mantle of prophecy when
she wrote:

> The moral and political elements of this state will
> almost surely make it the theatre of first test for
> the most radical questions.

Besides crystallizing these opinions in her mind,
Eliza Farnham gave herself two research assignments
before completing her book. Primarily to prove
woman's ability to endure the extremes of hardship,
she gathered information from several survivors of
the ill-fated Donner expedition which in 1846 was
caught in an early blizzard in the Sierras.[19] Ma-
rooned in the mountains, many died of exposure or
starvation while others yielded to cannibalism.
From John Breen, who had been a fourteen-year-old
member of the Donner party, Eliza solicited reminiscences, making a contemporary record of the
desolation and agony of this dread episode in the
westward migration. Published as an Appendix this
"Narrative of the Emigration of the Donner Party to
California, in 1846" would enrich her book.

To bring her work up to date Eliza also culled
information for what would be a supplementary

19. The Donner expedition, the subject of George
R. Stewart's *Ordeal by Hunger The Story of the
Donner Party* (Boston, 1960) has recently been used as
the subject of a narrative poem, *The Donner Party,* by
George Keithley, reviewed in *The New York Times
Book Review* (February 6, 1972), pp. 7 and 22.

chapter entitled "The Present Crisis in California." The Vigilance Committee, formed in San Francisco in June 1851 when venal judges and false witnesses had abetted crime, had been adjourned when it completed its task of policing the city and arresting, banishing or hanging offenders. Now in 1856 the Vigilance Committee had been revived to extirpate the frauds, crimes and corruption of a later date. Eliza's detailed and contemporary record would supply a source of prime importance for these popular tribunals of California. Her endorsement of this form of judgment was understandable if shortsighted. She saw little danger in a precedent that would one day lead to the Ku Klux Klan, but rather an experiment in self-government, "an expression . . . by the *people* of California, of their determination to be no longer wronged and disgraced by the worst men among them."

Indeed in 1856 Eliza Farnham held that "this is the commencement of an era of improvement in California . . . . Society will rise, because open villainy will no more strut proudly in high places . . . . The period of wild enthusiasm and insane hopes has passed over California; but a better is before her. In the proceedings of the last few months, she has proved her claim to the confidence of those who, in thinking of emigration, entertain other considerations than those of the mineral wealth of the country, or the chances it affords to speculators. Business will become better regulated, and labor more settled, as the population takes on a quieter character."

The explorer John Charles Frémont had recently been nominated by the Republican Party to exclude slavery from all the Territories and Eliza allied herself with his purposes which, she believed, would vastly benefit the Golden State:

> If the great cause with which Mr. Fremont is identified should happily succeed, this fall, the friends of California will, indeed, have cause of rejoicing . . . . We may look to his elevation as a means of giving her a right position, by connecting her with the Eastern states, and by preserving from the withering presence of slavery the territories which border upon her. . . . Plant slavery all over the broad plains that stretch between the Mississippi and the Sacramento, and there could be no vital circulation between the commercial, thriving East and that remote free state. Slavery ties the arteries of civilization. No life and vigor can travel eastward or westward through its dark dominion. May its black shadow never come nearer to the soil of California than it is today.

> But let the 'talking-wires' span free soil from the Atlantic to the Pacific, and let free labor, with its enterprise, progress, and intelligence, possess and build up Kansas and Nebraska, through which California will ultimately be connected, by railroad, with the East, and, in a few years, she will be garden of the Union. There is no prosperity to which she cannot attain.

XXXVIII

With this radiant vision of a golden West linked to a vibrant East by an as yet nonexistent transcontinental railroad, Eliza Farnham would conclude her book on California.

She had written much of it in 1851 and so she recorded the early phases in the State's development: the "breaking out" of mines, of squatting, of speculation. She did not complete it until 1856 and so she recorded the incredible changes that had occurred during the interim: "such changes . . . as half a century would not produce in many older countries. . . . Where . . . there was scarcely a mile of fence . . . continuous grain-fields . . . substantial farm-houses . . . upon the sites of . . . little canvas shanties" and in place of clumsy wagons "the best Concord or Troy coaches" on all the main roads. With her supplementary chapter on the revived Vigilance Committee and with a few footnotes she brought her eye-witness account up to the date of her preface completed at Santa Cruz, July 1856.

California, In-Doors and Out; or, How we Farm, Mine, and Live generally in the Golden State was published by the New York firm of Dix, Edwards & Co. in 1856, bound in cloth and priced at $1.00.[20]

20. Orville A. Roorbach, *Addenda to The Bibliotheca Americana, 1855-1858* (New York, 1939), p. 76.

The following February, *Graham's Illustrated Magazine* reprinted Eliza's report of the Donner party's emigration under the heading, "Perils of the Overland Route to California," explaining that "the following thrilling account of the adventures and sufferings of a party of emigrants who started for California by the overland route, is taken from Eliza W. Farnham's new and interesting work on California, just published by Messrs. Dix, Edwards & Co., New York."[21]

While the twentieth-century writer George R. Stewart was to characterize the Farnham version of the Donner story a "sentimentalized" defense of a woman member of the party, the earlier historian Hubert Howe Bancroft labeled her book "a pleasing picture of life on the Pacific coast."[22] It was far more than that. Eliza Farnham's mild addiction to purple passages and flowery effusions did not hide the facts or impede the flow of her narrative. Her book serves today not only as the fascinating story of one woman's pioneering in California but as a documentary source of no small importance.

Out of her western experience Eliza would write still another book, *The Ideal Attained,* a novelized,

21. *Graham's Illustrated Magazine* (February, 1857), pp. 113-126.

22. Bancroft, *op.cit.,* XX, 734; Stewart, *op.cit.,* pp. 385 f.

romanticized and discursive version far less successful than her straightforward narrative. *The Ideal
Attained* would be copyright by the author's only
surviving son Charles and published in 1865.[23] It
was a posthumous publication.

In 1856, partly because of her son Edward's
death and her divorce, partly to supervise the New
York publication of her book, Eliza returned to the
East. In June 1857 her character analysis, based
upon a phrenological reading, appeared in the
American Phrenological Journal, emphasizing her
"stoutness of character," her "breadth of affection," her "vigor and compass of thought. . . . She is
one of the strongest female thinkers and writers in
America; and . . . in many . . . spheres of action, she
has shown her stamina of character and strength of
mind."[24]

In the short period still allotted to her, Eliza
Farnham expanded those already wide spheres of
action. She used both voice and pen to elucidate
woman's potential, speaking before the Woman's
Rights Convention in 1858, publishing an ambitious
two-volume study, *Woman and Her Era,* in 1864. In
between she revisited California where she lectured

23. Eliza W. Farnham, *The Ideal Attained; being The Story
of Two Steadfast Souls, and how they Won Happiness
and Lost it not* (New York, 1865).

24. *American Phrenological Journal* (June, 1857), p. 133.

and served as matron of the Stockton Insane Asylum. During the Civil War she returned East and, active in the Women's Loyal National League, helped petition Congress for an amendment to abolish slavery and went to Gettysburg as volunteer nurse.[25]

In December of 1864, as the war was entering its last campaigns, Eliza Farnham died and was buried in the Hicksite Friends' Burying Ground in Milton, New York. In her forty-nine years she had encompassed many lives, not the least fruitful of which was her life in the Golden State. Out of it had come a book which — now reprinted for the first time — recaptures for a later age the hardship and exuberance, the vitality and stamina of a woman pioneer in El Dorado.

25. For her later life and her death, see *The New-York Times* (May 14, 1858), p. 5 and (December 18, 1864), p. 3; *New-York Tribune* (December 16, 1864), p. 4; *Notable American Women* I, 599 ff; Elizabeth Cady Stanton, Susan B. Anthony, and Matilda Joslyn Gage, eds., *History of Woman Suffrage* (Rochester, N.Y., 1887) I, 669. For details of *Woman and Her Era,* see also Helen Beal Woodward, *The Bold Women* (New York, [1953]), pp. 337-356.

CALIFORNIA,

IN-DOORS AND OUT;

OR.

How we Farm, Mine, and Live generally

IN THE

GOLDEN STATE.

BY

ELIZA W. FARNHAM.

It is a goodly land, my lord, of richest stores
And most delightsome ways.   The pleasant sky
Doth never weep upon't thro' all the sunny
Summer months.
    Ay, but knowest thou not, good Jacques,
That e'en with precious stores, and smiling skies,
And beauteous earth, there lacketh much.
                                    PERU.—AN OLD PLAY.

NEW YORK:
DIX, EDWARDS & CO., 321 BROADWAY.
1856.

MILLER & HOLMAN,
Printers & Stereotypers, N. Y.

PREFACE.

TO MY FEW PARTICULAR FRIENDS, IF I HAVE ANY SUCH,
WHICH THE GENERAL READER HAS PERMISSION TO
PASS BY, IF HE HOPE FOR SOMETHING BETTER FUR-
THER ON.

A CONSIDERABLE part of the book before you was
written in '51. The finishing of it was so long delayed that I had nearly given it up; but a strong
desire to complete what I had begun, and a resolution
not easily defeated, prevented my doing so altogether;
and within the last few months I have been so often
urged to tell my story of California, that, at length, such
as it is, it lies before you. If there appear to be dis-
crepancies between the early and later pages, you will
please bear in mind that, in many respects, there have
been such changes in the things and aspects sought to
be described, as half a century would not produce in
many older countries.

In returning to the work, I frequently felt an inclination to strike out from the MSS. passages which

were not truly descriptive of things as they now are, but, remembering that whatever has been true in our history would be equally interesting with what is so to-day, I have not erased a line of the early writing. The book may, perhaps, have a greater interest from this fact than if it had been written in a few consecutive weeks.

The personal experience related in it, extraordinary as it may appear, is as tamely stated as truth will permit; and my own has been, in many respects, not more novel than that of scores of my sex who emigrated both before and after 1848. Mine has included none of that terrible physical suffering which has fallen upon many women who had been tenderly nurtured. To the mental anguish, the racking anxiety, the unmitigated loneliness, the numberless humiliations, have not been added the hardship and destitution which have been the lot of many on their first arrival. The Goodness which overrules all, and fits the burden to its bearer, has spared me that, and though I can never recall, even momentarily, what I have suffered, without shuddering, and shrinking from the recollection as the victim who turns his weary eye upon the rack, yet I have to thank one who better knew my strength than I did myself, that some bitter ingredients were withheld from my cup.

Let me pass to say a few words on general topics,

and close.   Life in California is anomalous—unique—and a book which should faithfully describe it, must contain strange developments; tales and pictures, some of which would be set down by those who had never seen the country, and, perchance, by some who had, as exaggerations, others as falsehoods.   I am not conscious that a single passage in this volume deserves the application of either of these comments. The grotesque features of our life defy the caricaturist —the pathetic ones could derive no additional power to pain the heart, from the most exalted and tender imagination.   We are extreme in revelry, in gloom, in vice, in pleasure (not happiness), in sorrow, in munificence (not in meanness), and I feel that, so far from having exaggerated or embellished, I have, in many things, fallen greatly short of conveying the full impression which actual every-day facts make upon observing and thoughtful minds among us.   My best abilities would fail me in the task.   Only one of the masters—a Dickens or a Jerrold—could do that.

But such as I have been able to make it you have it;—the book long promised, and by some of you, I will please myself with believing, still desired.

Let it not be forgotten in the reading, that the California of to-day is neither in material nor moral aspect the California of 1851-2 and 3.   The exterior and the interior life are alike advancing.

In riding through one of her large agricultural vallies, a few weeks since, where, so late as 1852, there was scarcely a mile of fence to be seen from one end of it to the other, I saw now continuous grain-fields, of six or eight miles in length, with, perhaps, a dozen reapers, of the best patent, marching up and down, leveling the tall thick harvest. Comfortable, substantial farm-houses, or neat cottages, stand upon the sites of the little canvas shanties we used to see, and neat, often elegant vehicles, have taken the place of the clumsy coarse wagon of those times. You may travel in summer on all the main roads, from the north to the south, in the best Concord or Troy coaches, and be received, in the more considerable towns, at as good hotels as you will find at corresponding places anywhere in the Union. And even this great material progress is less expressive of the growth of the state than other signs at present visible in her condition.

The revolution in progress here at this hour will shortly have inaugurated a new and more hopeful state ; and there is little reason to dread that the influences from which we have hitherto suffered, will ever regather to such wanton waste of life and character as we have witnessed. The present is a war, not between parties or persons, but between the principles of good and evil. The latter of which has been so long in the ascendant, that it is not wonderful that common observers should feel there was no redemption for the country that bore it. They erred. There is redemption for California—as, indeed, there ultimately is for all people, however low, whose lives contain the progressive principle that distinguishes ours in free America—for her there is swift redemption, which it is idle and wasteful for the outcast and worthless to resist. It will be the result of her intelligence and true moral life, working together for a result, which is preordained to them. The self assertion they labor for, is as certain to follow the overthrow of villainy and corruption as day the night.

God speed the fearless souls who are striving for it.

E. W. FARNHAM.

SANTA CRUZ, *July*, 1856.

CONTENTS.

CHAPTER VI.

CHAPTER VII.

CHAPTER VIII.

CHAPTER IX.

CHAPTER X.

CHAPTER XI.

CHAPTER XII.

CHAPTER XIII.

CHAPTER XXX.

CHAPTER XXXI.

CHAPTER XXXII.

CHAPTER XXXIII.

CHAPTER XXXIV.

CHAPTER XXXV.

CHAPTER XXXVI.

CHAPTER XXXVII.

CHAPTER XXXVIII.

CHAPTER XXXIX.

CHAPTER XL.

CHAPTER XLI.

APPENDIX.

SUPPLEMENTARY CHAPTER.

CALIFORNIA, IN-DOORS AND OUT.

INTRODUCTORY CHAPTER.

VOYAGE TO CALIFORNIA.

THERE are few more difficult and disagreeable tasks than the vindication of one's-self
against charges and accusations so vague that
it is impossible to put them into a form
in which yea will be yea to them, and nay,
nay. I had determined, in writing this little
volume upon California, to give no heed to the
vulgar slanders that heralded my emigration
hither, and to obtrude no relation of the trials
that attended the wearisome voyage.

The one came from a coarse, but perhaps, in
many minds, an honest misapprehension of one
of the best endeavors of my life ; the others
grew, in my case, as they have in thousands of
similar ones, out of the opportunity possessed
by a brutal and tyrannical nature, to indulge

1

itself in paining and wounding to the utmost one which it could neither assimilate nor approach. And I should never have given expression to a word growing directly or indirectly out of either, but for the repeated and urgent solicitations of persons, who, by a generous vindication of me, when assailed, have won a claim to my consideration, which I feel it would be ungracious to deny, more especially when one considers how seldom the vindicatory voice is heard, when character is attacked, deeds misrepresented, or unworthy motives imputed to those whose conduct falls under discussion. But I must beg those who have acted thus nobly toward me, whether personal friends, or those even more to be prized (in this land), who, without personal knowledge, have believed me worthy of defense, to pardon me, if I dwell less on details than to their kindly feelings I might seem justified in doing.

I have ever felt a powerful repugnance to the intrusion of direct personal vindication upon the public. Only the rarest circumstances can justify such a proceeding to my taste or judgment ; and in the years that are gone by, it will be well remembered by those who were cognizant of the slanders heaped upon my private, as well as official character, while I was in a position which, according to the corrupt usage of our country, in some measure, extenuated the virulent industry and unscrupulous ingenuity of my enemies, that I was never over hasty in seizing the public ear for justification or defense. Bide your time, is a motto which fully expresses my feelings in relation to all such experiences. Time and a clean conscience are more efficient remedies for such wounds than any words of vindication, unless they could demonstrate themselves, which the very nature of all such cases forbids, and when one is blessed in the latter, and possesses self-respect and fortitude enough to await the former, there is the best assurance that the world's mean warfare will ultimately be turned aside, and that, at last,

" The victory of endurance born"

will crown your patience. Be pure, be just, be merciful, be true, and let the world say its say; it cannot wound the vitality of a character that embodies these attributes. And however new circumstances may try you, new environments make old proprieties seem their opposites, and alien hearts, filled with torturing suspicion, replace those that have overflowed to you in trust and love, there is in the consciousness of an unsoiled spirit an anchor to the soul, from which the wildest tempests of popular censure can never part it.

The voyage to California has been the beginning of suffering to thousands of quiet home-bred people, and the continuation of it to as many whose previous experiences had been more varied, so that having had no wonderful escapes, or startling adventures, it need barely be said of ours, that it was commonplace enough in the early part—made wearisome by the slowness of our vessel, and insufferable by the dreadful quality of the water furnished us nearly all the time after the first few hours out of New York. There were twenty-two passengers, including my two sons and their nurse. This person was a young woman, of about eighteen or nineteen, in whom, from her peculiar traits of character, and some circumstances in her previous history, I felt a strong interest. She was extremely ignorant of everything, which her own keen powers of observation, exercised in a very limited sphere, had not taught her; and being wholly unknown to every other person on board the vessel, was entirely dependent upon me for advice and guidance, in whatever circumstances should surround her.

We were but a few days at sea, when the steward begged her to assist in laying and clearing the tables, etc.; and upon her asking my consent, I told her that when she could oblige them, without leaving her own work undone, I was quite willing she should do so. I did this, because it is a principle with me to train all young persons, and my own children as well, never to refuse to accommodate others when they can do so without neglecting a paramount duty. But I soon found we were dealing with parties from whom no such faith or good-will was to be expected. The girl was gradually withdrawn, more and more, from my service and influence; her daily lessons, which Miss Sampson and myself were giving her, were soon neglected ; and we had not, I think, been more than a month or six weeks at sea, when it was made known that the steward—a lazy, lying, worthless creature—a mulatto, had proposed marriage to her. I expostulated very earnestly with her, but the captain, on every occasion, when allusion was made to them, encouraged it to the utmost.

There was a good deal of ill-feeling provoked between him and the passengers before we reached St. Catherine's, by his refusal to put into that place, when his doing so had been expressly stipulated in agreeing for passage, and when, in consequence of the bad water, it was a hundredfold more necessary that he should do so than we before imagined it could be.

A remonstrance, signed by all the passengers, save one, had been laid upon his table one evening when we were one or two days north of St. Catherine's, which he thought fit to heed so far as to change his course, and stand in, but with a great deal of profane protest. And as this paper had been drawn up by myself, and was sent in in my handwriting, it greatly increased the anger he had all along felt toward me, and which I had never allowed him to dissipate by abusing me, as he had the rest of the passengers.

Arrived at St. Catherine's, he took especial pains to make the position of his lady passengers as uncomfortable as it well could be, and as he never named women but to depreciate them in the coarsest terms, and was, in his best temper, destitute of that respect for them which argues somewhat of refinement in the rudest, and of nobility in the meanest, so in his ill-humor, he was restrained by no scruple. The coarseness he had exhibited on the voyage was now turned to malice ; but it could not greatly affect us. For our resources on that shore were confined to a single family (of which only the husband was American), and to the hills and vales adjacent to the anchorage, so it was comparatively a trifling matter what report he should give of us.

We were fortunate, too, in meeting at this place a party of English gentlemen, also bound to California, whose civilities contributed much to the pleasantness of our stay.

They had seen somewhat of the country before our arrival, and very kindly showed us its best points, as far about the anchorage as we could walk, there being no other means of locomotion within our reach.   We remained nine days at St. Catherine's, during which my unfortunate protegé resisted the urgent entreaties of her dark lover to go ashore and be married; and, before we weighed anchor, she made me a half promise that she would not marry till we reached California.   On our arrival at Valparaiso, however, she informed me that if I would have a nurse for the rest of the voyage, I must procure one there, as she was going to be married, and come up as stewardess.   I had before said all, in the way of remonstrance, that I could, and when she told me this, sickened at heart of the whole disgusting affair, I only said, "I have no power to prevent your doing as you please; I am grieved that you will be deaf to all the reasons I have urged against the step, and will disregard the doubts that you have confessed to me; but I can do no more."   I ought to remark, that between St. Catherine's and Valparaiso, almost the whole of her time was spent in the service of the ship. There were many days that we did not see her face; and this was the more unjust and oppressive to me because that was, in many respects, the hardest part of our voyage. We were without fire the entire time, though amply provided with all the means for having it—a very severe privation to the ladies and my children, as we could only warm ourselves by exercise, which the roughness of the weather often prevented the most resolute of us from taking.

At Valparaiso, the marriage took place at the house of the English clergyman, Rev. Mr. Armstrong. I engaged a Chili woman to finish the voyage with me, and took her on board the day before the ship sailed. The captain had been informed in the consul's office, by Miss Sampson, two days before, that I had made such an arrangement, and he expressed no objection to it; but knowing his willingness to disoblige me, I had twice myself consulted the acting consul, Mr. Morehead being absent at the time, as to any preliminary steps it might be necessary for me to take, and was

1*

as often assured that there was nothing whatever to be done ; that women left that country
as they did our own, whenever it suited them
to do so ; that the passport law applied only
to men, for the protection of creditors, but
never to females of any condition ; and that,
having arranged for the passage of a servant, I
was not even bound to notify him of my intention to take a second, when the first one left
my service.   The woman was on board the vessel, and seen by him engaged in my rooms twenty-four hours before he sailed.   When he came
on board the last time, he called the passengers upon deck, to answer to their names.
When all had answered, he inquired who that
woman was, and though he addressed the inquiry to no one personally, I replied that she
was my servant.

    " Have you a passport for her," said he.

    " No," I replied, " Mr. Samuels told me I
needed none."

    " Then she must go ashore," he said.   " I
should subject myself to a heavy penalty to
take her without one.   Mr. ———," addressing
his mate, " put that woman, and her things,

in the boat I came off in, and send her ashore."

" But," I said, " I will go with her and get a passport. I cannot go to sea without a servant."

" There is your old servant," was the insolent reply ; " you can have her. You can't get a passport under three days. Put her into the boat, I say," addressing himself again to the officer, " and send her off."

Then I said, " I will go to the consul's office and see if he cannot give me something equivalent to a passport, or get me one immediately without the usual forms."

To this he replied that he was going to sea, and should not wait for me if I were not back in time ; but I knew the depth of water the ship lay in, and what had been done to get her ready for sea ; and, judging from what I had seen before, I knew that I could go to the consul's office and back twice before she would get under way in the ordinary manner. But, to be fully assured, I asked the mate, who entered the cabin as I was putting on my bonnet, how long it would probably be before the ship would get under way, to which he replied, " In two hours and a half or three hours." This was the time I had calculated on; and as I could do no more than step to the consul's office, state the case, and get something that would deprive him of the power to refuse taking her, I felt entirely safe in leaving the ship for the time it would take me to accomplish this.

But as I was going over the side of the vessel, the former mate who had left her there, and whose good-nature and kindness to the passengers, especially to the females and children, had caused him much difficulty with the captain, came up, accompanied by one of the English gentlemen whom we had met at St. Catherine's, to pay our passengers a farewell visit.

On seeing me bonneted and shawled, Lieut. E. asked, in some surprise, where I was going, and when I had stated the case in half a dozen hurried words, he said, " Surely the man cannot persist in such a thing. Pray stay a moment, ma'am, and let me speak to him." I feared his intervention would be of no avail ; but as his position in the English navy assured me of his full acquaintance with life at sea, and as I knew he went in the most conciliatory spirit, I did wait, notwithstanding my haste, till I heard loud oaths and curses in reply to what he said, and saw him turn toward us.

" He is a madman," said he. " He will hear nothing. But pray command me, ma'am. Will you come with the girl in our boat, and wait on your consul at once ?"

I passed hastily down the ship's side, and we pulled ashore. We stopped but a moment at the consulate, but long enough to get a note to the Intendente and learn that the miscreant had no authority whatever to demand any paper, and that the very moment before going into the boat to go off, he had promised Mr. Samuels faithfully to do nothing to annoy us in regard to this matter.

At the Intendente's office, which was directly in our way back, we were told that the captain had said that he hated me, and meant to play this trick upon me ; and although the gentlemanly official assured me, in broken English, that I had no business with a passport for the woman, he gave me a slip of paper written hastily upon, which procured it for me at an

office two or three doors from his own; and
when I had paid all and borrowed three or four
dollars from the gentlemen who accompanied me, I had a single shilling left in my
pocket.

In twenty-five minutes from the time we
landed we were again on the mole, with all
that was required.   In an hour and fifteen minutes from the time we left the ship's side, we
were well out in the harbor in a four-oared
boat, pulling around the point, whither, the
men at the water side informed us, the ship had
proceeded.   I could not altogether suppress a
certain heart-chill when I saw she had left her
moorings in that short space of time; but Lieut.
E—— was so firm in the belief that he had
only shoved out of sight to startle and annoy
me, and I felt the dread that struck me to be
so nearly an impossibility, that until we cleared
the point, and looked full out to sea, I did not
really doubt that a few minutes more would
place me beside my children.

At this moment I can see that vessel as she
looked in the distance, as plainly as these black
lines on the white page before me—her gray

sails and ropes, her paler spars and yards, her black hull, already partially hidden from my view, are all fixed forever in my memory. She stood before my straining sight, a phantom vanishing so swiftly and surely, with the fresh, steady breeze filling her hollowed sails, that the hope with which I first caught sight of her died out of my heart in a moment, and a sickening, terrible conviction that she was gone, settled down upon me like the chill of death.

Beside that dreadful vision, I only remember catching the blank look of the faces about me, until we were again on the mole. I did not faint, for I am strong and resolute by nature ; but my faculties seemed stunned and scattered, and only when I found myself again on my feet, destitute, in a city of strangers, did they regather to my aid. It seems now like a horrible dream, that return to the shore ; and the landing and meeting people face to face, like the awakening to a worse reality.

I had advanced but a few steps on the mole, when we were met by an elderly gentleman of the same party to which Lieut. E—— belonged. We had experienced his kind regard for our

comfort, both at St. Catherine's and this
place; and when looking into my blanched face,
he gathered from that gentleman, in half a dozen
words, the fact that the ship had sailed with my
children, his quickly-suffused eyes and cordial
grasp of the hand removed in a moment the
suffocating restraint upon my feelings; and as
he drew my hand into his arm, and said, " You
must go down and see our consul; he is a very
kind, considerate person, and yours is absent,"
the stifling sensation about the heart left me,
and tears came to my relief.   I found the English consul all that Mr. T—— had assured me
that he was—sympathetic, manly, practical. He
told him where he would find a quiet house for
me to stop in; put an ounce into my hand to
provide for my immediate wants, and assured
me that, although I was in a strange city, I was
among a people who would not only not let
me suffer, but would spare me even the apprehension of it.   I never saw this good gentleman
after; but his name, face, and manner are preserved in my memory, and will never be forgotten.   His reception of a stranger in my condition
could not have been kinder or more judicious.

But I was not left to the painful desolation of a hotel. In less than an hour I was under the hospitable roof of the excellent clergyman whom I have before named, and by noon of the next day I was furnished with a wardrobe, bountiful enough to have supplied me for a six months' voyage. Surely the prompt liberality of those generous people could not have been excelled. Houses were opened to me and money supplied for my wants, and I was assured that my passage should be secured in the first vessel in which I could be comfortably accommodated, if the ship which had left me did not put back—a belief which several persons did not abandon till the third day. I never entertained it, and yet when they talked of its being so cruel and extraordinary a step, and said, again and again, that surely he never would go on, carrying little children away from their only parent to a country like California, I could not help hoping a little, and my eyes were often searching the distant waters for the gladdening sight. But she did not return, and I thank heaven that I knew too well the hard nature which commanded her to be disappointed thereat.

I grew calmer after a few days, and very soon
the suffering and anguish of some of the truest
and kindest hearts that my hard fortune had
made known to me, occupied me too much to
permit the remembrance of my own griefs.
How ceaseless, how much keener must have
been my distress, had I not been providentially
cast where there was such a work of mercy for
me to perform.   This is not the time nor the
occasion to narrate those sufferings.   They
were the result of one of those terrible trials
which, thanks be to Him who disposes all
events, are seldom inflicted on the heart of man
or woman.   Peace be to the surviving spirit
which was stricken by them.

For a whole month I was compelled to await
an opportunity to follow my poor children.
Meantime, how, I continually questioned, were
they faring ?   I knew there were feeling hearts
on board that vessel in the bosoms of both men
and women, and I knew that, above all, my excellent friend, Miss Sampson, would devote to
them the whole of her little strength ; but she
was an invalid, requiring care and nursing herself, and how could I suppose that a tender and

feeble child, who had, most of his life, had one person devoted to him, and often two, could receive from her the attention necessary to his health and comfort? It was this anxiety that chiefly pained me. I did not really fear that, once arrived at their place of destination, they would be permitted to suffer. None can sympathize with this anxiety but mothers whose lot it has been to rear such a child, inestimably dearer for his infirmities, and compensating all by rare gifts of heart and mind. I believe I have never suffered in my own person an injury which remains at this hour unforgiven; but I cannot yet find in my soul grace to forgive the cruelty which, I fully believe, caused my dear son days and weeks of agony. I cannot forget the paroxysms which brought great drops of sweat upon the brow, and blanched the thin cheeks, and whitened the quivering lips so often, during our first wretched summer in the country.

His brief life of physical pain and spiritual beauty and sweetness has closed, and, though I cannot forgive, I can almost pity, the wretch who has to recollect that he ever willingly added one pang to it.

I sailed from Valparaiso just one month from that dreadful day, on the Louis Philippe from Baltimore; and here again I experienced a continuation of the kindness which had attended me from the first. How gratefully it fell upon my aching heart in the slow days of that voyage, language cannot express. The friendship that dates from that time of gloom and grief; the delicate kindness that, without appearing to recognize any peculiar cause for its existence, never failed in its uniform flow; the gentle words of encouragement that came to cheer and lighten my seasons of deeper anxiety, will never be forgotten. It is when we are suffering thus and true hearts are near us, that we best learn their value. To all the lady passengers on board that vessel, and many of the gentlemen, and especially to her kind-hearted captain, I am indebted for innumerable mitigations of my weariness and sense of injury. If we did not sometimes encounter the evil side of human nature, we should feel less pleasure in the excellences that make the reverse. I had suffered from the brutality of a coarse, low nature, and was, therefore, keenly alive to all the consideration, tenderness, and respect that were shown me here.

We made San Francisco in thirty-eight days, and then were nine more in getting within the Golden Gate. That was the sorest trial of all. Every morning we believed that another would certainly see us ashore ; but one night after another witnessed our disappointment, until the eighth one passed. I was consumed with impatience, anxiety, and vexation. I could better have borne twenty days at sea, than those nine there ; but they came to an end at last, and we dropped anchor somewhere off North Beach, on the tenth evening, after it was too late to see anything, but two or three straggling lights shining dull through the fog that never cleared, and the rain that never ceased pouring. This, then, was California ; but I was too much engrossed in thinking of my dear children, and what had been their fate since they were parted from me, to entertain a thought of the wonderful country whose emporium lay before me, like a young giant but half-conscious of his power, or a single speculation upon my own probable destiny in it.

It was past noon the next day before I found them still on board the vessel, where the indefatigable Miss Sampson, who had chiefly taken care of them, aided by some of their fellow-passengers, still remained awaiting my arrival. Our joy at meeting was painfully qualified by dear little Eddie's feebleness, which had increased very materially since our parting. We went ashore almost immediately, if that could properly be called shore where tall men were wading to the tops of boots above their knees, and where the falling flood filled the atmosphere so, that floundering along with a strong man at each elbow, we seemed to be almost submerged, and felt thankful for so small a favor as having the upper portions of our persons bathed in a medium somewhat purer than that below.

At that period in the history of San Francisco, it was so rare to see a female, that those whose misfortune it was to be obliged to be abroad felt themselves uncomfortably stared at. Doorways filled instantly, and little islands in the streets were thronged with men who seemed to gather in a moment, and who remained immovable till the spectacle passed from their incredulous gaze. Bold-faced unfortunates, whose presence added infinitely to the discomfort one felt in those dreadful times, were occasionally to be seen in bar-rooms, or, perhaps, hatless and habitless on horseback in the streets, or the great gaming-houses that never were emptied of their throngs.

But I had no intention of attempting in this place to describe San Francisco as it then was. In the two months we spent in it, chiefly awaiting the issue of a suit which I commenced in the foolish hope of obtaining some semblance of justice for the outrage and wrong I had suffered, I endured a variety of annoyances and trials sufficient to make the place forever disgusting and wearisome to me, and I turned my face from it with a feeling of satisfaction, almost the first I had experienced in the country.

The plan of emigration referred to in the first page of this chapter, is sufficiently explained in the following circular. To the intelligent and candid it will require no defense, and to those who are neither, I think it unworthy myself to offer any. I may say, however, that since I have experienced the moral and social poverty of the country, I have felt grateful that my endeavors failed. It would be a painful responsibility, which I could never throw off, if I had to reflect that there were persons here through my instrumentality who were less happy or good than they might have been remaining at home. The illness which alone prevented the success of this plan, and of which I was therefore very impatient, I now look back upon as a blessing. There are none here to reproach me with their sufferings—no mourning fathers and mothers, or brothers and sisters to say that but for me their lost ones might have been yet with them. I fully believed at that time that a company of females could emigrate greatly to their own advantage and that of the country, and I still think so, but if ninety and nine had come unscathed through the dangers that must have surrounded them, and the hundredth had failed, all the good would to me have fallen short of compensating the evil.

To feel that one has saved a human spirit from degradation or ruin is a source of exquisite happiness, but to know that a single soul, however mean or poor, has had its downward way facilitated by one's influence, would be the bitterest of all reflections.

The guarantees required in this plan would have sufficed for almost any other country in Christendom; but the moral life of California is to the character what the seven-times heated furnace is to the ore of the metallurgist—only purity itself can come unwasted through it. I give the circular as the only answer I should feel due to any but an honest questioner, and as sufficient for such an one:

NEW YORK, February 2d, 1849.

The death of my husband, Thomas J. Farnham, Esq., at San Francisco, in September last, renders it expedient that I should visit California during the coming season. Having a desire to accomplish some greater good by my journey thither than to give the necessary attention to my private affairs, and believing that the presence of women would be one of the surest checks upon many of the evils that are apprehended there, I desire to ask attention to the following sketch of a plan for organizing a party of such persons to emigrate to that country.

Among the many privations and deteriorating influences to which the thousands who are flocking thither will be subjected, one of the greatest is the absence of woman, with all her kindly cares and powers, so peculiarly conservative to man under such circumstances.

It would exceed the limits of this circular to hint at the

2

benefits that would flow to the growing population of that wonderful region, from the introduction among them of intelligent, virtuous, and efficient women.   Of such only it is proposed to make up this company.   It is believed that there are hundreds, if not thousands, of such females in our country who are not bound by any tie that would hold them here, who might, by going thither, have the satisfaction of employing themselves greatly to the benefit and advantage of those who are there, and at the same time of serving their own interest more effectually than by following any employment that offers to them here.

It is proposed that the company shall consist of persons not under twenty-five years of age, who shall bring from their clergyman, or some authority of the town where they reside, satisfactory testimonials of education, character, capacity, etc., and who can contribute the sum of two hundred and fifty dollars, to defray the expenses of the voyage, make suitable provision for their accommodation after reaching San Francisco, until they shall be able to enter upon some occupation for their support, and create a fund to be held in reserve for the relief of any who may be ill, or otherwise need aid before they are able to provide for themselves.

It is believed that such an arrangement, with one hundred or one hundred and thirty persons, would enable the company to purchase or charter a vessel, and fit it up with everything necessary to comfort on the voyage, and that the combination of all for the support of each, would give such security, both as to health, person, and character, as would remove all reasonable hesitation from the minds of those who may be disposed and able to join such a mission.   It is intended that the party shall include six or eight respectable married men and their families.

Those who desire further information will receive it by calling on the subscriber at ————.

ELIZA W. FARNHAM.

The New York built packet ship Angelique has been engaged to take out this Association. She is a spacious vessel, fitted up with state-rooms throughout and berths of good size, well-ventilated and provided in every way to secure a safe, speedy, and comfortable voyage. She will be ready to sail from New York about the 12th or 15th of April.

We, the undersigned, having been made acquainted with the plan proposed by Mrs. Farnham, in the above circular, hereby express our approbation of the same, and recommend her to those who may be disposed to unite with her in it, as worthy the trust and confidence necessary to its successful conduct.

Hon. J. W. Edmonds, Judge Superior Court.
Hon. W. T McCoun, late Vice-Chancellor.
Hon. B. F. Butler, late U. S. Attorney.
Hon. H. Greeley.
Isaac T. Hopper, Esq.

Freeman Hunt, Esq.
Thomas C. Doremus, Esq.
W. C. Bryant, Esq.
Shepherd Knapp, Esq.
Rev. George Potts, D. D.
Rev. Henry W. Beecher.
Miss Cath'ne M. Sedgwick.
Mrs. C. M. Kirkland.

I was ill two months following the publication of this paper, and the time set for sailing was too soon after my recovery to permit persons, who wished to avail themselves of this plan, to make their preparations. Only three ladies, of more than two hundred who communicated with me, came out in my company. Two of these have returned with the means of living comfortably the rest of their days, and with unstained reputations, and the third is at this time a member of my family.

CHAPTER I.

To the struggling advocates of Woman's Rights, it may seem a hopeful sign of the times that one of their sex should put forth a book claiming to be in any degree descriptive of farming, especially when they make the delightful discovery that the writer speaks in a great measure from personal experience in the business. But it must not be forgotten that life in California is altogether anomalous, and that it is no more extraordinary for a woman to plough, dig, and hoe with her own hands, if she have the will and strength to do so, than for men to do all their household labor for months, never seeing the face nor hearing the voice of a woman during that time.

I could not seriously undertake to write even so small a volume as I intend this to be, on farming, without the etc., which the reader will perceive, has completely freed me as to my subjects. I also have an abiding faith that there is something in California besides its mines; some life worth considering besides that of the people who delve at the "dry or wet diggings," and pray, if they ever pray at all, that the sierras might turn into huge piles of gold-dust before their eyes. The mining life is constantly so much enlarged upon in all books, pamphlets, letters, and newspapers, that there will be no just cause of complaint, if not more than a dozen pages of so unpretending a volume are found devoted to it. There are many thousand souls in the country, at least the presence of so many bodies is *prima facie* evidence in support of the assertion, who have never seen the mines, who, notwithstanding their previous silence give a side to life too apt to be forgotten by those abroad, who look only for tidings from the diggings, and the amount of gold brought by the last steamer. My own experience places me in this class, and I am the more willing to speak for it, because a large portion of it is connected with an interest not less important to the State than her mines, which is far more delightful to those who cultivate it, and which must be a chief instrumentality in her salvation, if any such fate await her. At present, the indications in that direction are too feeble to promise any clear tendency.

In truth, I believe there is up to this time a very weighty opposite preponderance, the removal of which must, in a great measure, be due to a thrifty agricultural population, such as it is probable will shortly occupy most of the arable lands of this beautiful and fertile State. There is not another on the globe, perhaps, in which agriculture can be so successfully pursued—in which fertility of soil is united to a climate affording every security for the growth and the gathering of crops, and where so great variety of products can be grown without resort to artificial processes. It is the land of the vine and the olive, and beside them the most delicious fruits of the higher latitudes come to the fullest perfection. If half the stout hearts and strong hands, that every year leave home for the mining regions of California, were as resolutely directed towards her teeming vales and plains and hills, for here all are fertile, there would be an annual saving of wealth, health, life, and virtue, that would, in these respects, soon elevate her to a level with any of her elder sisters.

In most of the older States, some portion of the year, if not a very considerable one, is spent in preparing to meet the severity of winter. Here, no such preparation is needed. The season of growth commences soon after the first rains fall (usually in the latter part of October), and continues until some time in May, when the country is become a vast, rich meadow, wherein the hay is already cured and spread for the innumerable herds; and in which oat-fields, millions of acres in extent, offer a subsistence nowhere else to be found by animals who feed without the care of man. With such a climate and soil it will readily be supposed that the farmer may have always planting or harvesting in hand, and as the markets for home products, made by the legions of consumers who throng to the country, are the best in the world, it follows that there must be great lack of skill or industry if he do not thrive. But

notwithstanding all these advantages, his calling is not without its difficulties, among the
first of which may, perhaps, be reckoned the
newness of the climate and his entire inability
to get the benefit of any previous experience
in it.   He finds it difficult to believe that, other
things being right, the best season for planting
is after all the rains are over, when, the seed
once covered, not a drop of water will fall upon
it, except in dews, until it is fit for gathering.
Accordingly, if he be a Yankee, he uses his
utmost exertions to plant in the intervals
between the rains, and finds that every one of
any volume is succeeded by a vigorous growth
of weeds, which, if his crop be not put in in the
best manner, it costs him great labor to get
removed.   But a difficulty which he has encountered previous to this, unless he set out
with the amplest preparations for his business,
has been the getting of his implements.   He
has found but few in the country and those of
the commonest descriptions, and if he have had
occasion to call on an artisan for repairs, he
has been startled at the magnificent conception
of his profits, by which they measure the value

to him of their labor. He gets over this as well as he can, but finds a lasting annoyance in the want of fenced pastures. He turns his cattle loose at night in a field of a million acres, fenced, may be, on one side by the ocean, and elsewhither by mountains, and in the morning has a tour, pedestrian or equestrian, as his for tune permits, of, perhaps, several miles, before he is able to gather them to yoke or harness.

He contemplates some measure a little, perhaps a very little, out of the ordinary way, and, not feeling entire confidence in his own judgment, he would like to get the opinions of some persons more experienced in circumstances quite new to him. His first resort is to some of the old residents, not natives, but no trapper or frontierman ever became an attentive farmer, and he is vexed to find that Messrs. Smith, Jones, Brown, and Walker, if they all live in his neighborhood, have each a diametrically opposite theory. He appeals to the Spanish population next, and, if he chance to meet an intelligent man of them, gets some notions which, if he will, he may follow with profit; if not, "quien sabe," or "no sabe," ends the conference, and he returns to his ranch to learn from his own experience what he cannot from his neighbors.

Then he sends to San Francisco, Stockton, or Sacramento for his seed. He pays prices, a catalogue of which is an entertainment for his friends at home not less wonderful than the Arabian Nights; gets them home at charges for freights, carriage, etc., which make a harmonious second part to what has gone before; puts it into the ground in a state of mind which, if he be quite new to the business, is a happy combination of faith and hope, and awaits the result. Ten days—a fortnight, three weeks go by, and about the 23d or 24th day he is able to discover a few plants above the surface. The fourth, fifth, and sixth week do not more than double these few, and at the end of this period he begins to think it just possible that his seed is good for nothing. If he have time and faith, he ploughs it in and plants again, waits a shorter time than before, and, perhaps, plants again, it may be to fail finally, because of the bad article that he has purchased at such enormous prices.

If the exporter at home could be made to suffer, in one season, the loss and vexation that a single man, who has been so deceived, endures, he would yet have experienced no adequate retribution for the wrong he has practiced, if he had any reason to doubt the quality of his merchandise before sending it. By the time he has sown small seeds the third time over, he begins to think seriously of falling back upon his potatoes and barley, if he have any. The former, he knows, will not fail, if they have had anything like fair treatment, unless, indeed, the grasshoppers overtake them in their season of tenderness, in which case a few days cropping by them will save him the labor he has been dreading in the harvest.

Thus he gets on through the planting and growing season, each particular portion of which has its trials and vexations; but, at last, when the crop is ripened, the prices he gets atone for much, and encourage him to make trial another year, perhaps under more favorable circumstances, when his greater success insures his faith for the future. The difficulties too, which I have named, are diminishing every

year.   There is already an experience which it
is safer for the beginner to trust, than any he
could have found a year ago.   Implements are
more abundant and better, and mechanical labor less scarce than at that time.

The region of country of which I can speak
most confidently, is one in which farming has
been as generally and as variously tried, perhaps, as in any other of the State, and the
reader must not be surprised into a loss of his
patience, if, instead of a grave disquisition on
Agricultural Science, or its possibilities in California, he finds the subject chiefly illustrated
by my own and my neighbor's experience in
the peerless little valley of Santa Cruz, if valley it can be called, which is shut in by the
ocean on its southern and western limits, and
by mountains in all other directions.   The
region now known by the name of Santa
Cruz, is the country lying contiguous to the
old mission of that name, which is situated
on the coast, at the north side of Monterey Bay,
about seventy miles south from San Francisco,
and twenty miles north from Monterey.   Like
the site of all the missions, it is one of the most

beautiful spots to be found in the country. The old mission buildings are situated on a gentle height, about a mile from the shore, where the San Lorenzo—a considerable stream, coming down from the coast range—empties into the bay, to the left. They command a complete view of the bay, with its surrounding shores, while in front the blue Pacific stretches its endless waters, which roll in and break on the beach in all varieties of tone, from the alto of thunder to the sweet tenor of that gentle chime which, heard through the deep solitudes of the night, soothes and charms the soul.

The country about the mission is one of the most beautiful that can be imagined. Gentle and lofty heights, divided by valleys and open plains, make its chief features. Abundant streams of water, clear and cool as the embowered springs beside which we used to dream away the early mornings in the distant land of our childhood, course these plains and valleys, and, fringed as they are at frequent intervals with clumps of low-spreading willows, or smaller shrubs, form a beautiful feature in the miniature landscape dotted by them. The coast-range borders on the east and north, the table characterized by these features, at a distance of from five to twelve miles, and the lands lying between these great barriers, and stretching some twenty miles in length, were the old mission territory.

It was secularized in 1834, and since that time its property has become so diminished, that of the thousands of cattle and horses, only hundreds now remain; its buildings are fallen to decay, or have been renovated by covering the substantial old adobe wall with a flimsy wood-work, and replacing the ancient tile with the Yankee shingle. But the changes in its exterior are neither so great nor so lamentable as those that have come over the spirit of the place. The rooms in which the old padres taught the arts of civilized life to the trusting savages, are dismantled and crumbling; and, perchance, where the Indian first heard of the simple faith they commended to him, his descendants now hold those beastly revels, which, if they have not been introduced by the new population, show themselves

in their ugliest deformities among them, because the charitable, hopeful soul refuses to be
taught by the many bitter lessons to the same
purport furnished in the world's history, and
still hugs to itself the belief that the superior
race will be the exemplars of virtuous life to
the inferior.

The climate and soil about this mission are
peculiarly favorable to most purposes of agriculture and horticulture, and the lands in its
vicinity are being rapidly taken up by Americans
and foreigners, for those purposes. Occasional
droughts, which affect the crops of the inland
valleys, are less felt here because of the humidity of many of the mornings and evenings
during the summer months; the fogs, which
amount almost to rain, often rolling in from
the bay, and hanging over our fields from sunset till eight or nine o'clock next morning.
Then the unfailing streams—which make
glad the dry and thirsty land during the cloudless months, render irrigation possible, if one
chooses to resort to it, though I believe it is finding less and less favor with judicious cultiva-
tors, except for very temporary uses in appli-

cation to the small crops. It is never desired
for the grains or coarser vegetables.

With these advantages of soil, water, etc.,
a climate entirely free from the blasting winds
that are so severely felt at other points on the
coast, especially at San Francisco, we, who are
so favored as to have our lot cast in this exquisite region, consider ourselves specially fortunate among Californians, and are wont to con-
gratulate ourselves and each other, and also to
set forth to visitors the blessings we enjoy,
much after the manner in which men and women usually commend their own possessions
and privileges, and I think with quite as much
faith.

CHAPTER II.

On one of the most delightful farms—or, to use a term we like better in California—on one of the most delightful *ranchos* in this beautiful region, the writer sat down, eighteen months ago, with her two little sons, a female friend, and a farmer, with the intention of trying the chances of farming-life in California—a new life to me anywhere—but the very essence of newness in this strangest of all countries peopled by our countrymen, and made doubly strange by the new and startling aspects which individual, as well as general character, not unfrequently assume in it.

We had come down from San Francisco by sea—been landed like bales of goods through the surf, partly in boats and partly in the arms of the seamen, and had walked out to our ranch, which the farmer had visited the previous evening.   Behold me, then, landed, with Charlie trotting eagerly at my side, and a friend who had come down with us carrying dear Eddie on his back.   My friend, Miss Sampson, had staid upon the beach—partly because she was unable to take the walk, and partly that a careful eye might be kept upon the goods as they were landed.   See us, after a walk of two miles, on the 22nd of February, through clover and grass four inches high, borne down by the heavy dews that had fallen on the previous night, enter the casa of El Rancho La Libertad. There have been two men occupying it before our arrival, who are to remove in the afternoon or the next day.   Their household goods consist of a table—the roughest of its species—two or three old benches, three or four bowls, as many plates, and one or two articles of hollow-ware. The casa is not a cheerful specimen even of California habitations—being made of slabs, which were originally placed upright, but which have departed sadly from the perpendicular in every direction.   There is not a foot of floor, nor a pane of glass, nor a brick, nor anything in the shape of a stove.   The fire is made upon the ground, and the smoke departs by any avenue that seemeth to itself good, or lingers in the airy space between our heads and the roof, which is beautifully done in bas relief of webs, dressed in pyroligneous acid.

The dimensions of the entire structure are about twenty-five feet in length by fifteen feet in width at one end, and diminishing, by beautiful convergence, to about ten feet at the other. A partition of slabs, thrown across the narrow end, rather divides the house than makes a room, of which the other three walls are so imperfect that you may walk through them almost where you will.

When Eddie, and a satchel or two that had come along with the party, had been deposited, and a brief survey taken of the beautiful spot in which this forlorn habitation stood, the men returned to the beach, and the boys and I were left to the housekeeping. Such outward apparel as I would have laid aside, I found it much against my inclination to deposit in the soot and ashes that everywhere abounded; but after some search, I found means to get rid safely of bonnet, shawl, etc., and giving the

boys license to explore the course of the little
stream that babbled and brawled along its deep
bed, within twenty feet of the door, I strolled
out alone, to enjoy the exceeding quietness and
loveliness of the place—the first novel emotions
at finding myself the mistress of it, and to get
some idea of the capacities and resources of my
future home. I had been told it was a beautiful
place, but I was not prepared for the sort of
impression it produced.

It was one of those peerless days, such as
only a California winter affords, with a cloudless sky above the head, and the earth piled
with tenderest herbage under the feet. In the
deep seclusion of La Libertad I enjoyed that
silence and solitude which for a day one finds
so welcome a change from bustle and annoyance, such as had been our previous lot in
California. Only the song of birds, the bub-
bling of the stream over the roots of the trees
whose tops embower it, mingled with the glee-
ful shouts of the delighted boys, who are already
deep in the mysteries of its most secret places,
greet my ear. The beating of the distant surf
rather aids than breaks the silence, and by

ascending a gentle slope to the right, I look out
on a picture so filled with repose and beauty,
that while I gaze, the hateful stir of the world
in which I have lately been mixed up, seems to
die out of the universe, and I no longer remember it. For the hour, I forget that life subjects
the spirit to jar or discord, and am only conscious of the harmony that flows from the generous breast of nature into our own, when, for
a happy moment, she gets undivided audience
of it. Alas, alas! that lapse of time should
constantly separate such seasons further and
further apart in our lives!

On either hand, at a short distance from the
stream, rise hills, now beautifully rounded, now
more abrupt and stern, but all clothed with
richest herbage, which herds of cattle are cropping in silent satisfaction. Just back of the
house these hills approach each other so nearly,
that what is a broad vale below becomes a
deep ravine, with wooded banks, upon which a
dozen tall redwoods tower above their neighbors, and seem, to my wondering eyes, to be
penetrating the very clouds. In front, the hills
open generously to the right and left, quite

down to the large stream to which ours is a
tributary, and stretch around a broad sunny
vale that looks out upon the bay, over the gentle swell of land, much lower than the hills on
either side, on which the old Mission buildings
stand.   Beyond this, I gaze upon the sparkling
waters of the great bay, whose surrounding
coast is diversified by hill and plain, cloud and
sunshine, so exquisitely, that I deem it a fairy
scene, rather than a portion of the real, peopled
earth.   So bright is it, in its newness and un-
revealed deformities, so tender in its solitude
and purity, so holy in its beauty, overhung by
a sky whose pure blue seems made only to veil
the heaven we imagine above from that we gaze
upon beneath, I wonder, while beholding it,
that religious and devout thankfulness to God
does not continually ascend from the hearts of
those who dwell in so fair a portion of his
creation.

But a shout of "Mother, mother," calls my
attention from the dream of goodness, inspired
by what I behold.   I descend to the house, to
learn the important and novel fact that the boys
are hungry   No stores have arrived ; and there

seems, consequently, no lawful way of satisfy-
ing their wants. I tell them this; but Charlie,
who has hungered occasionally through some
four years more than his brother, is quick to
suggest that a slice each might be cut, without
sin, from the solid looking loaf lying upon the
table. Neither its complexion nor juxtaposition
make it very inviting to my housekeeping sense;
but as that is a faculty rarely developed in boys,
they experience no qualms, but take their
lunches, when I get them off with some difficulty, and are off again with a cup, to the brook,
of the wonders and beauty of which they have
poured forth a stream of narrative, exclamation,
and delight, as incessant as the noise of its own
waters. But, for me, the charm was broken;
there was no return to the world from which
they had recalled me. To the child-heart the
beautiful was a sufficing presence. It placed
above question all that enjoyed its blessed contiguity. Faith could not waver, nor hope falter
before it. Blessed season! when the visible
works of God suffice to give us faith in all that
is, and all that we hope shall yet be.

Neither the trees, the birds, nor the sunshine,

could tempt me abroad again. I sat down in
the ashes—not at the fireside, but in a remote
part of the room, to look at the reverse of the
picture : at the in-door world—a less delightful
survey than I had made without. I had failed
to secure a temporary home, as I hoped to be
able to, in the house of a good old couple in
the neighborhood—the fame of whose kindness
had reached me in San Francisco, and now had
to address myself to my own resources for
that purpose, the Spanish houses being entirely
out of the question, and the very few American
families that I have referred to being entirely
unknown to me. In my meditations I inverted
the black walls, turned them inside out, laid an
ideal floor, erected imaginary closets, etc., set
apart corners for bed-rooms, and was far advanced in my housekeeping, before I was interrupted by a call from a neighbor—one of the
prisoners of 1840—who, after many civil expressions of pleasure at seeing me and the
children, invited us to make his house our
home until we should be able to fit up something habitable of these ruins. Before he left,
I had a visit from one of the notabilities of old

California—no less a personage than Captain Graham, who, with his rifle at his back, and shoes down at heel, presented in his exterior a curious mixture of the hunter and the man of leisure. From these persons I learned many things that were interesting and important for me to know; and when they departed, it was with the understanding that I should repair to Mr. Anderson's house for supper and lodging that night.

CHAPTER III.

MEANTIME, the day had been a busy one on the beach, where the men and Miss Sampson, with only some crackers which they accidentally found, by way of lunch, had been busy looking after and handling packing-cases, boxes, barrels, baskets, bags, and parcels, as they were landed through the surf. I waited at the ranch until the early February night had nearly set in, when the two occupants of the old house returned, one of them kindly offering to carry Eddie for me to Mr. Anderson's house, in the mission. We had not been there long when Miss Sampson arrived, under the escort of our friend from the beach; and in due time, the welcomest event of the day, supper, befel us, to which we did such ample justice as might have shaken less large hospitality than the Californians had been accustomed to exer-

cise. While it was coming, Miss S—— and I
were comparing notes of our day's experience,
which she informed me had been very merry
with her, by reason of the tumblings, gather-
ings, scramblings, and quarrelings between
the surf and the men, in the boats and ashore.
Boxes had been burst, baskets, bags, and other
articles slyly set afloat by the former, with intent to their felonious removal to deep water;
and all these accidents had raised questions of
jurisdiction which only the most exceeding
vigilance could settle in favor of the little dis-
putant, who ran nimbly about, dodging the
great broadsides of his antagonist. Ocean was
awake and disposed to jocularity, and his little neighbor was fain to meet him in the same
mood.

As the goods were lying scattered in all
directions upon the beach, it was requisite to
establish a night police, which was readily
done with a large fire, a joint of beef, the two
men, and the innumerable blankets, quilts,
comforters, and feather-beds, that by one dis-
aster and another had been brought from their
proper places in the melée. In the morning

the removal to the house was to commence; and, as I am setting down facts for the edification and comfort of those who may contemplate placing themselves in like circumstances, I ought not to omit saying that it had cost us $25 to land every boat-load of goods, and was to cost $8 more to remove each wagon-load to the house, a distance of two miles. In the council of the evening it was agreed that, desperate as was the condition of affairs at the ranch, we must make our quarters there from the next morning. Our cares were to be there, and our homes must be with them. We repaired to it, therefore, immediately after an early breakfast next morning, and there our life in California fairly commenced.

Next day begins the transportation of the goods from the beach, the quantity of which leads the people to ask Tom, the farmer, if we are to open a store, to which he demurely answers, yes, as soon as five tons of the potatoes are planted, the farm fenced, and a house built. It being Saturday evening, one of the wagoners, after discharging his last load, politely sent in a message that he was to preach to-

morrow, and would be happy to see us among
his audience; a pleasure which, considering
the state of our household affairs, within and
without, we were not very likely to indulge
him in. Towards night we sent down a
pitcher to our nearest neighbor, at the little
mill a few rods below us, which she filled with
delicious milk for the consideration of three
shillings; and this, with the help of the crackers before referred to, some steak furnished by
our kind entertainer of the night before, and,
above all, of our incomparable appetites, gave
us a supper which epicures would seek in vain
at tables never so costly or profuse.

The Sabbath was well occupied in unpack-
ing and drying wet goods, in searching for the
first indispensable articles of use in our half
nomadic state, and in furnishing our bed-room,
which was a capacious white tent that had
been kindly loaned us, and which, under the
renovating, careful, and prolonged preparation
which Miss S—— had given it within and
around, became a really elegant chamber, notwithstanding there was a very large bed in
the midst on the ground, and a smaller one for

Charlie at the side. No one thought of looking after the men in this respect: they camped down upon any box, table, sofa, or chance row of chairs, that invited them, and were no more heard of till the early morning. Next day the remainder of our goods were to come up, and before its close, commenced a season that will long be memorable on this ranch, which we generally designate as the siege of the stove. Up to this time our obliging neighbor had baked the little bread we had indulged in; but now that the stove was come, we already began to feel a sense of independence and comfort in its possession, which, alas, was doomed to many chilling disappointments. As soon as it was unboxed, Tom, being the mechanic as well as farmer, was detailed to put it up. He commenced in the best faith, but had not proceeded far before he made the important discovery that in a fall the box had met with, some important plates, and perhaps a rod or two, had been fractured.

In our busy passages to and fro, during the progress of the investigation, we got occasionally a word of encouragement, and again of

discouragement ; but we never doubted that
perseverance and skill would prevail over all
difficulties, and that we should soon see and
feel the grateful presence of an article so
necessary even in our rude housekeeping. It
should be borne in mind that all these first
days were passed by Miss S—— and myself in
dragging out and exposing to the occasional
sun gleams whole cases of wetted linen, mus-
lins, and clothing. We were just at the fitful
closing of the rainy season, when half-hour
sunshines alternate with five-minute showers
all day. So that each night we had the exceeding satisfaction that housekeepers can
sympathize in, of feeling that we had toiled
hard through the day only to increase the confusion and multiply the disorder that already
distracted us. A line would perhaps be just
filled with sheets, table-cloths, and napkins of
snowy whiteness, when a cloud gathering over
the ravine would give us the alarm, and in five
minutes the " entire," as our Irishman had it,
would be gathered in undistinguished confusion and pitched into the tent, or, if that were
too full to receive them, into the sooty house.

When, at nightfall, we had yet no stove, and were doomed to the further discouragement of hearing Tom confess himself defeated, Miss S—— and our friend, who had been laying a floor, spontaneously resolved themselves into a committee on that branch of domestic order, and proceeded at once to their duty. Their labors were continued to a late hour, but finally failed, and I, last of all, also failed.

The interesting feature of these efforts was our entire dependence on the right adjustment of two or three bits of iron; their amusing one, was trying the same tricks over and over with them, placing them in precisely the same relation they had been unsuccessfully tried in some twenty times in the course of our efforts. On the third day, it was agreed that stoves could not have been used in the time of Job, or all his other afflictions would have been unnecessary. But our spirits were now so thoroughly tamed by it, and our demands upon it so humbled, that we agreed to come to its terms without further parley, and abandon the use of the refractory rods, plates, etc., which before had been thought indispensable to its perfect action.   No sooner was this done than the question was amicably settled ; and it shows how, often, difficulties that seem insuperable, are in truth more imaginary than real—that in an hour from this concession we had our stove well heated and its oven doing duty upon a generous pan of biscuit, very comforting to our eyes.   This was a great triumph.

3*

CHAPTER IV.

WHEN the house had been reërected around us, a door and some windows cut and glazed with thin cotton cloth, a second tent pitched, and sundry boxes, tables, bedsteads, chairs, etc., safely stowed within it, our thoughts began to turn seriously to farming, as, indeed, it was time they should, the first of March being now come, and finding us with dilapidated fences, no team, and a two years' sward, thickly covered with clover and other grasses, to be turned. The farmer had purchased an "Eagle" plow in San Francisco for $75, and got it safely here: but I thought he eyed it with looks of no great favor, when he had in remembrance the fact that his team might not be of the strongest, while the sward was of the thickest. Perhaps the most distinguished piece of folly of which we had been guilty was, allowing ourselves to be persuaded that it was better to come here without money. Having ample means legally deposited in the hands of a person in San Francisco, who had been some three years in the country, and knew this neighborhood well, we had, nevertheless, been prevailed upon by him to come empty-handed to our undertaking, having his assurance that anything we needed was to be had on a hint, and that it would commend us far more to the hearts of our neighbors if we wanted occasionally some favor from them, than if we went among them too independent. This assertion bore a sort of brotherly-love air that commended it to me, and beside, seemed' like probability in California, where money was more abundant than anything else man desired, and spent with a prodigality of which any description would convey but a faint notion to those who count sixpences at home.

So here we were, in that glorious state of dependence which was to be so happy a bond of union between us and those who were about us, wanting everything for putting in a crop, but seed, plow, and the labor of one man. Every day

was important to us; but it took several to can-
vass the settlement and get our wants supplied.
At length, on the 10th of March, two horses
and a mule having been furnished by the liberality of as many owners, the plow started. But
the turf was too heavy, and the furrow too
large for the team. "What will you do?" said
I, looking down the long field at the broken
furrow.

"Ah, sure, what would I do, but make another, jist."

"Make another?"

"Yes; I have already the irons laid by from
yon old one, ye see, an' I'll not be long knock-
ing the bits of wood together."

So here was another delay. Meantime, our
neighbor, Capt. Graham, had fallen ill, and having heard favorably of my skill in homœopathy,
had sent a pressing invitation for me to call on
him professionally, which, of course, I could
not fail to do.

A splendid saddle-horse having been placed
at my disposal by our neighbor, Anderson,
I mounted him, and was to be accompanied
by our friend who had remained with us up

to this time, on the mule. I knew nothing of his equestrian accomplishments, and set off, little anticipating the sort of day we were to have.

A mule, as everybody knows, is the personification of calmness. No excitement is ever apparent in his face; no glaring eyeballs; no distended nostrils; no threatening ears; no quivering of the sinewy limbs. He jogs along through life with the same motion of his long ears on the last day that they had on the first. He must be not only hardly, but skillfully pushed, if he is made to exceed the ordinary speed of his every-day motion; and he would never be able to shake off the self-contempt he would feel, if he allowed any but an experienced *caballero* to keep him quite up to that. Now, my escort on this occasion had an earnest, eager face, the keenest contrast to Jenny's quiet one. He was, moreover, quite a stranger to the equestrian exercise, while she was thoroughly familiar with her part in it, and he was without spurs, which again gave her an immense advantage in the engagement that was to follow. A skillful general would never have taken the field with such odds against him. But poor B——, he had all his skill to acquire. Sheik being in high spirit, I galloped away, and, turning to speak just before plunging into the river, which was swollen by the heavy rains almost to swimming, found myself alone. I waited a moment, and was first notified of their approach by hearing the huge stirrups of the California saddle banging against the ribs of the mule, to their great jeopardy as I thought.

I began to feel the amusement of the affair before they came in sight; but when they did, it became irresistible, and my mirth convulsive. The mule was jogging along with a face entirely free from the excitement that flushed and literally exhaled from that of her rider, whose exertions had heated him to a glow, and whose shoulders, now that he had pushed her to a trot, rose to the rims of his ears at every step. A few yards of such traveling gave Jenny her cue for the day. She knew that her pleasure would be the law of her movements from that time, and settled into a deep state of meditation accordingly. We crossed the river; and it would be tedious to relate how many times, in the course of five miles, the same entertainment was repeated—never, I must say, to the wearying of my risibles ; for as often as they came up to me and Sheik, waiting to be overtaken, so often the contrast between the condition, both external and spiritual, of the animal and her rider, appealed irresistibly to my sense of the ludicrous, so that by the time I had reached the rancho, where the professional circumspection and gravity were to be assumed, I was so exhausted that they came upon me without effort or attention. But the day was pretty well advanced by the time we had dined and the prescriptions were made, so that we set out for home with little more than half an hour of the sun.

It became, therefore, an object to make speed, and to this end I proposed to pass over my riding-whip for Jenny's benefit. But as Sheik was going home, and Jenny from it, the contrast between their movements became stronger than we had seen it in the morning. At length, by dint of pulling in Sheik and spurring on Jenny, I was enabled, holding by the tip of the whip, to give B—— the handle ; and now we were to be off in earnest. I gave Sheik the rein, and we soon found ourselves alone and beyond hearing as well as sight. So we halted again. After waiting longer than usual, we walked back, much against Sheik's inclination. to meet the laggers. They were coming slowly up, Jenny utterly refusing to break a very dignified walk, despite her rider's desperate determination that she should. I saw at a glance that matters were worse than they had been. I inquired after his welfare, and was answered by the most earnest entreaty to take back the fatal whip, for that the least application of it brought her to a dead stand. It was possible to keep her in motion without it; but if he tried to use it, she would spend the night on the road with him.

Accordingly we jogged on at such pace as Jenny's pleasure allowed; but missing the road that led to our ford, we got on one to which both were strangers, and strolled through a muddy lane and over a large tract of unfenced lands, up and down, to and fro, seeking in vain the ford which we knew to be safe, and which alone we dared venture in that high stage of water. We called at two or three houses for directions, but the occupants could speak no English, and we no Spanish; so that we could get only the general consolation that there was *mucha agua*, a fact we already knew too well. At length we struck off for a light in a direction hitherto untried; and after plunging and floundering in the mud and darkness for half a mile, had the good fortune to find a Canadian, who kindly showed us a ford that led directly to our house, which we reached just before nine o'clock, glad enough to see its cheerful interior: the black walls clothed, as they now were, with clean, light cloth; the stove open, with a blazing fire inside it; and a neat hearth and the clean-swept floor suggesting an idea of comfort and home I had not felt at sight of any other house I had seen. Next morning Jenny was in far better condition than her rider, who protested, with unaffected earnestness, that he would rather walk to San Francisco than attempt to ride her the same distance again.

CHAPTER V.

I LAMENTED my lack of skill with the pencil when our housekeeping was fairly under way, that prevented me from preserving a sketch of the casa. I shall endeavor to describe its internal appearance as faithfully as my memory will permit, after an acquaintance of eight months. We occupy the smaller of the two apartments into which the house is divided—the outer and larger being a store-room for trunks, boxes, furniture, etc., which the tents cannot receive. We have a rough floor laid in the apartment we live in, through the middle of which ascends a pillar, which we call Pompey's pillar since it has been covered with white cloth. Innumerable nails on all sides announce that trophies of civilization depend from them during the hours when dresses and the et ceteras of the day toilet are laid aside. Pompey's pil-

lar, with the help of a curtain on one side and
the foot of a bedstead draped on the other, subdivides this commodious apartment into a bedchamber and room for general purposes. In the
former, Miss S., the two boys and myself, have
our lodgings—Charlie occupying a bed made in
a sofa, between its back and the wall, which it
faces. On the other side of this wall, in the
outer room, the men have their beds or berths,
and the slabs being only clothed over on our
side, the fact of our having retired to our respective lodgings offers no interruption to
speech; neither does the intervention of the
outer walls if one party is out of doors; and
it is not uncommon for some of us to be per-
ambulating the immediate vicinity of the house
and discoursing to those in bed respecting the
whereabouts of a gang of cayotas, an owl, or,
perchance, a band of wild bullocks that have
come down to investigate the condition of
things at the ranch.

On the part of these latter gentlemen, there
seems an especial spite to be felt toward a
bower that has been erected against the end of
the house, for the delectation of a cock and two

hens which a kind neighbor has sent me by way
of starting us in the poultry line.   As the bower
style of architecture is not the most substantial,
it will readily be supposed that this one did not
withstand the assaults of the huge horns that
were poked into it, to the great horror of its in-
mates, and it consequently behoved, that occasionally, when the attack became too pressing,
some one should step out to the rescue.   Defense
was generally made with spade, plowshare,
billet of wood, or any other weapon that came
first to hand.   At last the besiegers were all
beaten off, save one, who, either from intense
curiosity or malice, persisted in these unfriendly
visits.   He was bold, too, as well as obstinate,
and generally stood till the enemy was close
upon him before he gave ground. The bower had
been repaired and left undisturbed for some time,
till one bright moonlight night brought down
the old marauder, whose hoarse roar announced
his coming while he was yet at considerable
distance.   At the first onset, the man hurled a
spade at his ribs which seemed sufficient for
that time ; he retreated for half an hour or so,
but finally rallied and came on again.   This

time, Tom, who had been long enough in bed to be very reluctant to leave it, started up so resolutely that we were assured some new measure was to be taken. He opened the door suddenly, seized a revolver that lay upon the closet within, and rushed around the house. We heard the report almost instantly, there was a dead silence of a single moment, and then a rush of hoofs and shouts of laughter that made the hills ring again. When he came in he told us that he had fired plump in the face of the intruder, who gazed at him with an astonished countenance, and then ran with his tail stretched horizontally after him like a rod of iron. The bower was afterward suffered to end its days peacefully.

But to return to our room. Its form was quite irregular, being fifteen feet in length on one side, and about ten feet on the other. The width, at one end, was ten feet, at the other fourteen, and the roof sloped down at the narrow end to the height of about five feet from the floor. It would astonish housekeepers at home to know that in this space we kept and used every day, after the first few weeks, two bedsteads of ordinary size, a sofa, a large dressing-table, a breakfast-table, six or eight chairs, a tolerably commodious closet, generally from sixty to eighty volumes on shelves about the walls, and four or five large trunks. In the space left after these were stowed, we received visitors, took our meals, made our butter, nursed our little invalid boy, and did the other household offices of the family.

The occasions of our appearing in full dress were fortunately rare; for when they came they stirred the entire ranch as only a wedding or some great festival-occasion could agitate a house at home. And then the weary rectifying and repacking when the exigency was over, made it seem very like 2d day of May among the New-Yorkers. A dress had, perhaps, to be replaced in a cavity somewhere in the bowels of a box of china; a shawl restored to some trunk that was beneath three or four others, and shoes, gloves, hats, veils, etc., to go in as many different places. I have one hint to offer, growing out of this experience, which we were slower to profit by than it now seems to me possible we could have been. It is conveyed in a word : Never remove a thing from a place where you have been accustomed to see it, in hope to get it into a more convenient one. I observed that whenever this was the case, I had a longer search than otherwise ; because, first of all, I searched the old place, and not finding it there, was never able to remember more than that I had removed it, and the consequence was that I had to hunt indiscriminately till. I found or gave it up.

CHAPTER VI.

WE had been but little more than a month
settled before it became necessary for me to go
to San Francisco, on which journey Mr. Anderson very obligingly undertook to be my escort.
Miss S. was to remain in charge of affairs at
home, and especially to take care of Eddie, the
great object of anxiety to us all, as his health
seemed to have failed since we had been at
Santa Cruz. The journey was to be made on
horseback, and the road for the first day lies
across the range of mountains that skirts the
coast. We set out with formidable preparations of lunch, fire-arms, etc., Mr. A. carrying
two revolvers, and each of our horses having a
satchel of provisions in addition to those of
clothing. A habit-skirt, which I was assured I
could not wear through the mountains, was
packed conveniently, that it might be put on

when we reached the inhabited regions on the other side. The road across these mountains is stern and solitary in the extreme. Portions of them are heavily wooded with the enormous red wood which abounds here. One tree especially is pointed out by the cicerone, which is said to be 403 feet high. The valleys and many of the gentle slopes are fertile, and produce the wild oat and some varieties of clover in abundance, but immediately succeeding them we get precipitous cliffs of shale, in which the mule-path is so deep that rider and horse are swallowed up, and so narrow that there is only room to ride through without brushing the sides of the chasm. On either hand you have heather wastes intermingled with flowering shrubs, many of which, in their seasons, are very beautiful. At this time all the more productive regions were sparkling with the flowers common to the country, chief among them the eshcholtzia, purple and blue lupin, columbine, white and variegated convolvuli, fleur de lis, white lily, and innumerable smaller flowers of exquisite beauty, with whose names, being no botanist, I am unacquainted.

Something more than midway across, after all sorts of scramblings up and down rocky stairs, and through brush that has nearly torn your hat from your head, and certainly your spectacles from your face, you are quite surprised to find your horse treading a wagon-track, and riding further on, you find in a large valley shut in by high hills, partly wooded and partly covered with oats and grass, a house and saw-mill. The proprietor of this valuable property is an emigrant from Ohio, who brought his family across the plains three or four years ago. He started with a company for Oregon, and says that when he reached the point where the California trail diverged, he let his oxen choose which they would take. They turned southward, and the consequence is that he is now the owner of one of the finest timber ranches in the country, whose wealth his children's children cannot exhaust. So inadequate and fantastical are sometimes the influences that produce to us the most grave results.

From the first summit eastward in this range, you get a magnificent view of the coast-table, the bay of Monterey, and the ocean; from the last you behold a portion of the bay of San Francisco, and the great valley of the Puebla de San José, lying spread as it were at your very feet—one of the most beautiful views conceivable. And as the eye dwells upon the fertile plains, in some parts thickly dotted with the ancient and picturesque live-oak, its branches laden with gray, trailing mosses, in others sparsely set with the same, and still others open and smooth as a shaven lawn, one readily imagines that the time is not long distant when from this mountain-top the famous pine-orchard view shall be rivaled. Cover the bay with sails and steamers, variegate the uniform green of the fertile plain with grain-fields, orchards, gardens, farm-yards, and houses; dot the sunny slopes with vineyards, and let the church-spires be seen pointing heavenward from among occasional groups of dwellings, and I know not what would be wanting to complete the picture, and make it one on which the heart and eye could dwell with equal delight. The valley itself, when you descend into it, though very pleasing by its smooth and open surface, is less beautiful to my taste than our own little rougher and brisker Santa Cruz. Advance a few miles from the foot of the mountain, and you have a monotonous level that lacks extent to give it grandeur—variety of any sort to give it everyday interest.

From the Puebla to San Francisco, a distance of sixty miles, almost the entire road is over a surface so level that you see the broad bay, that puts up between you and El Contra Costa, only as a belt of water. An occasional sail seems to be gliding along in the grass over the top of which you look. Yet a ride through the valley is one of the most charming in the country, so fertile is it—so adorned with the orchard-like trees that take on new forms in their groupings from every point of view by which you approach or recede from them. It only begins to be disagreeable when you reach the hills some ten or twelve miles from San Francisco, and grows constantly more so till you reach the same point on your return. Here the San Francisco winds meet you face to face, and search you like an officer of the customs. They grow more unpleasant till you enter the city, by which time you are thoroughly chilled and dampened by the humidity with which they have been charged. Your eyes, ears, nostrils, and mouth are filled with the sand they have hurled at you, and you just begin to remember that out of Santa Cruz one must expect to encounter many disagreeable things that one has entirely forgotten the existence of in that delightful spot.

San Francisco, I believe, has the most disagreeable climate and locality of any city on the globe. If the winter be not unusually wet, there is some delightful weather to be enjoyed. If it be, you are flooded, and the rainy season closes to give place to what is miscalled summer—a season so cold that you require more clothing than you did in January; so damp with fogs and mists, that you are penetrated to the very marrow; so windy, that if you are abroad in the afternoon it is a continual struggle. Your eyes are blinded, your teeth set on edge, and your whole person made so uncomfortable by the sand that has insinuated itself through your clothing, that you could not conceive it possible to feel a sensation of comfort short of a warm bath and shower by way of preliminaries. These, as water is very scarce (and, for the most part, very bad), it is, as yet, impossible to have in dwelling-houses, consequently, you give yourself up to a state of physical wretchedness, your self-respect declines, and you go on from day to day, hoping more and more faintly, on each succeeding one, that your moral nature may withstand these trials of the material, but feeling, if you are possessed of ordinary sensibilities, lively apprehensions that your friends will have cause to deplore the issue. Something like this has, at least, been my state when I have been compelled to sojourn for a season in that wretched place, and I believe it does not differ greatly from that of a majority of persons with whom I have compared notes. What sort of end the unfortunates, who spend their lives there, can expect under such circumstances, one does not easily foresee.

I must not omit to state, however, that the horrors of the visit I refer to were sensibly alleviated, in being shared by a most agreeable and gentlemanly fellow-traveler, who joined us on the road some forty miles above the city.

He was a member of the first Legislature from
Sacramento City, originally from Baltimore, and
almost the first man of real cultivation and intelligence that I had conversed with in the
country. We had much pleasant discourse on
various topics, speculative and practical, grave
and gay, absurd and rational, during which I
related to him an original anecdote which had
amused us, at the time of its occurrence, and
which he seemed to enjoy as much as I had :
One of our fellow-passengers, an Irishman,
had stepped into the Methodist church one Sunday, whilst we were yet in San Francisco,
where the members were holding some meeting,
in which all took part, relating their various
experiences, and the causes they had to be
thankful to Him who had brought them safely through all. It struck Paddy that the chief
thing which had been done for all these
brethren, was bringing them safely around
Cape Horn, and as he had gone through the
like experience, he sat down with devout face
and sober manner to listen. Presently a brother,
who sat upon the same seat, and who appeared to be taking an active part in the exercises,

turned to him and asked if the Lord had done nothing for him that ought to excite his gratitude.

"Yes," said he, promptly; "sure he brought me round Cape Horn, with studding-sails all set, alow and aloft."

"Ah," said the brother, "you have, indeed, much to be thankful for."

"I don't know," was the reply, "he gave us a pretty tight switching after we got around; he didn't let us away from one place for three weeks."

A few days after I reached home, I was speaking to a friend, who lived in Sacramento, of having met this gentleman.

"Oh, yes," said he, "I have attended his meetings several times."

"Meetings! what meetings?"

"He is a Methodist, and preaches in the church there frequently!"

I did not forget the story I had told him, nor his unaffected laugh at it.

CHAPTER VII.

WE spent but a single day in San Francisco, and on that the election for county-officers was held; as stirring a one as ever, I imagine, Gotham, or any of the Atlantic cities, beheld. One of the candidates for sheriff was a professed gambler, and keeper of a hotel on the Plaza, the bar and tables of which had been kept open for three weeks previous to this election. The canvassing for his office cost him $50,000, and he failed at last to get it, by reason, not of any bad odor that attached to him as a gambler, but of the idolatrous affection in which the southern and western men held his antagonist, the famous Jack Hays, of Texas. I was obliged to pass through the most excited quarters of the city several times during the day, and my serious belief was, that any honors awarded to Mr. Jack Hays after that day would be posthumous.

No man ever received such treatment at the hands of a friendly mob—now upon their shoulders; now hoisted upon the counter of some public-house; then pulled down, to be borne off somewhere else; now compelled to stop and address a crowd at this corner, and then borne, without ceremony or tenderness, to some other spot; alternately seized by the arm, neck or leg, by men in all stages of drunkenness, and all degrees of popular frenzy—poor Jack Hays seemed to me a man much to be pitied. He triumphed, however, politically, and his constitution triumphed, also, over the violence done to it; for he survives to this day to enjoy his hard-earned honors and emoluments.

CHAPTER VIII.

WHEN I reached La Libertad, I found a sad state of things. The farmer, who had complained of a sore hand before I left home, had been laid up ever since, and it was now in a dreadful state. Poor Miss Sampson, who had been nurse and housekeeper, was very badly off also, and I, with the fatigue of the journey and the unpleasant anticipations of having to repeat it as soon as possible again, was not in a condition to undertake the cares and labors that required some energetic hand immediately. Of course our farming was suspended—another delay, that threatened to be fatal to the business of the year ; but there was no remedy, except to cure the bad hand, which, as it was partly a matter of acclimation, threatened to be very tardy, as in the event it proved.

Now we had an illustration of how life in California differed from the same phenomenon at home. There, if a man fell sick, or became in any way disabled, his place would be supplied; here it was not to be thought of, because, in the first place, men of skill and capacity were not to be had at any price; and, secondly, because the capital which, at that time, would be required to employ any man for a few months, would have been quite a fortune, and, moreover, was in the hands of a friend at San Francisco, who exercised so generous a care of my interests, that he remains to this day the depository of it to the amount of several thousands, and, in all probability, will continue so to the end of his life.

To this gentleman I am indebted for what will make his name memorable to me and my children; toils that would have taxed the strength of a man—trials and humiliations which could have been better borne by a saint; anguish of heart, and despair, which, I pray, may never fall to the lot of another. I would not be bitter, but it is not in human nature to have suffered as I have, without sometimes remembering those whose selfishness or dishonesty caused it. A man who could prove recreant to a trust held for the dead and the helpless, must have capacities in his nature that one would rather not prove. We had already begun to suspect that his motives in withholding our money were less generous than he would have had them seem. In San Francisco, I had been unable to learn anything alarming respecting his solvency, but on the road home, it came to me with such directness that I felt constrained to return at the earliest day possible, and take any steps I might yet be able to take to secure myself and my sons from loss.

I set out after being at home eight days, and was three weeks away. When I returned, I found Tom plowing, with his right hand in a sling, and Miss Sampson sick in bed. Here was a state of things! I wished, then, for the power to be man and woman both, to add to my vocations of dairymaid, housekeeper, nurse, and physician, that of plowman. But not having that power, things were carried on as well as might be, each one endeavoring to do his best. To supply the failure of our own plowman, a neighbor was engaged. But the Irish notion of this art did not correspond with the Missouri one, which, according to Tom's account, consisted in turning the two swards together, leaving just half the turf unbroken. When five acres had been gone over in this manner, for ninety dollars, it was "consithered enough jist;" what else could not be done by ourselves should remain as it was. We were now busy, indeed. What with the sick, the infirm, the planting, the fencing, and the making of implements for the farm, there was little leisure on the ranch; even little Charlie found his tasks in driving Jenny and her co-workers before the plow. Three men, and, when they could be had, more, were employed in putting the seed into the ground.

In California, the relation that elsewhere exists between employer and employed is reversed. The man who does not know but he might make a hundred dollars per day at the mines is not likely to engage with you at two or three dollars, without causing you to feel, from time to time, the favor he confers by stay-

ing. Most of the floating laborers to be
picked up at this time, were either too infirm
in health to be able to go to the mines, or too
intemperate to trust themselves there. Invalids, or drunken sailors, were the staple of the
laboring community. And, except that one experienced, sometimes, intense annoyance from
their drunkenness and their ignorance of what
they were engaged in, it was not unamusing
to watch their attempts to adapt themselves to
new occupations.

"Keep that mule in the furrow," said Tom
one day, to the man that was driving for him,
who had been some fifteen years on the northwest coast.

"D—n the mule!" exclaimed the fellow, "I
could drive a whale well enough, but a mule is
a critter I never could manage."

One of this sort of men, whom we called
George, was a very waggish fellow, though a
dreadful inebriate. He was dirty, nearly naked,
and shaking like a paralytic when he came to
us. A few days of soberness brought him
around considerably, but still his clothes were
sadly dilapidated. One afternoon he presented

himself in the field, very decently clad in a sailor's suit of blue, which was at once recognized as the property of a man who had been with us before, and left his clothing to be sent for.

" Why, George," said Tom, " where did you get that jacket and trowsers ?"

" Isn't Mrs. Farnham a lady ?" was the reply.

" Yes."

" And can I be in the employ of a lady without being decently dressed ?"

Not another word was said ; the man and his new suit "vamosed the rancho" in a day or two, and were last heard from in the Sandwich Islands. At any hour of the day these men might be seized with the appetite for drink, and leaving the plow in mid-furrow, or a basket of seed wherever it chanced to be, they were off to the Mission, perhaps for one, perhaps for four days. This was not a pleasant way of going on ; but as no other was possible, it had to be endured. Not one of the most worthless of them would take less than $2 per day, with his board, for his labor ; and if he received less than three, he felt himself quite the patron.

During my absence, the little community had been thrown into great excitement, by one of those domestic tragedies that one would never have dreamed of in so quiet and secluded a little world. Capt. Graham's wife, a young and rather pretty woman, had absconded, whilst he was from home, taking with her their two little children, and, as report said, some $25,000 in specie. Strong sides were taken by the friends of the husband and wife; prosecutions followed, and the ill-feeling at length rose to a degree that provoked young Graham—a son by a former marriage—to fire upon his stepmother's mother, and shoot one of her brothers dead. This made it necessary for the young man to absent himself, which he did. Then reports were continually afloat, that Mrs. Graham was here or there; or that payment by her husband of a thousand or two thousand dollars would restore him his children; or that his son had been arrested; or that people hunting him had got upon his track; or that his children had been heard, on the night of their mother's elopement, crying dismally, along the solitary road that passed some ranch away to the south.

One could not but feel that, hard and rough as had been the old man's experience, this was the bitterest cup of all.

At length he was himself arrested, on his return from a vain search for his lost family, on the charge of being accessory to the murder which his son had committed. The country was searched far and near for witnesses, who might have overheard conversations between the father and son respecting their affairs; and when a great deal of time had been wasted, and expense had been incurred, it proved that the magistrate had no authority to make the arrest or examination, and, afterward, it was generally conceded, with what correctness I know not, that in consequence of the American laws not taking effect for twenty days after the date on on which the Mexican laws had been abrogated, there was no legal responsibility to the Commonwealth during that period, and that the murder having been committed on one of those days, the young man was not amenable for it. Where else, but in this chaotic state, could such things be?

CHAPTER IX.

OCCASIONALLY we heard somewhat of the attempts at farming going on about us, some of which were not a little amusing. Between the native Californian, the Missourian, the Yankee, the Englishman, the Irishman, there was a sufficient variety of animals, implements, and modes, to have wrought out some valuable information ; but I do not know that the world is the wiser, or the journals the richer, for any of the experiments. We sometimes got descriptions of their progress, dissertations upon soils, plows, harrows, rollers, and modes of planting and gathering, that, attentively listened to, would have made scientific farmers of Miss Sampson, myself, and Charlie ; but our heads were so crammed with cares and plans, that I fear we were often but indifferent listeners.

One of our borrowed horses had been called for one day, by the owner, under an unpleasant impression that he had received some material injury, as he said, right over the heart. The man, who was not so sober as he might have been, came with a revolver to enforce his demand. He left both the field and the revolver after him, and sent the sheriff in his stead, who, after a short parley, also went away, taking only what he brought ; then the owner returned, departed again, and was again succeeded by the sheriff; but still the team was kept going till nightfall, when the animal was delivered to his vexed owner, who certainly was entitled to consider the treatment he had received very slender thanks for the use of his animal. I was not made acquainted with these events till they were over ; and although they give evidence of a shameless unthankfulness for substantial favors, I remember that they made but little impression on us at the time. They were so much in harmony with the general spirit of things, that we only looked on their amusing side a few moments, and presently forgot them. They represent well the harum-scarum life we

led, the disregard of opinion or feeling into
which we degenerated with such fearful rapidity, that in the moments when I realized it, I
sometimes feared we should never recover our
old standard again. Trifling as they are, they
exemplify, better than pages of essay, the California of '49 and '50. No man appeared desir-
ous of abiding by the laws, unless the law and
his pleasure were one, and the courts seemed
to be little more guided by it than individuals.
Yet that there were few serious difficulties
growing out of this disorderly state of affairs,
was, no doubt, chiefly due to the fact that the
great body of the population had an occupation
open to them which promised abundant returns
for their labor ; and there are few men, even
among the bad, who would not rather work for
a liberal reward than be criminal.

In California, crime has been in very low
ratio to population, if we take into account
the character of a large class of emigrants
from Australia, the absence of executive force
under the law, the influence of that pursuit to
which the people of the State were given up,
and the unblushing front which some of the

most debasing vices have worn among us. This condition of things, however, must constantly grow worse, as the disappointed and consequently desperate class increases in numbers, until the excessive evil work its own cure, either through the summary measures of the Lynch law or the gradual growth of organization and order in society. If these shall rise with sufficient vigor from the present chaos, the State may yet be saved those appalling features which many of the good and thoughtful among her citizens have dreaded would stain her history. For this, she must greatly depend upon the kind of emigration she receives. There is but a feeble self-regulating power in a population engaged to so great an extent in mining, and having so temporary an interest in the country they occupy, as that of California. I believe there is not, at any one time, more than half the population, inclusive of women and children, who contemplate remaining in the country, and who, consequently, act with reference to any but the most transient interest in her affairs. Half the incumbents of public stations at any one time, purpose leaving the country as soon as their term of office shall have expired; and the spirit of self-sacrifice is not so broad or generous in these persons that they will forego any personal advantage for the good of a country which they do not regard as their future home. Thus the reputation of republican office-holders has received no lustre from these shores; but especially have the legislative and judicial functions suffered irreparable and lasting disgrace from a very large majority of those who have exercised them. Facts, that would have astounded and outraged any other community, were published on credible authority in respectable journals of the State, near the close of the session of the last Legislature, touching the public conduct of some of its members, without exciting any show of indignation—without even making the day's talk which the development of villainy in high places always produces in a self-respecting community.

It is the interest of all persons who are not abandoned in character, to preserve sufficient public order to admit of their callings being peacefully and profitably pursued. Hence we have occasional exercises of Lynch law, very wholesome in their influences, but so far from reaching the root of any disorder, that they are to the social body what the excision of a portion of a gangrened limb would be to the natural one. They carry the patient over his present difficulties, but leave the evil by which he is afflicted to spread itself through his entire system. The men who unite to hang a gambler at midnight for some outrage he has committed, put a check for a time upon other persons, who but for it might disturb the peace. They accomplish their purposes, dig their gold, finish their trading, or whatever they are engaged in, and are off, perhaps, before a like necessity again occurs. It matters little to them whether those who come after them have to hang two or four instead of one. Thus it is that public opinion only conduces to the most superficial public order, which is also only desired for the most selfish purposes. There is no deep stake in social welfare, and consequently no action that reaches its springs.

Meanwhile, like other Californians, we were much more engrossed with our private interests and concerns than with any of a public character. Our crop, which was coming on remarkably well, as I thought, was attacked by hordes of grasshoppers about the middle of June, and not less than half the entire planting was destroyed in the course of sixteen or twenty days. It would be difficult to imagine anything more vexatious or trying than the watching of such a destructive process. After all the labor had been performed, all the care borne, and the prospect of a large and very valuable crop had flattered us in some degree out of our weariness, it was indeed a trial of one's equanimity, to see millions of worthless insects consuming the fine growth which had promised so much. This was a result of the late planting. Had we been able to finish a month earlier, we should have escaped with little or no harm. Some of our neighbors suffered with us; but the sort of indifference to all results of personal effort which characterizes the earlier settlers, was an effectual balm to their wounds. They smoked and drank no less, did not lessen the diameter of their vowels, or ride their horses a whit slower.

There were also other enemies to our peace and prosperity : these were the immense herds of huge cattle, which, now that the grass had lost its freshness, were intent upon the appropriation of whatever invited their appetites. The ranch was under my own personal charge for some three or four weeks of June and July, the men being absent sawing lumber for our contemplated house at Capt. Graham's mill, about six miles away.   Before they left the place, a boy, some fourteen or fifteen years of age (the son of a neighbor who had recently arrived from Illinois after a very severe journey across the plains), was engaged to ride Jenny about in pursuit of intruders, and so relieve me from any care out of doors.   The domestic economy of La Libertad, however, did not suit this young gentleman's ideas of health and comfort, his condition requiring the use of tea or coffee at breakfast, dinner, and supper ; and as we substituted milk or water at all the three meals, he departed on the second morning, leaving Jenny tied to the fence, where she remained until it appeared beyond question that her rider had deserted his post, when she was released, and Charlie and I took the field against the besiegers. How we toiled, raced, watched, and kept up an active preventive service on the outskirts, not one of which was impregnable, this narrative can never adequately convey.

The eminence on which the new house was to be placed, commanded the entire field, and there, like a great but prudent general, whose peaceful staff consisted to-day of Lamartine, with his Graziella, to-morrow of Whittier or Bryant, and again of Wordsworth, or Barrett, or Sterling, or the more practical Jerrold, I had my station, sending out, when it promised to be sufficient, the small private force which was at my disposal ; and at others, when the emergency grew pressing in several quarters, or the attack was vigorously pushed in any one, abandoning my post and mingling in the thickest of the fight. My staff, though not an active, was an invaluable one to me. The peacefulness of the fisherman's island, when he gained it after a storm, enhanced what I enjoyed after a victory; the repose of favorite passages in the Excursion was rivaled by the exceeding duietness of the skies and earth on which I gazed; and the Lost Bower differed only in its minor features from that I mourned, and mourned more bitterly under the unbroken sunshine of California than I had found time to under the rugged and varying skies that had overhung my native land.

After several days of this sort of skirmishing, I willingly resigned my post, and let it not be reckoned dishonorable that my successor was an Indian. He was a gentleman in his way—after his light and knowledge. I hired him at two dollars per day. He was to catch and saddle his own horse, walk to and fro between the rancherie and the house, and for the consideration of an occasional lunch of *carne y pan*, and sundry supplies of biscuit and gingerbread or other delicacies to his *mujer*, who was *malo*, was to relax his dignity so far as to cut us a few sticks of wood occasionally of a morning. This gentleman occupied a seat distant from the ranch about seventy or eighty rods, and as his house gave him a view of most of the field, he fell, after the first day or two, into the habit of remaining at home until the cattle were fairly into the crop, when he would run lazily up, walk them out, and set out on his return. Once, and only once, was I guilty of the rashness of urging him to quicken his steps, when thirty or forty bullocks were rushing into a distant part of the field. He laid his hand upon his heart, and protested, in the blandest tones, that señora must excuse him; for running made his heart beat *mucho*. In this way he divided the care with Charlie and me for eight days; and, notwithstanding the $16, duly paid, sundry little bags of *arina*, various small stores to the wife, and the disappearance, at the same time, of an entire piece of goods belonging to Miss Sampson, he always casts upon me, when we meet, the kindly patient glance of an abused benefactor.

Beyond laying up a rail or two, it was out of the question to think of this personage repairing the fences, so I was compelled occasionally to summon one of the men from their sawing. As I was setting off on this errand one day, señor informed me that a grizzly bear

had been caught the night before at San Augustine, a rancho at the foot of the mountains, and
that I could see it by riding up there. This
was an opportunity of seeing a native of California which I could not at all consent to lose.
He informed me that thirty or forty, *hombres*
had gone up to bring him down to the Mission,
and that he was to be fought with a wild bull
next day. The reader must bear in mind that
all our communication was in Spanish on one
side and English on the other, and that whenever a discourse was to be delivered, I stationed
myself against the side of the door, Spanish
dictionary in hand, and made the best I could
of it. At the end of each sentence, the inquiry
entiende? or *sabe?* was propounded in the lowest possible tone, followed by the universal *sí*
in a corresponding tone from myself. The bear-
story was the longest and most difficult passage we had; but at length, by the aid of the
dictionary and certain signs, it was all related
and comprehended, whereupon I set off to in-
tercept or hunt the escort. Arrived within a
mile of San Augustine, I met an old hunter,
who informed me that the game was coming

on, and that I would see it better at the Mission, as it was so lashed and bound in the innumerable *riatas* wherewith they had secured it, that one could judge nothing of its size or proportions. I accordingly turned back, and when I reached the Mill, took another horse from Mr. Graham's *caballado*, and rode post with the farmer in pursuit of the bear. When we were three miles on our way, we met a man who told us that it was dead of the heat and the lassos, but that by pushing on briskly, we should be in time to see it entire. The horse I was on need have had a rider of wrought iron; but for the sake of seeing a grizzly, one would not mind a little shaking; so we put him to his speed, and about a mile from the Mission met his owner with a bottle of spirit in his hand and another in his head, who politely pronounced me a fool for my pains, and told me that the "*bar*" was already cut up and laid out on his own skin! "He was small," he said, "and of no account, anyhow." Thus ended my first bear hunt.

CHAPTER X.

THE sawing of the lumber was completed about the 1st of July; and on the evening of the 4th, after joining in the first celebration of that day ever had in Santa Cruz, I had the lines stretched on the ground, marking out the foundation and plan of the house. It was to be thirty-seven feet front by twenty-seven feet deep, with fifteen foot-posts, and a wing thirteen by twenty-one feet, with nine foot-posts at the east end. A piazza six feet deep was to cross the entire front, including the wing, and project, with a balustrade, from the second story of the main building. It seemed to me a great step taken, actually to see my future house defined on the very ground it was to cover. It was more real than any plan on paper could have been. Here I stood in the parlor, there was the dining-room, yonder

the bath-room, here a sleeping-chamber, and, in
the pleasantest yet most secluded corner, removed from all noise and bustle, my library.
Already, in imagination, I saw its walls lined
with the contents of my well-stored boxes, and
felt the quiet, happy days stealing by, which
should be to me days of delightful reunion with
those who, alike in life and in death, were my
companions and consolers. I felt the friendly
strength and hope they would impart already
flowing over my soul, forgetful, in that first dream,
of the days and weeks of toil that must be performed before I could invite my guests or sit down
with them ; for—let not ladies lift their hands in
horror—I designed supplying the place of journeyman carpenter with my own hands. In due
time the lumber began to arrive, and we welcomed each huge wagon with its contents as
elsewhere we would the most beloved and honored guests.

On one occasion a difficulty arose between
one of the drivers and Tom, and in the set-to
which was to decide their respective pretens-
sions, the American, who was a Kentuckian,
had nearly destroyed an eye for his antagonist

—the "gouging" faculty being in a state of active development in that gentleman. His employer and patron looked coolly on while the engagement was progressing, and after it was over said a few words, not of consolation to the half-blind man, who was not certain, at the moment he heard them, whether his eye was in its place or in his enemy's hand. At the succeeding election this gentleman lost the office of county judge, to which he aspired, by one vote, which the enraged Irishman had the satisfaction of feeling he had cast against him. He is now planing and sawing boards, instead of enjoying the honors and emoluments of that position which has fallen into far worse hands. Thus is the balance of life often adjusted in these new regions.

In due time, with the labor of three Sonorians, the site of the building was leveled, the sills cut, hewn, and drawn, and the work pretty fairly under way. Miss Sampson and I had rejoicings every evening over the progress of the day, and made innumerable anticipatory arrangements of rooms, furniture, etc., and of visits to be received in that house from distant lands, and the friends of long ago, which, alas! are not yet realized, and much I fear me never will be. My first participation in the labor of its erection was the tenanting of the joists and studding for the lower story, a work in which I succeeded so well, that during its progress I laughed, whenever I paused for a few moments to rest, at the idea of promising to pay a man $14 or $16 per day for doing what I found my own hands so dexterous in. I often found it necessary to go in and refresh myself with a morsel of bread and a cup of milk, or a glass of the delicious water that ran down among the shady willows, and on these occasions the affairs of the house were discussed, the dinner, the supper, the breakfast, and Charlie's progress at his studies reported (for the invaluable Miss Sampson united to her functions of housekeeper and cook that of teacher also), and, above all, full returns furnished of the fleas that had been captured since our last interview. These bulletins were often such as would surprise ladies who never resided in a country infested with these troublesome insects, such as the following, for instance:

" How many fleas do you think I have killed, dear, since you went out ?"

" Twenty."

" Twenty ! Fifty-seven, besides twenty-five in Charlie's bed."

Next time the report would, perhaps, be thirty, fifteen, or forty. The last method of killing I found the safest and most expeditious. We provided a basin of scalding water, and the story was soon told. If homœopathic pharmacy had included the use of any property of this insect, we could have furnished the North American Continent with mother tincture of it.

I ought not to omit mentioning that I commenced my new business in the ordinary long dress, but its extreme inconvenience in displacing all the smaller tools, effacing lines, and flying in the teeth of the saw, induced me, after the second day, to try the suit I had worn at home in gymnastic exercises. It is the same that has since become famous as the Bloomer, though then the name had not been heard of. When I had once put it on, I could never get back into skirts during working hours. I usually gave myself half an hour before sunset to bathe and dress, and was generally so weary, that when supper was over I could not too soon get to rest. No night was ever too long, and no bed too hard for me to sleep soundly on, till it was time to rise to the toils of the succeeding day. Eddie's health had improved materially before this time. He spent most of his days, when the heat was not too great, at the new house, watching its progress, wondering at my achievements, and gathering incidents to report to Miss Sampson and Charlie, in the brief visits he occasionally paid to the shanty. It was my greatest pleasure to see him pleased and interested, and to kindle his hopes of happy days in the new house. The agonies he had first suffered on our arrival were, I hoped, forever over; and we all loved him so much, that no pleasanter idea could be associated with home than that of his happiness in it.

CHAPTER XI.

IT was very vexatious, that when we had the frame partly erected, there came another call to San Francisco, which I felt constrained to heed, notwithstanding the intense annoyance of leaving home under such circumstances, and the fear I felt, amounting almost to certainty, that the wearisome journey would prove, as its predecessors had, a fruitless one. It certainly was far less agreeable, in all outward respects, than the previous ones had been, the country having now lost the fresh and beautiful appearance it had when I had last passed through it; and the roads being covered with dust, beaten to such a fineness as one sees no where but in a country that has long droughts. My annoyance was greatly increased at this time by my having to take Tom away from the farm and house, no other escort being obtainable.

From the Pueblo, we had a slight detour to make to the mission of San José, twelve miles distant, on the east side of the bay. The previous day's journey over the mountains had so disordered Sheik that I found him traveling very badly—a circumstance to which I was less indifferent than I should have been if I also had not participated in its fatigue. After some four or five miles, it was proposed that we should exchange horses, as Bill was going with his usual ease and freedom. If Bill has not been formerly introduced, I beg to state that he was a small roan horse, with one crop ear, who had plowed some two months of the season, been " to the fore" in nearly all excursions, and, on the day before this memorable one, had borne, great part of the way over the mountains, a burden of nearly three hundred pounds. Bill was made much upon the model of a large Canadian pony, and having, as I before said, an ear cropped, had a sort of ruffianly look and bearing, that forbade his aspiring to be a lady's horse, unless under the most absolute necessity. I was, however, very willing to mount him on this occasion, having before proved him both easy and free. The exchange conduced greatly to my comfort, and we were within about a mile of the Mission at noon. Here a decent respect for appearances demanded that my saddle should be replaced upon Sheik, and, accordingly, we halted, that the exchange might be made. Bridles and saddles were to be transferred, and Bill was left ungirthed while I was getting remounted. His bridle lay upon the ground, and the riata was wound about his neck.

"I am afraid," said I to Tom, as he stepped across the road, "that Bill will give you trouble if you let him go away from you."

"Oh no," he replied, "he is going to nip at that green spot, jist."

But when I was in the saddle, and the man, with bridle in hand, approached him, Bill stepped indifferently forward, as if being caught or not were the same thing to him, only he would put it off a little. We had a steep hill to ascend, with the bank rising abruptly at the side of the road. I went moderately forward, keeping him between me and it, looking as unsuspicious as possible. I already begun to be oppressed with sore doubts that my entrée would be a less impressive one than we intended it should be.

"Cap him, madam, where he is," said Tom, in a half suppressed voice, afraid to speak louder lest he should show a clean pair of heels at once.

Now I knew, although the reader probably does not, what to cap him meant, and accordingly pulled Sheik's head in, to cut off his passage between us and the bank. This brought him to a decision at once; he fairly took the road, and left his rider to make his way as best he could. The mid-day sun was very warm, and only an Indian, or some poor unfortunate miner, could take foot-exercise on the road without disgrace ; but here was my escort on foot, and I a little in advance, creeping along, not to lose any possible chance that might offer of taking the graceless runaway, who jogged on impudently before, cropping the dried grass, and when I advanced too near, starting into a trot, at the imminent peril of leaving saddle, as well as rider, behind him. Tom was still below when we had gained the height, and I made a sign to a Spaniard, who was riding toward us, to throw his lasso, which was gathered in his hand, upon the offender's neck. He made one or two motions, that were just sufficient to set him off on a gallop, whereby he relieved himself of the saddle, and us of any further effort to capture him.

Hope now was quite gone. There was no chance of a display of horsemanship, whatever else might be before me, and I rode along, sympathizing, as I never before did, with Mrs. Raddle, in her unfortunate dash up to the wrong door, and with the less celebrated victims of numerous like calamities. With the additional burden of the saddle, Tom was left quite behind, so that when I entered the Mission, he was not to be seen. I had been referred to a gentleman, whose house I was to inquire for, and seeing a man, with a very large gold chain, sitting under the porch of one of the old adobe buildings, I rode near and accosted him. He was taking his siesta, however, from which it seemed not easy to rouse him; for the disquiet of the place would have banished light sleep But his was too sound to be broken by my speaking within three yards of him, or by the incessant jabber of half-a-dozen Indians over a carcass of beef which they were dressing at not more than twice that distance from his chair, or of a deal of noise that issued from a party of three or four who were engaged with a living animal a little further on. I was about turning to seek some more wakeful person, who might give me the information I sought, when a horrid noise caused me to raise my eyes, and the tide of blood pouring from the throat of the struggling brute in the street, made the earth waver, and the sunshine turn to darkness before me. I had never witnessed the shocking spectacle before, and coming suddenly upon me, weary and heated as I was, it was near proving an overmatch for my firmness. I resolutely held myself up, however, burying my face, to shut it out, as effectually as possible, and mentally resolving that I could be pleased with nothing in the place where people permitted such horrors to be enacted in the public streets.

When the sound died away, and I raised my head, I observed that the attention of a young

American, who was sitting on a fine gray horse, was attracted to myself and Bill, who had followed me close into the street, and was now standing beside me. Suspecting something wrong, he began to gather his lasso, and make ready for an attack. I was about to put myself in the way of the vagrant, when the horseman called to me to let him pass, for he should be better able to throw the lasso if he were running. Accordingly they started by the road we came in on, where Tom soon met and turned them back. Bill dashed past me, and through the lasso, which was thrown on him a few yards before us, and, turning a corner, was fairly off to the plain. This performance had awakened the sleeper, who now politely escorted me to the house I inquired for. Here I was ushered into a room wherein the evidences of female taste and refinement soon encouraged me to forget the shock I had experienced without. A tumbler of roses, an India work-basket, with a bit of muslin, and a gold thimble lying beside it, gave assurance of the presence of a home deity not often found in California, and which I certainly had had no idea of meeting in this place. Scattered books, and those of the best, too, raised my hopes still higher, when the lady entered, and was introduced as Mrs. B———, the wife of my gentlemanly entertainer, just arrived but a few days before from home. Indeed, I was delightfully surprised to find in this secluded place so sweet a woman—so perfect a lady. Before we were half an hour deep in talk, news was brought us that Bill gave his pursuer a chase of three miles, and at last was driven into a corral before he could be captured, and that the fine American horse had come in bearing on his bloody sides marks of having been hardly pushed to overtake the fugitive. The pleasure we should have felt in his newly-discovered fleetness, was materially lessened by the consciousness that a constitutional roguery was at the bottom of it.

The Mission of St. Joseph, San José, or, as it is irreverently called by the Yankees, St. Jose's, is a beautiful spot, at the foot of the hills that skirt the bay of San Francisco on the east. No mission in this portion of California is better preserved, though most of the buildings

here are more or less dilapidated.   Its orchards
and vineyards, however, are flourishing, and
here, for the first time in California, I saw
abundance of the fruits that were cultivated
by the old padres—pears, apricots, olives, pome-
granates, figs, grapes, and apples—the last most
inferior of all.   I had seen nothing in the country more refreshing and beautiful than the
stately orchards, with their stores of fruit.   We
spent the night here, apparently much to the
satisfaction of the fleas, and the next morning
returned to the Pueblo, without losing Bill,
who conducted himself with becoming quietness during the remainder of the ride to San
Francisco.   Here, however, he escaped, and set
out for home one evening, about eight o'clock;
and, as Sheik was tied to the other end of his
riata, he conducted him quietly out about two
miles on the road homeward, where, after a long
search, and a panic of anxiety on my part,
they were found jogging on, Bill leading, with
the entire length of their rope stretched between them.

CHAPTER XII.

My present journey was not altogether so fruitless as the previous ones had been, and so, after the end of a week, I set out homeward, with better courage than I had before felt on leaving this detestable place. A light wagon having been procured, to give Miss Sampson and Eddie, neither of whom could ride on horse-back, an occasional airing, we started, with Bill harnessed, for the first time alone, in it. For the edification of ladies who cannot travel without the complement of trunks, bonnet-cases, etc., I ought to have mentioned that these horseback journeys precluded any re-spectful transportation of millinery or mus-lins; and, consequently, I was reduced to the necessity, on my arrival at each stopping-place, of walking out in a riding-hat, or bor-rowing a bonnet—a considerable difficulty,

which I did not find it easy to get over, the size
of heads varying so greatly. Once, indeed, I
had a bonnet carried at the sash of my escort,
but a long and fast ride proving very unfriendly to ribbons and flowers, I did not repeat the
experiment. On the pr esent occasion, having
my usual equipage only, I preferred mounting
Sheik, to ride out of the city ; also, if the truth
must be told, I was quite willing that Bill
should perform his first antics, if there were to
be any, without my participation.

The three miles of sand to the Mission were
passed over in such a manner that he was white
with foam before he had half done them, and
seemed to me to be shrinking away to nothing.
The wheels ran from four to eight inches deep
in the sand, and at every bank or bush he made
a desperate effort to sheer up and brush off the
frightful incumbrance that followed him. His
eyes glared, his nostrils quivered, and flanks
trembled, under the fright and excitement, as
if a grizzly were at his heels, instead of a
little peaceful four-wheeled vehicle ; but Bill
was a Californian, and had never seen the one,
while he might often have encountered the

other. Ten miles out, I took a seat in the wagon, and Sheik was made fast behind. We had left San Francisco at two o'clock, and at five o'clock were twenty miles out, with Bill ready to lie down in the harness.

" What can we do ?" I exclaimed, in despair, for Sheik had never had a strap or band over him, and, though a gentlemanly, noble fellow, it seemed to me the wildest idea to think of harnessing him for the very first time then and there. Nevertheless, Tom proceeded to do it. I alighted, and the harness having been taken from Bill, led him away to the side of the road to await the result. He appeared to me to have fallen off from a very passable condition to a mere skeleton in those three hours. I expected to see him lie down before we should get another start, not to rise again for the night, if ever. But while I was laying these comforting probabilities to heart, and dreading every moment to hear the crash of the wagon at Sheik's heels, the change was going on very quietly with him. When he was harnessed and fastened into the traces, he was first led a few steps, then the man taking his seat, started with the reins in hand.   To my infinite relief, he at once moved off, making only one or two trials to twist himself out of the shafts.   They now came up, and I took my seat, Bill having first been made fast to the back of the wagon. Away we went over the smooth, hard road, and, but for a certain doubtful aspect of Sheik's generous face and long, slender ears, one would not have known but he had been driven through from the States.   Poor Bill was now the only unfortunate one of the whole party.   To add to his afflictions, he had fallen lame of a sore foot, and had altogether so miserable an appearance I dared not look back at him.   We pushed briskly on, however, paying little heed to him, and at nine o'clock had left forty-five miles between us and San Francisco. I thought it a miracle, considering the uneducated condition of our horses, but was too glad to get to rest to revolve it much in my mind after getting to my room.

There were still ninety miles between us and home by the wagon-road, and it certainly was a triumph to have ascertained that both horses would travel in the wagon if necessary.

Next night we reached Murphy's ranch, eighteen miles from San Juan, where we were kindly entertained, and where I was delighted with the good sense, good heart, and good looks of the proprietor's daughter.

Our weary horses did not get so well over the ground to-day. We had only reached the beautiful valley of San Juan at 3 P. M. Here I would have stopped till next morning, but my impatience to reach home forbade the idea, and, after visiting the orchard, where I had a lively discourse with a Spanish boy, the only *old* Spanish youth I have ever seen, we resumed our journey. An American had told us that we could find comfortable quarters at Castro's rancho, about eighteen miles further on, and thither we bent our way. It was nightfall before we reached the neighborhood he had indicated, and after dragging wearily on till it seemed as if neither of the animals could possibly get over another mile, we descried a light which appeared to be twice that distance away and quite off the road. There was no choice but to steer for it, and stop at it, too, whether it was *the* rancho or not. When we reached it,

which we succeeded in doing partly by following, in their zigzag course over the plain, the
dim ghosts of three horsemen who were bound
thither, also, we learned that Castro's ranche
was still two miles away, but that we could
stay there for the night.

On the ground, under the corridor that ran
along the old adobe building, two immense
fires were blazing, around which were gathered
twenty or thirty men and women, and several
mules and horses. Being thoroughly chilled,
and having no desire for the contiguity of these
gentry, biped or quadruped, I declined the invitation to a seat among them, and passed on,
hoping to find a fire in the house. But there
was only that in the kitchen, at which I sat
down when a chair was brought me.

The Yankee housewife thinks, now, I ought
to have been very comfortable ; for the kitchen,
in her land, is a bright, cheerful place to enter
from the chilliness of a dark night. But this
was not a Yankee kitchen. The apartment
might have been eighteen by twenty-four feet,
lighted only by a door in day time, and, at this
hour, by the fitful blaze of the wood-fires, built

upon a sort of brick range that ran across the end of the room. In the corner, at one end of this range, a dirty Indian girl was making *tortillas*—the bread of the country. She was kneading a large lump of dough upon a stone bench, slightly hollowed toward the centre, beside which stood a very ill-favored basin of water, into which she occasionally thrust her hands. Beside her, upon two adobe jambs, which rose some fourteen or eighteen inches above the level of the range, lay a huge circular plate of iron—a rude griddle. Some time after I entered, during which the kneading was vigorously carried on, some lighted sticks were placed under the griddle, and the tortillas began to take shape for baking. They were flattened dexterously in the hand to an extreme thinness, and thrown upon the iron, where two or three minutes sufficed to bake them.

At the other end of the range, a buxom, merry-faced girl was superintending a pot of *caldo*, and another of *frijoles*, with an apron before her so excessively dirty, that I involuntarily reached my hand out to stay it when it fell too near the cooking. Five or six other young women were sitting or standing about, and several more were passing in and out to other parts of the *casa*. A merrier set could nowhere be found; they chatted to me in Spanish, and laughed if I failed to understand them. They laughed when they could not understand my English. They examined my riding-hat, habit, whip, rings, watch, pin—every thing, in short, their eyes could see, and put on whatever they could detach from my person, trying its effect with a critical and generally an approving eye. There was such simplicity and hearty good-nature in all these tricks, that I could not feel annoyed, although I was both very tired and very hungry, and could think of nothing so comfortable as getting a good supper and lying down.

After what seemed an interminable delay, I was called to supper in a long, spacious room or hall, at the upper end of which stood two beds. The long table occupied one entire side near the wall; but the cloth, to my surprise, was laid on only a small portion of it, with plates for but half a dozen persons. The two proprietors were seated at it, and a younger man, also, but no female. When we were seated, the senior señor threw each a tortilla from a stack that was piled on the cloth near his plate, and, helping himself, signed to us to do likewise. The supper was delicious. The mercy of Providence, in the shape of a fasting stomach, enabled me to forget the filthy apron, and the long hair and suspicious-looking arms of the Indian girl, and I made ample amends for the fast that I had observed since morning, relieved only by a few half-ripe pears, and one or two fugitive biscuit, that had eluded my previous searches in the satchel.

Of course there could be little conversation at supper, but I conveyed, in answer to their inquiries, very explicit information that Tom was not my husband; that I lived at Santa Cruz, and was on my way thither from San Francisco; and, in return, was informed that they were *hermanos* (brothers), not *marit*, and that the young people were their nephews, nieces, and dependents of all sorts.

The supper was a far more palatable one than I believed it could be. The *caldo* was deliciously flavored; the tortillas very sweet and crisp; and everybody knows the *frijole* so well, that praise of it would be quite superfluous. When we had supped, I retired again to the kitchen, and here I found all the young people taking 'their evening meal, quite informally, seated upon the earthen floor about the room. Two or three large toilet basins, placed in various parts, contained the food, from which each supplied his or her plate at will; and my cook, with the formidable apron, washing the dishes as they were handed to her; an operation which she performed in a very summary manner, by dashing a handful or two of water over the plate, tilted on the edge of the kettle, and, shocking to tell, wiping them on the very apron! Until that moment I was determined on waiting breakfast next morning. But now the neat table-service, and wholesome cleanliness of La Libertad, rose so palpably before me, that on retiring to my room I directed Tom to have the horses ready and call me very early in the morning.

" I will go home to breakfast," I said, " it is but sixteen miles."

The sleeping-apartment was in the second

story, to which I mounted by a sort of ladder,
constructed by tying bits of wood, upon two
poles, with thongs of green hide, and placed
against the sill of the door. The chamber was
the entire size of the building, and was used as
clothes, store-room, and granary. Two beds
occupied the nearer end; wheat and barley the
remote one, and sides of leather, old barrels,
boxes, broken chairs, etc., the intermediate
space. Zarapas of all styles were pendant from
the roof, rafters, and walls. I objected to the
door, as lacking all means of fastening, but my
solicitude was promptly removed by the intelligence that six or eight persons were to share
the apartment with me. I certainly did wish for
a curtain of some sort; but my extreme weariness
suggested that the curtain of irrsistible sleep
would divide me from all the world in a very few
moments. The bed was not of the freshest,
though everything upon it was snowy white;
but my sleep was unbroken till the words, " the
horses are ready, ma'am," sounded loudly in my
ears next morning. With infinite difficulty, a
pint bowl of water was obtained for my ablutions,
and I soon descended equipped for departure.

The good-natured girls gathered about me to say adios; one tried on my riding-habit, and another solicited me to leave a ring with her; but these little ceremonies were well got through with by the time the bill was paid and all was ready. As I crossed the yard, the Indian girl was washing one of the iron pots with a high colored handkerchief she had worn on her head the previous evening; perhaps the same process served to cleanse both. I offered a silent thanksgiving that home was so near, and passed on.

This, then, was a Spanish rancho and the manner of life in it. These people were the owners of a great estate here, and another up the coast, on which were hundreds, if not thousands, of horned cattle and horses. Not a drop of milk nor an ounce of butter could be had in their house. Their chief articles of food are beef and beans.

Of the wheat grown on their lands they make a kind of coarse, flour which they use in porridge. The tortilla can only be made of fine flour, which they have always imported, though occupying one of the finest wheat countries in the world. The simplicity of their external lives is quite in harmony with that of their natures. No ungratified want or cankering ambition, shorn of the power to achieve, consumes them, and though the same lack of material refinement in almost any other people would argue a positive coarseness which could not fail to distress a stranger, their whole manner, though familiar to a degree, is so evincive of kindness and respect, that there is nothing left to dread or doubt as to their motives. They are a simple-hearted people, whose contentment flowed out in acts of continual hospitality and kindness to all who came to them before their peaceful dream of life was broken in upon by the frightful selfishness of the late emigration. It is difficult for us to imagine contentment in the idle, aimless life of these rancheros, or cheerfulness in the dark, dirty, naked houses they inhabit ; but they have sufficed for them, and it must be confessed, that their domestic condition does not, in most parts of the country, promise any very rapid improvement from the example of their new neighbors.

CHAPTER XIII.

WHEN I reached home I found that sad rava-
ges had been made by the cattle in the potato-
field, and our neighbors, who had kindly undertaken to look after it, had become quite dis-
heartened in their task. Poor Miss Sampson
and Charlie had watched and chased to the best
of their small ability in this way, but their success had been only partial, and of the wreck
left by the grasshoppers, a second had now been
made almost as discouraging. A cherished asparagus bed, which had been my pride since the
plants first showed their heads above the ground,
all my melon vines, all the tomatoes, all the
squashes, all the beets, had disappeared, and I
was no better reconciled to the loss of them by
recollecting as I did, when walking over the
ruins, that the same ground had been four times
planted that season, to be finally stripped of
the only crop that had ever promised to reward

my labor. The timbers of the house were standing as we left them, the only substantial satisfaction I found in reviewing the entire place.
Work upon it was resumed with the liveliest
interest, and went on far more successfully
than I at first believed would be possible. By
the time I had been home a week, I found myself so much at home in my working costume
that I was no longer watching the various approaches to the house, lest I should be caught
in it. If I saw a man coming, I did not stroll
away to the shanty, to keep out of sight till he
was gone, or to change my dress. This was a
great victory.

The approach of the rainy season was our
great stimulus—our terror, indeed—for when
that set in, the shanty would be afloat. So we
worked from before the sun rose till after he
was set, almost every day, having no holidays
nor pleasures, except an occasional visit to the
pear-orchard—the courtesy of whose liberal proprietor, if I were a poet, I would celebrate in
pomological verse—and a half day on the anni-
versary of the founding of the Mission, when
we went down with the boys to witness the

ceremonies, and customary recreations of a bear and bull-fight. What particularly amused Charlie and myself in the festivities of this day, was the sight of the church choir turned out, after the rites were over, into a street band. Their instruments consisted of a bass and kettle drum, two violins, a triangle and a banjo. The performers, all Indians, appeared to have suffered in some recent encounter; for every head was more or less damaged, the eyes, foreheads, noses, and cheeks, being badly battered, and patched; doubtless a reverent, but certainly not a very reverend choir! We staid to see the combatants pitted and almost refuse to fight, and having examined the bear at our leisure returned to resume our labors.

CHAPTER XIV.

I HAD been some two months on the farm before I attended religious services. There was no Protestant church organized till late in the summer, but the numerous Methodist brethren met at the school-room, and heard preaching every Sabbath from some of the many *locales*, of whom, as a Missourian told us one day, there was " a right smart sprinkle about *hyur*. One Sabbath morning, which seemed, if possible, calmer and brighter than the bright summer mornings of this Sabbath clime, I set out with Charlie to find the meeting. He had explored the highways and byways of the Mission before, and so was prepared to conduct me at once to the place, which we found to be a small room, sufficient to receive, perhaps, thirty persons, with seats arranged upon three sides of it. When we entered, the Sabbath-school was just over, and some fifteen or twenty misses, who had attended it, were awaiting the commencement of the services, to which but few adults were yet gathered. There were some beautiful faces among them, and nearly all were characterized by that freedom, strength, and self-reliance that belong only to the children of the Western States, and to the ruder conditions of society in which they are born and reared. Their styles of dress were as various as their persons, agreeing in only one feature, that of skirts falling to the feet. Hideous bonnets, of all fashions, which their grandmothers might have worn, deformed their heads and concealed their fine faces; gowns pinned at the waist in front; monstrous shoes, or may be none at all, showed the want of supplies in the country, if it also argued some lack of taste in its inhabitants. The materials were very inadequate to the uses of civilization; the power of compelling them to serve it even more so, and these children, in their ancient and incongruous dresses, were a curious spectacle to me. But the law of compensation did not fail them, for I was equally an object of interest to them;

and the undisguised manner in which they gratified their curiosity, was a triumph of nature more destructive of my equanimity in that small room, than it would have been if shown upon a larger stage. Some of the seats afforded a better view than others, and these were accordingly taken in turn. Meanwhile, the congregation was gathering, and when some twenty-five or thirty persons had come together, and one or two hymns had been voluntarily sung, a brother offered prayer, in which, among other requests, he desired the Lord, if any one had come there to be seen, to put better thoughts into their hearts! What a reproof of meek brown organdy dress and straw cottage! When the prayer was closed, he announced his text in the words, "Now abideth faith, hope, charity," etc. He said that no doubt the text was familiar to most of his hearers; that they had often heard it preached from —so often, that may be they would think there couldn't be any new sermon made on it. He knew it was true; it had been preached on a great many times, but for all that he considered it one of the texes that would bear frequent examination. His sermon, though pronounced in the language of an illiterate man, did not lack good common-sense or moral tone. " Is our souls sot heavenward ?" he exclaimed ; " if they be, we shall move on the road to it ; but some folks, talking of going to heaven and hoping to get there, is like a man at home in the old States saying he hoped to get to *Kelly-ferny*, while all the time he sot still."

This energetic and zealous denomination is here, as everywhere else, the first to take up the outposts of new society. There is already a flourishing congregation here, with a regular preacher, who has relieved the local brethren from any further exercise of the function of teacher, much, I presume, to the relief of many whose consciences overruled their tastes.

The position of an earnest religious teacher in California must be one of the most trying and difficult. Among an overwhelming majority of the population, vice carries so unblushing a front, and, with all classes, the pursuit of wealth is so absorbing, that one need have great confidence, to ask the attention of men, thus occupied, to a subject so far removed from their thoughts as religion. For, if elsewhere it is separated in common minds from life and its daily concerns, here they are so divorced, that it seems a weakness or a madness to think they could ever be united. And when wealth is gained, and somewhat of the eagerness of pursuit is abated, the abundant enjoyments furnished in the external world, the numerous gratifications of sense, and the constant incentives to a purely outward life, flowing from nature, in the genial skies and generous earth, will, I think, dispose the heart to receive most readily the faith which sits most lightly upon it. Asceticism belongs to a more rigorous clime, and less friendly aspect altogether, than this land offers. Even Puritanism, tough and tenacious though it was, would have been shorter lived had the Mayflower landed her inflexibles on this laughing coast. The rock-bound shores and inhospitable soil, the wintry skies overhanging the sterile mountains and stony vales of New England, were far more favorable to earnestness in the religious as well as the working life of man than ours will ever be. And yet one must believe that all the true ends of life will be as well and certainly served in so magnificent and generous a country as in the other. One must think that a faith less exacting and more kindly than this one of the unswerving and tenacious old fathers, honestly held and faithfully lived up to, would serve the need of man.

The repulse which religion suffers at the hand of this generation, cannot come so rudely from the next, because then it will be checked by the kindred influences of home, of greater civil and social order, and some degree of individual self-respect—influences which come but feebly to her aid in this time of struggle.

One feels here that the peril of new society is more imminent and sensible than could be dreamed of amid the quiet and order of older conditions. It is not barbarism alone that one dreads ; for barbarism, which is a negative condition, may be innocent and comparatively pure ; but here one fears a far worse condition —a condition in which all the knowledge and art of civilized life shall be made to subserve the most corrupt desires, in which wealth and power shall be the servants of dishonorable motives, of frightful lust and greed, and in which any sort of merit may be driven shrinking into a corner, ashamed almost of its own character, and trembling at the restraints itself imposes.

I am aware that there are persons in the country who see and feel nothing of this ; who are unconscious that any frightful portents darken the moral atmosphere about them ; but these are persons who, happily, or unhappily, are incapable of foreseeing results; who, like the blind and deaf man, can sit quietly down at the base of the volcano, and remain unapprehensive till the rivers of fire flow down and consume him. Such persons may make very comfortable companions for the quiet watches, but must not be trusted when the winds threaten or the skies lower.

CHAPTER XV.

One of our neighbors, whose garden I rode to see, a few weeks after it was planted, told me some time after, that he expected to realize $900 from his crop. As there was only a small cabbage-plot visible and a few potatoes, I said, " then you have another piece planted besides the one I saw?"

" No," he replied, " but there are six hundred cabbages there, and I reckon they will bring a dollar and a half apiece."

This was California farming and reckoning both! I do not know how the event corresponded with his calculation, but I know that several enterprises, of little greater magnitude, resulted in profits that would surprise our plodding neighbors at home as much as this amused me. Thus, one man leased three acres of land, and was to pay the proprietor one-fourth of the product. He planted potatoes, and in the fall paid his landlord a thousand dollars, and put three thousand into his own pocket. Another, who had planted some ten acres of his own land, sold fifteen thousand dollars' worth of produce from it.

We had no such fortune to anticipate ; but when the time for our harvest came, we set about it with the very subdued hope of having enough left us to pay for the harvesting and to plant the next year. The sacks that we spent many evenings in making, and which were to us, in-doors, one of the most tedious features of the year's labors, we did not reckon in the account. All day I was on the roof of the house shingling, and at night engaged till a late hour in this interesting manufacture, or, when it was not very pressing, in reading aloud to to those who were so engaged. Our choice of books included fiction, poetry, history, philosophy, and religion. Occasionally, we attended the day or evening worship of our Methodist neighbors, or looked in upon the Temperance meeting, where once an indirect invitation to speak so alarmed me that I did not venture back to acquaint myself personally with their proceedings, but contented myself with watching the results as they appeared in the persons of some of our neighbors and in the vicinity of the drinking-shops.

One fine morning, after a slight evening shower had added fresh stimulus to the very iron of our hammers, I received a call from a stranger, who introduced himself as Mr. C——, of a town in the southern portion of the State—an acquaintance of a much-valued friend. In a few moments we were in the midst of a discussion on Swedenborg, to whose opinions my visitor was attached—the new philosophy generally, and the absence of both the old and the new from California life. Getting interested, I laid down my hammer after a few minutes, took off my nail-pocket, and, the carpenter being absent, descended the ladder with the help of my visitor's hand. This was early in my experience as a roofer. Afterward I could go up and down alone with perfect freedom and ease. When I reached the ground, I did not apologize for my dress, because, novel as I knew it must look, I felt assured its fitness would be appreciated.

We discussed our region, which Mr. C——
justly admired, while he praised his own for
its beauty, fertility, and superior climate. We
descended to the shanty, where I saw the pre-
vailing attraction to him was our little stream
murmuring and gurgling along its cool, shady
bed. The pleased ear he lent to its song, led
me to ask if the country he had praised so
much were well watered. "No, madam," he
said; "that is our only misfortune. At this
season, all our water is carted from five miles
out of town!" It is possible, I suppose, for
one to get used to so disagreeable a fact; but,
in thinking how it could be done, I was painfully reminded of skinned eels, and I also felt
devoutly thankful that with all the confusion
and destruction we had suffered, such a bountiful external world was about us.

Only in one respect had the elements been
unkind to us. Tom, who was away to market
with a quantity of potatoes, had shipped a
variety of articles for finishing the house, as
well as some other stores: shingles, zinc for
leading the gabled windows, paints, oils, tur-
pentine, molasses, sugars, seed-wheat, lamp-

shades, stove-fixtures, brooms, dried fruits, and, most important of all, a second Susannah, an importation from Sidney. The vessel arrived, and with it a letter, advising that Susannah should receive great care, as, although she was a traveled pig, she was not yet amphibious, and the Santa Cruz surf, if she came to a full experience of it, might prove too much for her. The next day the things were to be landed, and when the young man, whom I sent down to receive them, returned late in the afternoon, he reported the zinc, paint, oil, molasses, and numerous minor articles, lost in the surf. This was certainly provoking enough, but Susannah had not started yet, and there was hope, therefore, that she might be saved when her turn came.

Next morning another boat-load was capsized. She was not in that, but was let fall from the next one, and washed ashore, where a humane carpenter opened her box and resuscitated her; a deed which I would recommend to the notice of the Humane Society, if there were one here. On my last journey to San Francisco, I had seen an animal of the same kind, for which the owner had paid $100 ; and Susannah was so much superior to that purchase, in proportion, carriage, and disposition, that when the peril of landing was over, my other vexations lost much of their edge in the exercise of so dignified a proprietorship. She lives to be the pet of the outdoor force of the rancho.

There had, however, been one loss which it was difficult to bear with any degree of equanimity—that of our zinc. We had counted the days of waiting for it, as we had laid the last shingles that could be put upon the window roofs without it ; and now it was at the bottom of the bay, and we could get none again within four or six weeks, unless some one should be dispatched expressly for it. It was proposed to cut up the tin pans, pails, etc.; and they were just about to be gathered, as an offering to the god of storms, when it luckily occurred to the carpenter that he might find some large tin canisters at the Mission. He immediately set off on the hunt, and in an hour or so was seen returning through the brown, waste-looking fields with a burden which glittered and shone encouragement to us from beneath the sun.

We had had no heavy rain as yet, but the new moon, we were assured by the old Californians, would bring it with her, if any were coming before the next quarter. There were about six thousand new-made unburned brick lying in the field below the house, and these we watched, trembled, hoped, and feared for whenever a cloud darkened the horizon. Our neighbor, Capt. Graham, who was occasionally passing to and fro in the examination of a quicksilver mine which he had discovered, or believed he had, a little way up the ravine, at length advised us on a Saturday afternoon that rain would fall that night " for sure." The potato-harvest and the shingling were at once left, and the brick taken earnestly in hand, to be put in such a shape that they might be covered as securely as possible. As the Irishman was still absent, I took my share in this lady-like occupation also, and so industrious were we, that an hour before night we had done all that the fresh and plastic condition of our material would allow. The Sonorians worked bravely on a stout cup of ginger tea and a piece of new bread.

After all the sun went down as clear as on any mid-summer eve, much more, I think, to our annoyance than if it had been attended by a train of watery clouds. We accepted the promise, however, and went to rest weary enough, but quite tranquil in mind, leaving our brick uncovered, for him to shine upon next morning, which we all agreed he certainly would do, if he expected us ever to trust him again.

About two o'clock I found myself under the patter of a gentle shower, which seemed to be feeling its unaccustomed way through the dry roof of the shanty. But my first thought was not of ourselves, nor our beds, nor clothing, nor books, but of the brick. The men in the outside apartment were soon aroused, and set off with an india-rubber tent, blankets, overcoats, green hides, boards, ropes, etc. The rain increased after they started, as if, having got its enemy afoot, the battle should not want spirit. We remained within, counting the drops till they became streams, and wondering what tenacity of form the clay possessed, and whether every stream would be sufficient to melt down a brick in half an hour, or two hours, or a day, if it should continue. About daylight, report came that all was secure as could be under the circumstances, and that no damage had been done—a great consolation, which went far to sustain me while I was dipping the water from the stove-hearth; taking soundings in the flour-barrel; draining a tub of dried apples, which were getting a premature soaking; removing a sack of sugar from under a funnel-shaped aperture in the canvas roof of our out-kitchen; and experiencing sundry pleasant surprises prepared for me that night, which the long, dry months had taught us to forget. The rain continued to fall until about nine o'clock; and, by that time, had so thoroughly effaced anything like neatness or cheerfulness from our environments within and without, that the gleam of blue sky which smiled upon us soon after, and rapidly widened to a broad laugh, was joyously welcomed. The afternoon shone gloriously over the freshened earth. Even the blue sleeping bay and the slow heaving ocean seemed to share in the general revivification. Animate and inanimate nature were gladdened, and the earth seemed to feel a new and mightier pulse in her broad bosom. One could imagine the eagerness with which the thirsty roots and swelling seeds would meet the descending element of life ; and feel, as under the warm suns and gentle rains of a rare March day at home, that being would be bliss again, in the exuberant life that would soon embrace us.

But to me, under my numerous burdens and the weariness I had borne, nature was no longer the sufficing minister she had been in earlier days. Her frowns no longer filled me with ecstatic terror ; her smiles no more gave me the delight of the olden time. I lived upon her bosom, and beheld her beneficent operations ; her half-secret processes ; her sterner and tenderer beauties ; all her pomp and glory ; all her meekness and patient love, and felt my life little affected by them. A few acres of potatoes, a few thousands of brick and shingles, and the four walls of a house that should separate us from the winds and clouds, could shut her out of my soul for the time ; could so weary and subdue my spirit, that it settled

down in abject bondage to them, and almost
forgot that it had ever nobler relations, greater
freedom, more joyous life.   I remembered the
devout gratitude I had always felt, that only sin
could destroy in the soul, that loved nature, its
true affection.   I could turn to pages in which
I had recorded the overflowing thankfulness of
my heart that this love would ever be mine,
unless I willfully perverted my own powers—
unless I, with more or less consciousness, resigned it for something not merely less noble,
but positively unworthy a clear-seeing soul
And now, with continual external struggle—
with a spirit defiled by no subversive indulgences—with aspirations for good no whit
lower than those I had cherished when she was
to my ardent hope and faith, the chief source
and minister of the joy I should know on this
side heaven—the visible throne of God—the
type of his majesty, strength, faithfulness, and
bounty—now my eye was dimmed to her pure
glories; my ear dulled to her sweet tones ; my
heart indifferent to all the tenderness with
which she cherishes, as a loving mother, the life
that dwells in innumerable forms in her bosom.

It is a painful consciousness to have fasten
to one's very life of life, and chill the heart
with a sense of decay which its own growth
hastens, to divest life of one of its chief sources
of interest, to dry up one of its brightest fountains, blight its greenest vallies, cloud its
purest skies, and spread, between the soul and
the external world, a mist that dims the one
and chills the other till it no more longs for
the approach that once delighted, no more
rejoices, no more wonders, but dwells, side by
side, with the sources of profoundest emotion,
stilled and indifferent as that face from which
the flush of happy being has been struck forever. The spirit will not consent that its attributes die out under a weight of cares and
labors that are borne for paltry or purely selfish ends, but

> " In some good cause, not in my own,
>   To perish wept for, honored, known,
>   And like a warrior overthrown ;"

this was sweet service in the battle of life ;
such as could well soothe the bitter moments
which all generous natures must feel when
they find themselves thus cabined, cribbed, con-

fined, and such a lot is all the more bitter if
there be none to understand and share its
agony of hopelessness, its rebellious conflict,
or gather from the future some gleams that
promise escape.

As the year of this experience drew to a
close, I seemed to feel myself passing irrevo-
cably to a condition whereon

> "Hope's moonlight never shone,
> And faith's white blossom never waved."

Despair of the future plucked from me whatever was consoling and strengthening in the
past.   All its toils, trials, and triumphs, became
valueless, removed so entirely as I was, from
everything that could remind me they had had
value to any, and hopeless as I felt that true
moral relations would ever offer to the poor
remnant of my better nature, that I might
bring out of this battle, like opportunities of
use worthy of itself or its past.   The isolation
of this period was its most disheartening feature.   Shut up in my narrow house, with the
interest and sympathies which had been wont
to embrace classes, communities, humanity,
chilled and driven back upon myself; unable

to approach the social life about me in the way of co-operation or enjoyment, or individuals in the relation of serving or aiding, because their wants were not those to which I could minister, I was, most of all, unhappy in finding myself circumscribed in all action to my small family circle and my private interests. The least endowed and cultivated woman in the community was more valuable to it, if she had health and industry, than I had power to be.   Her fitness to serve society in its primitive conditions, to supply its first wants, made her superior in the things wherein excellence can be practically tested, and gave her sources of happiness, which, surrounded as I was, I could not command.

I learned from this experience how that which is most highly prized in advanced conditions of society, may, in another, be brought to a market where no demand is.   There is little in the condition of California society, up to this date, to engage the higher orders of female intelligence, and, among all earnest women of this class whom I have met, there is a universal feeling of being sadly out of place,

a feeling which I fear visits sometimes, more
or less, the good of all classes. The necessities
to be served here are physical; washing linen,
cleansing houses, cooking, nursing, etc., and I
would advise no woman to come alone to the
country who has not strength, willingness, and
skill for one or other of these occupations;
who has not, also, fortitude, indomitable resolution, dauntless courage, and a clear self-respect which will alike forbid her doing anything unworthy herself, or esteeming anything
to be so, which her judgment and conscience
approve. She will, at best, have many days
of anxiety, many weeks and months of misgiv-
ings; and dreadful doubts will hang about her
at times, suggesting the fear that she has taken
a step fatal to her future in placing herself in
relations so unsustained, so depreciating. She
will feel, in the moral atmosphere which sur-
rounds her, such taint, such infection, that she
will scarcely hope to find the integrity and
purity that would inspire trust; she will feel
herself in an enemy's country, where she is
to watch and ward with tireless vigilance,
and live, unless she be very happily circum-

stanced, alone, entirely alone, and bear her trials in silence. None but the pure and strong-hearted of my sex should come alone to this land.

CHAPTER XVI.

But the keenest of my trials in it, thus far, was now likely to pass away; for a friend was coming to me. A note, two months and a half old, reached me one evening bearing the joyful news that an old friend, a beloved one, a woman of genius, yet in very many things thoroughly practical, musical, witty, independent, affectionate, had reached San Francisco, and, at that date, was anxious to hear from me before engaging in any occupation. But as she did not know my address her letter had lain in the office in the city till a friend found and conveyed it to me. I immediately forwarded an answer to herself, a note of instructions to Tom, who was still there, and one to a friend who resided there, in order to insure the finding of her if the cholera had not swept her off, or she had not gone to some other part of the country during those weeks.

By the return mail (our communication with the world beyond the mountains was *hebdomadal*) came answers, saying that she had been found, had accepted my invitation, and would be down with the man.

The arrival of her Majesty at any town in the Irish corner of the realm could not produce greater agitation than our little *rancho* was thrown into by this announcement. It would have been an event to know that any good woman was coming into the neighborhood, how much greater, then, to receive a friend into my own house to be of us and not belong anywhere else? The appellation by which we called her was Georgie; but dear Eddie, whose joy was greatest of all, because Georgie could tell stories and sing, unable to give our sound of it, adopted one of his own, Geordie, which found greater favor.

Tom's long delay, before those joyful tidings came, had been a matter of wonder which every subsequent day tended to increase to impatience, and, finally, almost to wrath. It

was the one thought and theme in the morning—at table—at work—in the evening—in
the night. The potatoes and brick sink by
their own weight quite out of view. If it
rained I thought not of them but of the travelers; if the sun shone I considered how it would
permit them to advance, and rejoiced for that
reason.

Every evening, from the roof we cast weary
glances in the direction of the mountains, and
every night left us to wonder and inquire more
impatiently, Why don't they come? At last!
The night had been very wet from dark till
daylight, and the rain continued to fall after
daybreak. We had been obliged to dispense
with our second bed and bring the stove in to
occupy its place, and I was just contemplating
the dismal scene with a view to directing my
first efforts as judiciously as possible, when
down rushed the carpenter from the new
house, where he slept, with the astonishing
words, "here they are." We could scarcely
have been more surprised if we had not expected them.

I sprang from the door, disheveled as I was,

and the moment I came in sight, around the corner of the house, was greeted by one of Geordie's old-fashioned laughs—so downright —I had not heard one of them for five years. She alighted from the saddle with the help of my hands, and, the next moment, struck me aghast with the words, " We have been in the mountains all night without fire, food, or shelter, except the trees !"

Such a bustle as we were thrown into by this reception of a guest so wet, so chilled, so starved ! The table was but three feet square, and the seven of us, who had been at home, filled it closely enough, for convenience or comfort; but when it was spread there was no room to get away except by going to bed or sitting on the stove. The breakfast was gotten through, in some way, I am unable to remember how, except that Miss Sampson was everywhere at once, making everybody comfortable, finding inconceivable places for wet garments, conducting the drippings into snug out of the way channels; supplying a cup of chocolate here, and a round of bread there, keeping up a good fire, and bringing out dry clothing from hidden trunks and secret places, which I think she scarce could have remembered but for the extraordinary stimulus given to her faculties by this arrival.

Breakfast over, came the narration how they had waited so many days before starting, that Geordie had been out of patience as well as ourselves; how they had started with three horses besides Bill, who was now missing; how Geordie, not having been on horseback in the country before, had been very weary; how, nevertheless, they had pushed on after leaving one horse on the road dead, or nearly so; how they had been overtaken by darkness in a great ravine in the mountains, from which, when they got into it, they were unable to get out; how Bill, with all the luggage, shawls, etc., packed on him, escaped them there and they had not seen him since; how, at first, they stopped down in the ravine near the creek, but how Geordie, hearing strange noises, and fearing wild animals, more especially grizzly bears, with which the mountains were thickly inhabited, in a moment of terror, rushed through the brush and blackness, some eighty or a

hundred feet up the steep breast of the mountain, and took refuge near a tree which she
hoped, after feeling around it she might be able
to ascend, in some manner, upon the approach
of danger. How, then she sat under its dripping boughs, and listened, and shivered, and
trembled with cold and horror through the entire night, more exposed and terrified than her
lamented friend had been years before on that
memorable night on Ben Lomond; how, after
a weary, aching age of darkness, day-streaks
shone over the mountain-top, and they set out
for home; how she was now here, glad enough
to see a table, small though it was, and a fire,
though in a small room; how, finally, they had
not tasted food since breakfast the day before;
and how, between traveling, and fasting, and
watching, she was ready for food, rest, and
sleep, to which last, after innumerable alternate
dozings and rousings, to say something that
would not wait to be said later, of the olden or
the latter days, she at last succeeded in addressing herself, notwithstanding the intense excitement and stir of the little dark confused house.

Meantime, just as Tom had equipped himself

in an oil-cloth suit, to return in pursuit of Bill, one of the men led the graceless scamp up from the field, where he had found him quietly feeding—packs, satchels, parcels, and all, safe.

His arrival relieved Miss Sampson and myself of some anxiety ; and, after allowing Geordie a short nap, which was all I could indulge her in, we sat down to one of those seasons which, if they are delightful to persons enjoying the ordinary relations of life, would, it may well be supposed, be a hundred fold more so to me, after my desolation and loneliness. It is not literally true that we sat down, for Geordie continued reclining, and I sat upon the bedside, bending my head low, to avoid contact with the tester, which hung upon ropes and temporary rails, and was so laden with the dust and soot that had sifted through the roof, that touching it was next to wearing sackcloth and ashes. My spirit was not so clothed that morning. I felt strong and rejoicing.

There were endless tidings to be heard—as Geordie had left home a year after my departure—of coteries ; of societies ; of individuals ;

of late books; of reform movements; of successes and failures; of marriages, births,
deaths; of Eastern friends, and the Western
set—in short, of the thousand persons, events,
and subjects in whom and which my interest
was almost painfully revived by the presence
of one fresh from among them. The association people, the anti-slavery folks, the prison
reformers, the phrenological set, the criminals in and out of prison, the poor friends
and the rich ones, the obscurities and the
celebrities, were all asked for and reported
of. As yet, there was not time for talk; and
we ran confusedly over authors, editors, washer-
women, reformers, prisoners, doctors, clergy-
men, judges, artists, poets, shoemakers, female
medical colleges and practitioners, Homœopathy, water-cure, spiritual knockings, Swedenborg revelations, Davis ditto; the World's
Fair; the Catholic movements, including
Brownson's latest performances; her own
voyages and adventures hither, together with
mine; and whatever else we could remember
at so short notice, that was new to either—and
there had been enough in the five years' expe-

rience we had had apart, to occupy a good portion of the happy day.

I was no more alone now, nor lonely; for, what with personal reminiscences, discussions of social, religious, and moral questions, and analyses of character, we had few dull or silent hours

CHAPTER XVII.

THE new house was driven on with all possible expedition; for the rainy season was now coming in earnest. But there was another and almost as momentous an enterprise in hand. Our Irish Tom, who said he was a millwright and mechanic in general, as well as farmer, and who proved himself a "Jack at all trades and good at none," had rented the old mill below us, which only wanted a new dam and some slight repairs within, to put it in running order. It was a poor, rude affair enough; but such as it was, it seemed likely that if it could be set to making flour, it would furnish us with something more desirable than the sour stuff we had been getting from San Francisco at $40 to $60 the barrel. It was calculated that a few men might start it in five or six days from commencing. So we suffered our flour-barrel to draw near to an alarming state of emptiness while it was going on; and thus the success of the work became a question of the most intense interest.

For it constantly failed. Word was always coming up to us, that at noon or at evening the dam would begin to fill, and then we watched and waited, and measured the little handful of water that always stood in the centre of the muddy basin, to see if it increased. But it always turned out that it leaked in some unexpected place, and the water would rise only to a certain line, and then, the leak constantly increasing itself, would fall again. Thus eight, ten, twelve days went by. The flour-barrel was empty, and Miss Sampson and I in a state of despair. This, however, was nothing novel in our experience; for we were always destitute of something essential to comfortable housekeeping. Either the beef, or the tea, or the sugar, or salt, or molasses, or flour, or butter, was out, or the cows staid away, or something that we had sent for in time to save ourselves from want, was lost in the surf or stolen from the beach.

Thus we went on. And now our hope of bread was in the little mill; and we had watched it so long, that at last, when the gathered waters were turned upon the wheel and it was fairly in motion, the entire population of the rancho rushed with acclamation to behold it. And darling Eddie's little hands were not the only ones that were clapped with rejoicing.

Meantime, two rooms in the new house had been finished to the extent of being partitioned and floored, some nice rag, as Eddie called it (calico), stretched upon the walls, and a carpet laid. Overhead were loose boards upon the joists. After this was accomplished, removing commenced, and a forlorn man or woman might be seen at almost any time of day straggling up the hill with a parcel, satchel, basket, trunk; or armful of crockery or books; or a chair or small table; or a picture, with or without a frame. And so we gathered gradually our " plunder" into the " mansion," and the household followed slowly—first Charlie, then Geordie, Eddie, and myself; and last of all, Miss Sampson, who had swept and dusted the old place so many, many times, that she felt a real affection for every inch of the black boards, and could, I think, with very little persuasion, have been brought to think it quite comfortable, with a window, a tight floor and roof, and new, fresh walls, which would not have been making, as she insisted, a new house of it; for the same rafters might remain, and Pompey's pillar be left standing.

We removed the week before Christmas; and our first invitation to dine out, in California, came a day or two after, to go to a Christmas dinner, about three miles from home. Our host was a neighbor, who had been kindly assisting at the dam, and who had sustained himself under the protracted labor, by such free application to the bottle, that his manner of inviting was of the funniest; but he assured us that if we would come, he would keep sober himself, and that if he did not, we might entirely rely on his thrashing any person who should be rude to us, and sending us home the moment we should intimate a wish to go. He would send horses, mules, wagons, to convey us—a camel or elephant, if he

owned one—escort—anything his rancho afforded.

We could not reject so cordial hospitality,
and accordingly promised to go, doubting,
almost, if our doing so would be remembered
till he got home. But on the day, came the
horses and escort, and we went. And because
I despair of doing the dinner or the party any
justice in description, I must content myself
with saying that they gave us a better notion
of the life of the country than a month's
Christmas at home would.

CHAPTER XVIII.

THE winter, so far, was one of the finest that could be imagined. A day or two of rain would be followed by weeks of bright sunny weather, that shone down upon the green earth and blue waters, converting them into a fairy world. Tom had commenced sowing his wheat immediately upon the completion of the mill, and had gone on until some twenty-five acres were sown, and more than half of it before the first of February.

Geordie and I, without any escort, had taken two or three rides, to see the wonders of the locality, expecting that every week of fine weather would be the last before a flood. Those were delightful rides; for, alone in the valleys, or on the hillsides, or in the grand gloom of the majestic forests, there was nothing to check that free interchange of thought and sentiment to which our natural frankness inclined each of us. In our lives there had been sadness and struggle enough—as in what earnest life is there not?—to give us a keen and abiding interest in human happiness, events enough to give character to our experience, and enough of triumph and failure to make the basis of our respective theories, which in many points differed so essentially as to give rise to prolonged and animated discussion.

The rights and position of woman were a theme of endless talk—Geordie standing upon the platform of the Worcester Convention, and I upon one of my own, the limits of which, at some points, lay considerably within hers. She always insisted that my theory and practice were at war on this question, as I actually did many of the things which her party demanded freedom to do, and yet would not subscribe to their demands. It was in vain I protested that necessity prescribed my practice, and only reason, taste, and conscience, my theory. I was scarcely credited with honesty in this matter, there was so formidable an array of suspicious circumstances against me.

See how imperative were some of the necessities that demanded sacrifice of convenience and ease, as well as theory. Our " annals were not vacant" of such incidents as generally fall to the lot of settlers in new regions, where the right of " squatting" upon other people's property is held to be one of the " inalienable" privileges of a freeman. It behoved me to look sharply to our little domain, when this spirit " broke out" among us.

The advent of each distinct phase which the rage for gain has assumed in California, is, with characteristic energy, termed, in the unwritten histories, " breaking out." Always it is said, " when the mines broke out;" then, " when the squatting broke out;" and, when the notable " flour speculation broke out."

What we called the " hill farm" was an especially tempting spot, by reason of its fertility and beauty. A fountain sprung from the grassy slope of a little elevation upon it, of sufficient volume to turn a small mill—the purest water. One or two pretty sharp hints had been given me respecting it, and I thought it necessary to put up something upon it which the law would accept as a house. After a great deal of labor—persuading, entreating, hiring—some lumber was got upon it, and I went up every day for the most part of a week, to press forward the getting up of a shanty. From the spot I selected for it, there was a beautiful view of La Libertad in its quiet, snug beauty; the coast range, and the intermediate country for several miles below, with all its shades of green in grass and foliage, its silent herds, its streams of pure water, coursing their way from the hill to the sea, visible only at rare points, but traceable in almost their entire length by the richness of the foliage which clusters on their margins. I took luncheon with me, and had always some convenient-sized volume (bless the duodecimo) which filled my moments of occasional leisure with greater repose. There my presence was necessary to insure the execution of a little job, which was the chief means I had of saving myself from robbery. If I had sat down in my library, or parlor, or kitchen at home (all which were kept in two rooms) it it would have been at the risk of half that had been left to me and my children.

A very vexatious circumstance occurred on one of those days, which made me wish that a prohibitory tariff had been laid upon Irish economy and Irish ways before I had suffered from them. There was a tall, lank, thin-visaged, Albino-white horse, with blue and pink eyes, which I occasionally mounted for short tours over the home premises. I rode him up one morning, and, when I got down from the saddle, found that the *riata* had been left at home. Upon this, Tom pulled the bridle off before I could understand his purpose, and giving him a blow with the gathered reins started him off with the saddle on. I remonstrated, but he answered that he would go straight home to Bill; and, indeed, he did go out of sight toward home, but, when I went down at sunset, he had not been seen at the house. Of course, my saddle was gone. Many days afterward, we heard of it, cut and mutilated, passing a rancho about ten miles up the coast, in possession of some Indians.

CHAPTER XIX.

" How sweet it were, hearing the downward stream
    With half-shut eyes, ever to seem
    Falling asleep in a half dream."

As the winter wore on, and the season of
planting approached, Geordie and I having concluded to enter upon " agricultural operations"
for the year, began to consider what were the
first steps to be taken. In January we planted
the first potatoes, and from that time till the
last of April we were steadily engaged in the
garden or fields. The serene skies and warm
sun under which we toiled, the pure air we
breathed, the mild winds that blew about us,
and the intense repose of the cool, refreshing
nights, gave us health and strength, and
for a time we both enjoyed the freedom and
freshness of that unconventional life. We repaired fences, and ditches, and water-courses,

superintended the mill, did " a turn or two" at
the plow occasionally, and kept up a constant planting of various garden-seeds, with
immense toil, by which, I regret to say, we
were little benefited—most of the seed having
either failed altogether, or been so very slow in
coming, that one or two subsequent crops were
put in the same beds, so that when they did
appear, we had parsnips, carrots, and onions
growing on the same ground, and not enough
of all to make one crop.   But this sort of discouragement did not fully overtake us till we
had somewhat exhausted the novelty of our new
calling, which was not nearly so soon as would
have been supposed.   Occasionally, we got an
hour's help from a visitor, and, in one or two
instances, whole days from gentlemen of leisure
in the neighborhood.   In this way our grape-
vines were set.   In this way, also, we made an
excursion up the coast for strawberry vines, and
returned with each a good-sized parcel at our
saddles.

When weariness overtook us, the earth was
beneath for a bed, and the warm, bright sky
above for a canopy.   Life looked a curious spec-

tacle from those quiet points of view. One or two plows moving slowly in the distance, followed by scores of white sea-gulls, gathering the worms it unhoused ; hundreds of blackbirds wheeling and chattering just above us ; and, higher up in the still and sanctified blue, a buzzard, lying lazily upon his outspread wings, were objects that rather aided than interrupted the wondering retrospect one could not but fall into at such times.

Were cities, with their din and clamor, a dream ; or had we, indeed, been at some time atoms in the great mass we now dimly remembered as heaving and surging in its eternal restlessness ? Were there really such things as railroad cars and steamboats, whirling men and women along their accustomed ways, as the wind does the dry leaves of autumn ? Could it be possible that hurry and confusion were still anywhere on the earth that was so full of repose about us ; possible that people were anywhere swallowing hurried, leaden meals, and rushing off to narrow counting-rooms or noisy manufactories, with no blessed earth to stretch their weary limbs upon, nor blue heaven to pour serenity into their souls, nor birds, nor sighing winds, nor chime of sea to drive the din of the stirring world from their ears? One could easily forget that one had ever been an undistinguished grain of that great shifting sand-mountain, in the magnitude and power to which one grew in those times.

World's fairs and conventions, reform meetings, political agitations, even Hungarian revolutions, seen at this distance through so quiet a medium, seemed too exciting to be conducive to life. We grew large in that calm state, and seemed able to look back upon those yet remaining out of it with a sort of "poor-things" sentiment; and, indeed, it was a sustaining possibility, that we could sometimes believe the quiet we had attained to be good also, though it might be of the less-exalted sort; which one could never for any moment forget, because there was ever a consciousness—not always uncomfortable—that it was purely sensuous. We did not rise, but sank to it, rather, nature's sweetest welcome inviting the exhausted frame to repose—her gentlest lullaby soothing the senses.

It was so clear, from these blessed, short experiences, how the country should have suffered the curse of a contented population. They were steeped in it as their brown, sharp hills are in the long summer sunshine. It flowed to them from the heavens, and the earth, and the winds, and the waters. They

"Breathe but peace, and ever peace."

No wonder those who dwelt in such a paradise should esteem any effort of theirs to add to the enjoyment of existence quite superfluous, and think the mere continuance of life blessing enough without adding luxuries to the beef and beans that would support it. The same condition seems to have sufficed to the foreigners that settled in the country previous to the discovery of the gold. They have adopted the habits and entered fully into the native life, seeking nothing superior to the old rancho style —a dark, dirty, adobe house, windowless, swarming with fleas, the ground in all directions strewn with bullocks' heads, horns, and hides, and guarded by an immense troop of worthless dogs, who rush around all the corners as you approach, with furious barking, but slink away with every particle of self-respect and courage frightened from their demeanor at the raising of a whip.

CHAPTER XX.

My fame as a *medico* having got somewhat abroad, it occasionally happened that I was called away from my digging and planting to treat some case of rheumatism, tinea capitis, or other not invincible disease. The miraculously small *remedias*, aided, as they sometimes were, by a few magnetic passes, and always by grave looks and oracular shakes and nods of the head, were, in most cases, very effective.

These visits afforded both occasion and opportunity for me to become better acquainted with many of the features of life on the ranches —that condition so extraordinary to us Anglo-Americans. The absence of that grand characteristic of enlightened Christianity—respect for woman—is painfully apparent in these rude houses. Running into the order of life and all its minor arrangements, it presents, at every turn,

something disagreeable, repulsive, or shocking. Among the common people, a man never
walks by the side of his wife, mother, or sister;
does not eat at the same table with her; does
not consult her in any of the things wherein
she is chiefly or alone concerned; and, in short,
assigns her the position of a humanely-treated
slave.

As a consequence, the females are extremely
ignorant, and, lacking the freedom of equality,
generally incline to take that which license
gives. In their domestic affairs they drudge
through the little labor they think it worth
their while to bestow upon home comfort;
wash the linen at the nearest stream; sew and
do ornamental work upon their own wardrobes
(they love colors); dress prodigally for church
and the fandango; visit by whole families, and
receive visits; but seem destitute of emulation
and, as nearly as humanity can be, without
rivalry.

The out-door arts are little further advanced
than those I have spoken of. Their plow con-
sists of a forked branch of live-oak, so shaped,
that one arm makes the beam, another the share,

which is round and only pointed with iron, and another the handles. To this the oxen are attached by a rude yoke, strapped upon their horns, and a man or boy walks or rides before them to keep them in place. I used to see, but never fully appreciated the value, of this service, until I was one day approaching a rancho on a professional visit, where a young don was gravely riding up and down a small field before a huge pair of oxen that were dragging a plow, and an Indian boy behind them. When the young caballero saw me, he struck spurs into his horse, and dashed off to give me admittance at the bars, whereupon the cattle left the furrow, and perambulated the field in whatever direction seemed to them good—the poor Indian behind having no control whatever over their movements.

I believe I have not yet said what ought not to be omitted respecting the horned cattle of this country—that they are among the very largest and best of their species. They have immense depth of chest ; long, straight, well-made bodies, and the largest horns ever seen— some of them measuring five feet across at the

widest curve. A size nearly as great as this
is not rare. The cows lack beauty in this respect, their horns partaking of the size and
shape of those of the ox. They yield, however, a good quality of milk, and if kept and
milked after a civilized fashion, would, I am
persuaded, make very good dairy cows. The
modes generally adopted, however, are such
as would make our Orange County friends at
home despair, if they were obliged to put their
dairies under California regulations.

The cows range the open country during
the rainy season; and those which are to be
milked, are " taken up" when their calves are
from three days to as many weeks old. The
calf is tied either to a post or fence with a bit
of green hide, or put into a corral. The
mother lingers near it for a day or two, and
then goes to feed, returning at night or morning; the custom with the old inhabitants, both
native and foreign, being to milk but once a
day. This process is performed by lashing the
head of the animal, if she be at all wild, to
the fence, or to a post set for that purpose,
and her hind feet to each other. If she be

quite gentle, and well used to it for years, the rope is only thrown about her legs. Sometimes it is even permitted to drop to the ground ; but whatever its use may be, it is never dispensed with. Milking, without it, would be too exciting and perilous a business for people who love labor and adventure so little.

As the season advances and the herbage dries, the milk, of course, fails in quantity. Then the calves are turned loose to run with their mothers, and you might famish for a cup of milk in a country where thousands of cows are ranging the plains. Indeed, it is rare to find milk at any season in the Spanish houses. A master of a vessel that was lying for cargo a few miles below our beach, said he sent a pail up to the nearest rancho one day for some milk, and was quite surprised to have it come back full. When he called to thank señora, she told him she would be glad to have him send every day for all that he could use; for it would save her the trouble of making it into cheese—and such cheese !

CHAPTER XXI.

WE had been some two months without milk, and the talk of getting up cows had been so unavailing, that one evening, grown desperate, I ordered horses to be got ready at sunrise next morning. I determined to turn out myself, rather than be without milk longer. As the plain where the cattle ranged was skirted with brush and timber, to which, in the chase, they might take for shelter, I was apprehensive that my riding skirt might encumber me, as I was to drive the cow on Sheik, while the man carried the calf on Bill. After a long discussion of the difficulties of the enterprise, it was finally agreed that the only safe plan would be to ride and dress *à la monsieur*.

Miss Sampson, who was never known to want a thing but she found it, mustered, after

a considerable search in a chest of clothing she
had in charge for a nephew, a proper suit,
only, as the clothes were all new, there was
an over-smartish look for what I had in hand.
And then the difficulty, always a capital one
with me, was to get a hat. One was found,
however, which, by dint of tugging and straining, was drawn down sufficiently to feel tolerably secure, and we set off before sunrise.
Not having crossed the Isthmus, nor ever before tried the style of riding generally adopted
by ladies making that journey, I was surprised
and annoyed to find myself feeling less secure
when mounted than in my own saddle. We
stepped out, however, and I should have felt
no uneasiness but for the fact that, to avoid
being recognized, I had left my spectacles off,
and could not tell, at twenty rods, whether it
was an ox or a man approaching; and I felt
the smallness of my hat so sensibly, that I was
certain I should lose it long before I did. We
had to pass between two houses, very near to
one of which, the breeze into which we were
galloping lifted it gently from my head and
bore it to the ground. I involuntarily raised

my hand to my head while the lost sombrero
was being restored to me, to conceal the comb
and twist, which is not the usual style of hair-
dressing among the caballeros I was counter-
feiting; and, notwithstanding that I should
have shrunk from the eyes that might have
looked at me then, almost as from lightning, I
rode the next quarter of a mile in convulsions
of laughter at the thought of how they would
have opened upon me, had they witnessed my
misfortune.

When we reached the plain, we readily
found a young calf, whose mother bore the
mark we were authorized to take up; and
Tom, after considerable effort to get him upon
Bill, who would not stand for him to mount
after the calf was laid over his saddle, came
up and threw him across my Arab's shoulders,
intending to ride up and take him off after
mounting. But to this also Bill objected; so
there was no way but to mount him, willing
or unwilling, which, after several trials, Tom
succeeded in, to my infinite relief; for it was
impossible for me to keep my eyes from wandering in all directions, or to control the beat-

ing of my heart when anything moving at a
distance suggested the possibility of encountering a stranger at such a critical time. When
this difficulty was overcome, and we turned
our horses' heads homeward, I, in full faith
that the victory was complete—the unnatural mother turned away from her captive calf
and walked off to join the herd that was
feeding on a height half a mile distant.

There were but two alternatives, either to
abandon the calf or follow her, which I accordingly did. I turned Sheik and gave him the
rein, upon which he stretched himself in gal-
lant style. It was an older business to him
than to me, and I soon found he understood it
much better. I therefore gave him his freedom, and he followed her like her shadow,
wheeling when she wheeled, slackening when
she slackened, quickening when she quickened
her pace; in short, changing his movements
so entirely without control or purpose of mine,
that in the excitement of the chase and of
keeping my seat, I forgot the annoyances I
had suffered—the small hat, want of spectacles, possible neighborhood of strange eyes;

indeed, I think the presence of numbers would have seemed to me, just then, an insignificant circumstance.

The cow was perverse, and Sheik liked the fun, so we did not'reach the ford till Tom had twice or thrice led the way, and as often returned to the top of the bank on finding that we did not follow. At length she gave up the battle and walked quietly after her calf, so that in about an hour we all reached home safely, with feats and adventures to relate that gave a fair relish to the breakfast I found awaiting me.

While I am on the subject of horned cattle, it may be as well to state that, except in the large cities and towns, there are no markets, and the only method of supplying one's-self with fresh meat is by the purchase of an animal on foot. A Spaniard, who is in want of a few dollars, gets on a horse, lasso in hand, and goes off in pursuit of a beef, which he will sell, when caught, at almost any price. If he suppose beef may be wanted at some house, he drives the beast thither before him, with another tame one, perhaps, made fast to the same *riata*. He proposes to sell it first for twenty-five,

then for twenty, then for an ounce, and, last of
all, parts with it for ten or twelve dollars;
winds the rope about its feet to throw it, cuts
its throat, mounts, and rides away. In a week
or so, perhaps, comes another Spaniard to
look at the head or hide to see if they bear his
mark, and a long dialogue ensues in English
(such as it is), on one side, and Spanish on the
other, between him and Tom, the result of
which is, that neither knows anything more
when they part than they did when they met,
except that the stranger hears the price paid
for the animal, and also from whom it was
purchased, if Tom happen to have that knowledge himself.

When the slaughtering is over, fresh beef
abounds, and the flies run riot for a few days;
but the great purity of the atmosphere neither
favors putrefaction nor the development of
their larvæ, and, after a succession of roast-
ings, boilings, and stewings, you settle down
to salt meat till the next slaughtering again
distracts you with an over-supply. Sometimes
a beef is obtained without going through all
these formalities ; but it requires the skill and

knowledge of older settlers than we are to dispense with them.   Thus, before the harvest in
the fall, we had defeated all the four-footed intruders upon our premises except one red cow,
whose resolution and tenacity of purpose were
truly astonishing.   Turned out, she came as
faithfully back as the sun with the morning;
she was always there, and, feeding well when
the other cattle were picking scanty supplies
on the dry plains, was in excellent condition at
the time, when our patience was sufficiently exhausted to lead to extreme measures against her.
Then it was thought best to have her appraised,
as there was no brand upon her, slaughter her,
and, if the owner came, pay him what she might
be adjudged to be worth.   Before doing this,
however, Tom thought fit to call on a neighbor, who was a functionary of the town, and
take his advice.   He promptly discouraged all
such proceedings as we had contemplated ; said
he thought the ear-mark was that of a Spanish
woman who lived two or three miles away, and
that he would send to her respecting it.   The
cow was driven from the field for the hundredth
time at dusk, and has never since been heard

of. Next day our obliging neighbor sent us up a piece of the best beef, and when Tom, soon after, inquired about the red cow, he replied: " Yes, the old woman sent a couple of Indians to drive her away. Did you not see them ?"

CHAPTER XXII.

I HAD sent to New York for fruit-trees, but, while waiting their arrival, was very glad to avail myself of the privilege kindly given me by my neighbor at the orchard, to get scions of such as were growing there. So, one fine morning, after a pleasant rain, Geordie and I set out, accompanied by Tom, to see what we could find there that was desirable. We had never before left the farm in costume and red top boots, but it was so wet now, that it was idle to think of going, and on such an errand, in any other garb. We had but two houses to pass, and could enter the orchard from the rear, so if a few persons did see the elephant out of his cage, we did not care.

Tom had a spade and some ropes, and he soon separated and bound up as many young pears and olives as we thought we all could carry. But when we were fairly off with them, it seemed very desirable to take along some of the prickly pear that was growing in a huge unsightly hedge on the bank of the river. The burdens were laid down, and a new arrangement made, by which Geordie and I took all the trees, and Tom staggered off under a mountain of the thorny cactus, to which his frieze coat proved but an indifferent armor. Many a hearty, but, I fear, heartless, laugh had I, toiling along, with Geordie plodding gravely at the other end of the pole, at sight of the wriggling and shifting by which I knew he was seeking to displace one thorn at the hazard of inserting half a dozen others in fresh places. But this exercise was confined to the first portion of the road; for experience, which teaches lessons with miraculous rapidity under such circumstances, soon warned him that any state of things that was, was better with him than any new one could be.

We passed a young lady from Missouri on the road, apparently not long from her slumbers, who was struck into a state of such profound astonishment at sight of the procession, that I could not fail to be deeply concerned for her mental soundness, till I saw her some time after in the apparent enjoyment of all that nature had bestowed on her. The intenseness, the utter *abandon* of her stare, I never saw equaled.

Geordie and I set the trees and cactus, the thorns of which, perforating our boots and gloves, so annoyed us, that before they were half planted, we abandoned the half mile of hedge we were at first resolved upon setting along the stream, and voted them ugly and undesirable.

The sun was very warm, and obliged us occasionally to desist from our labors, a circumstance which gave me some disquiet, as Geordie's inordinate appetite constantly drew her thoughts toward the house whenever her hands were unoccupied. On this day, however, we were to dine on Captains Cuttle and Bunsby, two hardy old members of the barn-yard family (only we had neither yard nor barn), and I restrained her by representing the weakness, almost sinfulness, of dulling the edge of an appetite by lunching, with a holiday dinner in prospect—the first dinner of fowls in the modern history of the rancho. So we beguiled the time by discussing the attractions of labor—which she, with a painful lack of heroism, insisted was much diminished by hunger—the abounding plenty of the country, and other collateral subjects, until the last tree was planted.

Then we set out, uninvited, for the house.

The clock was at two, and but for the spread table and savory odor, Geordie would have felt herself sorely aggrieved by the delay. Miss Sampson explained that Captain Cuttle had proved very pinfeathery, and that while she was exercising the requisite care in his case, Mrs. MacStinger, in the person of the gray cat, had seized upon the defunct Bunsby, and so lacerated his neck and breast, as to spoil him for roasting. So the two were a fricassee, to which we did ample justice, and would have done more, had we not been, in transcendental language, so much more to them than they could be to us.

CHAPTER XXIII.

ONE of the most insufferable nuisances to the farmer in this country, is the wild mustard that everywhere abounds, and grows to a size that literally verifies scripture. It began to appear among our wheat when it was from six to fourteen inches high, and gave us incredible toil in the removing. Geordie and I first attacked it in the strong confidence of inexperience, but we were not many days at it before the hope, that had made us first reject the offer of help, failed us, and we were quite willing that Tom should search the rancherie and neighboring huts, which he did every morning, sometimes successfully, sometimes otherwise.

This was very severe labor—more so than digging, if that were possible. I failed at it first, and was obliged to leave the field to Geordie and the Indian—a soft-spoken, per-

suasive old fellow, who, if left alone, would
stand erect by the half hour watching the
blackbirds, the clouds, the plows, the Mission—
anything that he could make himself believe
was worth his attention, and he would bestow
it very cheaply. Geordie would work with
him till she was tired, and then lie down in
the furrow for a nap, the grain being a delightful couch, at once clean and soft. The sleep
was generally broken by some adventurous
bird swooping a little lower than his fellows,
and screaming within a few yards of her ear,
when she would rouse and address herself to
the battle again. At last her old compatriot
gave out, and she was left quite alone. This
seemed too severe, and it occurred to some
lucky brain among us that we might get a fresh
start by inviting a few of our neighbors to share
our toil for an afternoon—in short, by making
a bee.

So notes were sent out to some eight or
ten gentlemen, informing them of our forlorn
condition, and appealing to their humanity to
aid us. They all presented themselves on the
appointed day, and, notwithstanding that a

smart shower drove us in some half hour too early, we overturned a great many sturdy enemies during the afternoon. And yet, a great deal was left for us to do, and we had many a weary day in the great field before we gave up the hope of exterminating the hateful weed. But the wheat is now harvesting, and it is still very abundant among it. On some of the lands, where it now abounds, there was not a stalk to be seen before it was cultivated; on others, it covered the sward, and grew to a miniature forest.

The wheat of this year was sown broadcast about sixty pounds to the acre, and the growth is so enormous, that it is nearly impossible to harvest it. The heads measure from five to eight inches in length, the average is between six and seven; fifty of them weigh a pound with four or five inches of the straw attached. The yield has not yet been ascertained, but the harvesters generally think it will average from eighty to one hundred bushels per acre. This is one evidence of the energy of California soil.

The spontaneous products are equally astonishing. The forests are the most gigantic on the continent, if not on the globe. On the rancho of Captain Graham, about five miles from the Mission, is a tract of forest in which the trees are of enormous size. Their immense proportions and towering height fill one with awe and wonder. On all sides of you rise immense boles, whose altitude is reckoned by hundreds of feet, and whose diameter is from ten to twelve, fourteen, and eighteen feet at the height of a man. One known as " the Big Tree" measures three hundred feet and nearly nineteen across at six feet from the ground. Yet people in looking for it, not unfrequently pass it, so unnoticeable is it among its towering neighbors. These trees are of a species of cedar—the redwood of the country, of which its lumber is chiefly manufactured. From the straightness and freedom of its grain, large quantities are split into boards for fencing, lathing, etc. It gives off, when green or damp, a black dye to whatever is brought in contact with it, and hence is very objectionable for floors, closets, bedsteads, etc. When undressed, it also fills the hands with fine splinters, which it is very painful to leave or extract, as I often found during my term of apprenticeship last summer.

CHAPTER XXIV.

THE great labor of seed-time, in which Geordie and I had yet to bear our part, was the potato planting, which was in itself less disagreeable than the preparatory step of cutting the seed. In the old shanty, which we had all abandoned except Miss Kilmansegg and her eight golden-legged little chickens, there lay, when we began, about nine hundred *arobas* of potatoes. Day after day we sat in the dark, dirty place, over this disagreeable pile, with hands muffled in old gloves or new gloves, white rags or colored ones, just as chance permitted, but always the same hands. How wearily they spun out! How dirty and distasteful the handling! When a day came for planting, we rejoiced to rush out into the open fields, and, with basket on arm, or sack suspended by a strap over the shoulder, march up and down the furrows, laborious though it was.

Geordie and I always made a procession in getting off to any distance—she invariably falling some six or eight steps behind with her spade, hoe, or whatever it might be, swinging as a walking-stick ; and there was always about her, in these walks, a plodding, matter-of-fact air that irresistibly amused me, when, as it often happened, I was compelled to turn back to address her. In her air, look, and manner, there was something that seemed to suggest that it was a very old business with her, and that she was mentally comparing the prospects of this year with those of some cold, or hot, or wet, or dry season, of years ago, or estimat-the comparative expense and durability of modes of fencing, the utility of improved plows, harrows, scarecrows, etc.

Our planting began in April, and continued till the third of May, the day on which we commenced the previous year ; and as, beside this advantage, we have better fences, no grass-hoppers, and not a tithe of the cattle that then consumed our potatoes and patience, we are greatly encouraged in our labors. We reckon ten acres each of our own planting—we putting

the seed in the drill, while Joe followed with
the wonderful plow, which, in every succeeding step of the process, took a new shape. In
this one it had become a broad, wedge-like implement, which, dragged along the middle of
the ridge between the drills, turned the soil
both ways into them. Occasionally the boards,
which were nailed on either side to give it this
form, would split away, and then, when we
looked for Joe, we saw him at the end of the
furrows, hammer, axe, or saw in hand, repairing.

The rapidity of this mode recommended it
greatly to us, who were so impatient to see it
over, but did not meet the approbation of some
ease-loving neighbors of ours—gentlemen from
Arkansas, who took a gentle undisturbing interest in our affairs, and discussed them, while
reposing in the sunshine, in heavy red flannel
shirts, outside boots, worn up to the knee, and
with commodious pipes in their mouths. In
those days they "allowed" that California was
no better than other countries, and the proof
of it was, that they could only get twenty dollars a week and board offered them for driving

an ox-team. They wanted thirty, and this being refused, spent the days reclining, for the
most part, in the sun against their house, or the
mill, or a fence, their feet elevated to the height
most conducive to that perfect ease which such
gentlemen of leisure court.

The scarcity of labor, and the indifferent
quality of those who seek employment, are, at
most seasons of the year, among the chief difficulties of farming in this country. If your
hired man go off any evening to get drunk for
two or three days, or any morning with a gun,
to spend half the day in pursuit of a deer which
he never overtakes, or a flock of migrating
geese which always fly a little too high for a
shot, you are to be very complaisant on his return, and receive him as if he had done you the
best service.

The dryness of the winter had induced many
of our neighboring farmers to plant early.
Some large crops were put in in February and
March, while others determined, according to
the Spanish custom, not to plant till the rains
were over. The result proved the wisdom of
the latter plan ; for each rain, on this fruitful

soil, brings a rank crop of weeds which it is extremely laborious and tedious to remove. This year, several early crops have been plowed in, and the ground has been replanted in preference to attempting to keep it free from weeds.

It is found, also, that the rains harden or crust the surface of plowed land, so that it requires to be afterward broken up and mellowed.

CHAPTER XXV.

THE great disappointment of this season was the loss of my trees, which were delayed so long on the Isthmus, that they were as dead when they reached us as Mr. Scrooge's partner. Geordie and I lamented and groaned over them, knife in hand, cutting carefully here and there, to see if, by chance, any lingering sign of life might be discovered, and denouncing the Express people, whose extraordinary pretensions to punctuality had beguiled me to entrust so perishable and invaluable a charge to their care. We set them in a choice spot near our vines, and watched them for three months hopefully, since which time they are only heard of in some despairing moment.

Up to this time the difficulty of getting trees to the country in such a condition as to insure their surviving the transit, seemed insuperable. Nearly every undertaking of the kind, which I have heard of, has failed as mine did, either from bad management in packing, or delay in the journey. A short time will, no doubt, make what is now so difficult perfectly practicable. Meantime, the primitive experiments are very costly.

The native and cultivated fruits of the country are so rare and excellent, that one desires very much to have trees growing. Only the pear and grape are found in any quantity in the old Mission orchards in this part of the state. The apple, olive, fig, pomegranate, and apricot, grow well, and were sparingly cultivated in most of the orchards; but the apple is a natural fruit, which, inferior at first, has declined with age, so that it would be esteemed, in an older country, unworthy to cumber the ground. There are many varieties of pears, all excellent, and some, I think, superior to those we have at home.

There are fewer fruit-bearing vines and shrubs than in the States of the Mississippi Valley, very few berries, except strawberries in certain localities, no plums, pawpaws, haws, persimmons—no nuts except the hazel, which grows very sparsely on its bush.   There is an arbutus, a beautiful tree for lawns, which bears a bright red berry that may be eaten, but is not palatable.   There is, in short, no substitute for the numerous delicious fruits we used to gather in such profusion in Prairie Land.

CHAPTER XXVI.

Some twenty to forty miles up the coast is a region famed for strawberries, to which we determined, in the winter, to pay a visit, when the fruit should be ripe.   When we were very weary, we were used to borrow encouragement from this anticipated holiday, which at length dawned upon the last day of May.   We set out —a company of four—Geordie, myself, and our gentlemanly neighbors, Messrs. G. and K.   We had an extra horse on which to pack our provisions, camp-furniture, etc.; were well mounted and appointed in every respect, except that the loss of my saddle had necessitated the borrowing of one; and I was not at all suited with it. It was a Spanish, or California side-saddle, made for the rider to sit facing the right hand—the fashion of all the native women in these Spanish States.   Except in this respect, this saddle is altogether superior to ours; and I was told that it could be ridden nearly as well on one side as the other.

But the experience of the first fifty rods contradicted this assurance. It was impossible for me to ride off a walk with any dignity; and as I considered myself responsible for a certain style, I protested against the sacrifice of my pretensions to any such mean necessity, and insisted upon being properly equipped before we left " the settlements." Accordingly, we stopped about four miles from home, where a good-natured neighbor furnished me with an American saddle, in which I found myself something freer. Then, when I first tried my horse's gait, I condemned him, and an exchange had to be made.

Mr. K., being an old campaigner, had been elected captain by acclamation, and he proposed to surrender, for my comfort, his own steed, which I at once christened Randolph, because in color and some other characteristics, he resembled a horse so named that had run away with me in the streets of San Francisco a few months before. He was a frisky, dashing-look-

ing fellow, with easy gaits and a kindly spirit ;
but before we had gone far, after remounting, it
was perceptible that the saddle did not fit his
back. Thus there was another (a third) dis-
mounting and remounting, at which Geordie,
looking comfortably on from her reliable old
roan, laughed triumphantly. My wrathful pro-
phesy, that retribution would overtake her before we reached home, only brought a merrier
shout and some bantering words, from which,
as soon as I was once more in the saddle, Randolph and I absented ourselves without ceremony.

Ten miles up the coast, we passed the last
habitation for forty miles. We called, and were
treated to a pitcher of delicious milk—what
New Yorkers would call cream—and some excellent radishes and turnips, some of which were
added to our camp-stores. After a chat of half
an hour, in which Mr. W—— related to us an
adventure he had recently had with a grizzly
bear, in the hills near his house, and described
the method of capturing and killing the seals
and sea-lions that were tumbling and bellowing
on the rocks, not fifty rods distant, we again

rode on, not much cheered by what he told us of the scarcity of strawberries, but fully resolved upon taking our full holiday, whether we found any or not.

Randolph's back occasionally protested, with the kind of wince one does not like to feel in a spirited horse, and which I was the more interested in observing, from his being a stranger and having times of treading very gingerly under me, and at the same time, of looking about his head and his ears, as if he were on the point of taking terrible fright, and leaving everything behind him. But he had a broad, round, good-natured face, and he did not belie his physiognomy. So we went on without further trouble, after some very careful arrangements for his comfort.

The country at that time was glorious in herbage and flowers. From about four miles above Santa Cruz to the last rancho, it is less beautiful than below; but the bold coast, and the great variety of forms made in its outline by the gaps, fissures, arches, and broad gateways, through which the rocks admit the surf, and about which, on the detached fragments and great bases that project from them, the tremendous seals congregate for their sports and social shore-parties, make the seaward view sufficiently diversified and interesting; while on the right, the hills that swell into very considerable heights, offer you smooth curves and slopes of exquisite beauty, sometimes covered, and again richly flecked with golden, purple, scarlet, and pink flowers; among which the yellow lupin—a very beautiful shrub of large size—the low purple, and white lupin, the mallows of bright pink and rose color, and a flaunting euchroma, twin brother to my old friend of the prairies, abound. Innumerable smaller flowers, of almost every imaginable color, lie below these showy dwellers of the plain, and shade the bright hues more softly down to the grass and herbage which, on the high lands, bear already the first tints of maturity in their tops.

As we advanced northward, we began to get the wind very fresh in our faces, charged with the spray thrown up by the surf beating against miles of broken rock and solid wall, that bound the shore for a long way above us. What with the slow start, the frequent changes, the visit at the rancho, and the stopping to look at seals occasionally, the afternoon was pretty well worn away by the time we had traveled twenty miles; and the captain proposed that we should go into camp at the first locality that offered us the requisites of wood, water, grass, and a lee.

We reached such an one about four o'clock. It was a narrow valley between two considerable hills, opening seaward, over cliffs eighty or ninety feet in height, and landward, up into the stern, sterile mountains, that come down here in a sharp spur from the coast range. The entire valley was not more than two acres in extent, and covered with a luxuriant growth of wild oats. We alighted, and in half an hour had a generous fire blazing before us, with a thick clump of shrubs at our backs, which were also almost a roof for us. I had never camped before; Geordie had, in crossing the Isthmus; so the edge of the novelty was taken off to her; but we felt such an escape from the care and labor that had borne so heavily upon us at home, and enjoyed so keenly the old holiday

feeling that light those rare seasons in childhood, that we did not require the stimulus of
novelty to make us happy.

The event of the evening, after the horses
were staked out, the fire made, and the blankets spread, was dinner. Good Miss Sampson
had roasted, carved, and packed those moral
antipodes, Dombey and Toots, in two small
jars. We had a ham, bread, butter, cakes,
nuts, raisins, brandy-peaches, and last our turnips and radishes, not the least desirable of
our stores. It was first proposed to dine upon
two courses; but there seemed a certain pro-
digality in this which prudence discouraged,
so we agreed to disembowel one of the jars,
and reserve the ham till next day. Mr. Toots
was accordingly produced, and portions of him
served on the small tin plates, which constituted
the chief part of our dinner-service; but he had
fared so hardly in life—having been the fag of
the entire poultry-yard, and the unhappy recipient of so much [fowl] treatment—that,
after the first few morsels, the flavor was voted
bilious, and the ham taken in his stead.

This was really nice; and as we sat about

the warm, bright fire, and saw the chill mist
driving over the hills before us, and heard the
surf madly chafing at the foot of the rocks,
we felt much of the cosy comfort of a snug
home. As the night threatened to be damp,
and I was mentally wondering how Geordie
and I were to sleep with nothing between us
and the fog that occasionally shook out his
gray wing, and again folded it, revealing mo-
mentary glimpses of blue sky and golden clouds,
far above us, our Captain threw out some
hints about the practicability of making a house
that should serve us for a shelter. We liked
not to be too earnest in commendation of the
proposal, lest the difficulty should prove greater
than it seemed to be; but he assured us that
nothing could be easier, there being a small
axe, plenty of boughs near at hand, and among
us all an abundant supply of blankets to cover
it with. When dinner was fairly over, both
gentlemen set themselves diligently to work,
and in a short time we were completely sheltered from both wind and fog in a little lodge,
which, though of small dimensions, quite sufficed us all for a sitting-room during the even-

ing, and Geordie and me for a sleeping-chamber
and dressing-room. It was larger than our
state-rooms at sea had been ; and though we
could not stand over four-and-a-half feet in it,
we could sit very comfortably *à la Turque ;*
while, by the light of the great fire, I read the
Chronicles of Clovernook, what time the hills
resounded to shouts of laughter, and the seals
on the rocks responded in an occasional bellow,
as if the Land of Turveytop were a familiar
country to them, and the Asyoulikeans old
friends, whom they were glad to hear of
again.

We read till a late hour ; then we talked till
a later one, inspired by the incomparable book
—by the novelty of our situation—by the stern
majesty of the darkness which brooded over us,
and let loose the wings of thought, and un-
sealed the fountains of memory—so that the
life of the past seemed to have compressed
itself into those hours. At last, Geordie in-
timated a wish to go to rest, whereupon the
gentlemen, having renewed the fire, betook
themselves to their blankets and saddles, and
in five minutes she was as sound asleep as if

she had been at La Libertad in our own chamber.

I could not sleep! A very long time had elapsed since my spirit had unfolded so free a pinion as it did that night.

My whole past life surrounded me. The earliest recollections of those years whose radiance the darkness of my human world could not dim, when the earth seemed a succession of flowery vales, and slopes, and sunny fields; when the clouds never stayed a moment too long to charm me, and even the little flash of unfriendly winter was welcome for the exceeding loveliness of the spring he ushered in; when every day was an age of delight, and every peaceful night a foretaste of heaven—all rose as vividly before me as if they were not memories but passing realities.

The hopes, the triumphs, the disappointments, the griefs of each successive period arranged themselves there—the former sanctified, the latter softened, by time, till they seemed more nearly assimilated than the wishes and purposes of a single day, in the latter period of sterner conflict, are. I have heard many persons, whom experience has instructed and saddened—as, indeed, what worthy spirit has she not?—express the painful want of satisfaction with which they reviewed their early successes. To me, such expression seems tantamout to a confession that their early ambition was false, their pursuits unworthy, and their triumphs, therefore, vain, ephemeral, and unproductive of good to their after lives.

Childhood is so inestimably blest, where nature is its nursing mother. My early hopes had been inspired by her; my victories gained at her bidding; and I thanked the great Father devoutly, as I lay there in the silence, that I scarcely could recall one which had not made me a happier child, a better girl, a more earnest woman. In the watches and battles I had used to have with the vermin that destroyed my ducks and chickens, my victories gratified the best affections I knew—for these were all I had then to love; and when I pressed a rescued one to my heart, life seemed brighter and worthier: I grew stronger and more resolute with every such experience.

When later I succeeded in removing obstacles that clouded my highest aspirations, and realized in successive years what had been the ideals of those that went before, I felt each victory to be a step toward a higher life ; and now I could review them with no bitter consciousness that the struggles by which they had been gained were vain, or themselves fruitless. Each had contributed to my womanhood. Each had helped on my interior life ; and I felt religiously thankful that I could then recall no one that had retarded my progress. Are not the internal experiences of like natures like, under all external circumstances, however various? Do not the truly good always advance in their own souls, however they may appear to the world to stop by the way, or even to retrograde ?

Day breaking over the hills, revealed a broad hollow, scooped out quite across the summit of the one opposite us before I slept. In a few minutes, it seemed, the sound of voices woke me to full light. The night had been very damp, as the dripping eaves of our lodge fully proved ; but there was great relief, on finding ourselves all afoot, in ascertaining that no one had taken cold; the more that our friend, Mr. G., was in very delicate health, and wholly unused to sleeping on the ground. Our ablutions were made at the spring. Breakfast was over; the sleeping arrangements converted to sitting ones; the dishes cleaned and packed; Messrs. Dombey, Toots, and the ham bestowed in their respective quarters; watches pulled from under our saddles (which, for the untraveled I relate it, had been our pillows), wound and compared, and still, as the fog hung along the coast, we waited a little, and fell back upon the immortal Chronicles again for an hour or so; when, the mist clearing, there came to us from the blue sky, the dry air and the fleecy clouds it bore gaily inland from the still-shrouded main, an irrepressible desire for movement. We were off from Oatnook unanimously and swiftly.

The horses were as impatient as ourselves, and when we had reached the sandy tract over the hills and descended to the beach about a mile from our camp, they literally flew along the hard sand. The delicious breeze, the great surf rolling in and dashing its spray among their feet, seemed to inspire them, as it did us, with overflowing life. We scarcely broke a gallop for five miles, except in crossing the clear streams that fall over the cliffs, and run their short course of a few rods through the sand into the sea. One could not fail there to understand the anguish of that exquisite song,

> " Where is the sea, I languish here !
> Where is my own blue sea,
> With all its barks in fleet career,
> And flags and breezes free ?"

The hills rise abruptly from the beach by a rocky wall, varying from forty to one hundred feet in height ; the face of which presents a variety of strata piled upon each other as perfectly as if done by the art of man. The hard slate, near the base, is worn in places into caves of considerable depth and dimensions. Occasionally great fissures open an escape for streams falling from the tops of the hills.

Leaving the beach, we rise by an inconsiderable ascent to an open country, where the coast-range sweeps abruptly back some two or three miles from the spur we had passed. This was the most beautiful region we had seen since leaving Santa Cruz, and, indeed, very like it. Gentle hills were divided here, as there, by gulches running seaward from the mountains, but so open and luxuriant as frequently to deserve the name of vallies. In the distance we saw the low sandy point, in the neighborhood of which were the strawberry-beds, and, nearer, a hut, upon one of the swells, which indicated that we were upon one of the large grazing ranches into which the whole of this portion of the coast region is divided.

I omitted to mention that while encamped in Oatnook, we received several calls from Spaniards homeward bound, from these ranches, who all told us that there were no *madusas ;** and one young *Caballero*, who had been at La Libertad twice, with beef to sell, assured us, with friendly earnestness, that there was *no nadita.*† These men had been up to mark the year's addition to the great herds that range those untenanted plains and hills. Every year

* Californian for strawberry.   † Not one.

this is done.   Three, or four, or five men go up,
driving before them as many horses, which
they ride and drive alternately on the way,
and use while there in herding the cattle. The
herds are gathered to the corrals, which sometimes are complete yards, and at others, have
only two sides—a deep gulch answering for a
third, and two or three horsemen for the
fourth. They are near water, close to which
the *hombres* camp—that is, build a fire to roast
their beef by—and there they live till the *roder*
is over.

Near the hut we were approaching, was also
a large corral, where this process had been
going on, and many of the fat-shining cattle
were yet lingering on the plain around. At the
sound of our horses' hoofs, they raised their
heads, snuffed the air a moment, looked wildly
at us, and took to their heels. Their timidity
helped to remind us that we were away from
the habitations of men, and gave further zest
to the sense of freedom with which we flew
over the plain, scattering them to the right
and left.

The Captain had dashed out a few yards

ahead, when suddenly he pulled up, with the cry of "here they are, and plenty of them," and the next moment was half knee deep in a sand knoll covered with strawberry vines. We all alighted, and several handsful were gathered, some of which were ripe, and large enough to give us a correct notion of their quality, which is unlike any I have seen at home, but very like the garden strawberry of Chili. The fruit is firmer, and more deliciously flavored than those we have in the old states; and, when full grown, three or four times larger than the largest there. These beds, however, were small, and had been pretty thoroughly plundered; so we mounted, after an impatient inspection of them, to push on to a more fruitful spot, and one, also, that would furnish a camp

Mr. K. and I stepped out in advance, to select a camp; and, as the country before us was dotted with lines of timber growing upon brooks or rivulets, we were confident of not having to go further than we chose. Coming upon a height, we saw a corral across a large gulch, through which ran a lively little stream.

We were descending to it, with eyes open for any advantageous location, when suddenly four or five buzzards rose from beneath a clump of trees on its bank. Here we saw the brands and bones of a camp which the Spaniards had left the night before.

"Why, there is beef," said Mr. K., "hanging under those trees—the best kind—that those fellows have left to the buzzards; and a new coffee-pot, too. We must take some of this along," and the next moment he had his knife deep in the choicest part of the choicest of *five* nearly entire quarters of young animals that were hanging upon the boughs. "This will make us a splendid dinner," said he, "and I shall cook it in a way you have never tried. You will see how nice it is. I must *cache* this coffee-pot till we return. And then we will push on and have something cooking before those lagging folks come up." They were still out of sight when we had reached a beautiful valley, some two miles further on, near which were acres of strawberries. We had unpacked, unsaddled, and were just about starting to the beach for muscles, when they came up.

We found the shell-fish too small to take, but there were exciting prizes in the shape of numerous shells, and curious forms of animal life, which the advancing tide disputed with us at that time, and we submitted the more readily, for remembering the experience of the ancient Dane, and the fine steaks that would soon be awaiting us. To these we repaired, after innumerable solicitations from the Captain, who assured us that a more propitious time for beach-ranging would come when the tide was out, and our dinner disposed of. While it was cooking, we received a call from the female population of a neighboring rancho, six miles away. They were seven in number: an elderly woman, a middle-aged one, a young girl, and four children, one an infant.

The mother was a fat, happy, careless person, even for a Californian. The sight of her face would have been a blessing to the distracted mothers among our care-taking countrywomen. We asked if these were all her children. To which she replied that she had many more.

How many?—and she held up all her fingers, and then snapped them, as if she would defy

twice that number to disturb the calm contentment of her life. They had been gathering
strawberries, which they offered us, in civil exchange for which we gave them nuts.

They assured us it would rain, and hospitably
invited us to their *casa*, where we could get
milk in plenty, if nothing else. They departed just as dinner was ready—a meal which we
enjoyed exceedingly, not only because of the
sharpness of our appetites after a long fast and
ride, but of the exquisite flavor of the beef,
which was simply roasted upon a stick before
the fire. How it shamed the elaborate arts of
French cookery! It is the trapper dish. I
recommend it to the attention of epicures.

The evening was very threatening, and as we
had been housed the last night, it was not to
be thought of that we should pass this unroofed.
So when the dinner things were out of hand,
the erection of another house was commenced,
and as there was plenty of drift-wood, spars
and yards, that had, perhaps, once, floated in
frozen Russian seas, or on the blue Egean, and
been thrown, at last, into this little cove,
whose frolicsome waters now lock in wintry

imprisonment the hardy navigators of the north, and again bathe the flowery shores of the fragrant " summer isles," our architecture lacked not honorable and fitting material, and went swiftly forward to completion. It was christened Strawberry cottage, on the strength of our expectations, which we had not yet sought to realize. Its perpendicular capacity was greater than that of Oatnook ; otherwise it showed very similar proportions. Before dark, a store of wood was gathered, and I was again appointed to conduct the entertainment of the evening, which was to consist of that noble sermon of Channing, on " the Church." The reading, and running comments, occupied us until ten o'clock, when we retired, agreeing upon an early stroll in the morning, on the beach. There were no seals that night, or if there were, my sleep was too deep to be interrupted by them

In the morning, there was a long discussion on the expediency of rising early or late, first, between Geordie and me, but, finally, extending to the lodgers outside the blankets. It was ended by reference to the Noctes Ambrosianæ, wherein I found a speech of the beloved old shepherd, so triumphant in the affirmative, that my hearers were afoot before I had fairly done with it.

But we found none of the poetry, beauty, and freshness, so vividly described in it; for the morning was damp, above and below, gray, thick, and uninviting. When the fire was replenished and the breakfast put in the first stage of preparation, Geordie and I walked quietly to the beach, with our coarse bathing-towels, and having doubled a jutting ledge of rock, about thirty rods north of the lodge, we tried the *matutin*, so much to our satisfaction and refreshment, that the steak à la trapper cooled while we *ploutered*, and the Captain, when we returned laden with magnificent shells, expressed his entire disapprobation of going sea-*fairing* so early in the day.

The morning began to be rosy before we had finished some selected passages from the Noctes, and laughed at some special pleading from Mr. G., and then we betook ourselves to the strawberry beds, with a deep, precious sense of the rare freedom of coming and going at will, of lounging, sitting, reading, eating, riding or walking, at the bidding purely of our pleasure, for another whole day. By the afternoon, with intervals of rest on the cliffs, or in the lodge, as fatigue or caprice prompted, we had gathered several quarts of fruit, and a number of beautiful shells. A ride up among the hills, or to the *rancho* was talked of, but finally abandoned, and a quiet, grateful mood settling down upon us, I drew Sterling from the book-satchel, and passed it to Geordie, who opened at the Sexton's Daughter, and read on in her appreciative and varying tones. We listened, at whiles, with glistening eyes, and a keener sympathy, with all the variety of hopeful, anxious, tender, and religious emotion, than we should have felt elsewhere, and were silent after its close.

" I wish," at last, said the reader, " that some one would tell me what I or this poem lacks, that, loving it as I do, it yet never quite satisfies me. There is always left, after reading it, a painful impression which I cannot explain."

" It may be," said I, "that the human excellence so beautifully portrayed, and fervently enjoined in it, partakes of the long-received theory of constraint and self-denial, which you reject. It is the virtue of the old life, somewhat, but not altogether, freed and irradiated by the light of the new philosophy!"

"I do not know," she replied, "that that is the origin of my difficulty, though one could certainly have rejoiced in further revelations of the freedom which such a spirit as Henry's might be supposed to have a foretaste of on the threshold of the spirit-world. I think, however, this does not give rise to the feeling I speak of, and I am unable to suggest what may, as well as to describe its exact character; but that comes from indolence, or a careless kind of distraction in which I suffer my mind to remain on some subjects. But I like to be free to do just that if I please—free as we have been these three days, to be still or move, to stand or walk, to sit or lie, to speak or be silent, to think or muse, without constraint or a sense of being inharmonious. That only is freedom to me which is so to my inner sense."

"But, happily," I said, "all persons do not feel the want of such freedom at this time, or we

should be a world of abject slaves. To most
natures, freedom from outward constraint is
the largest liberty they desire; and even that,
is so much more than is wholesome for the
masses, high as well as low, that the most
radical of us must rejoice that the idea of a
truer freedom does not take hold of the popular mind."

" There is use in error. Much error and
some truth have brought the world to its
present condition, which could, at any moment, be made worse by the sudden spread
of truth, for which mankind is not prepared."

" Yes," said Mr. G., " the very fact that we
have arrived at our present condition by ex-
perimental wisdom, proves a use in error, or in
partially-developed truth, which seems to the
age looking back upon it, to have been gross
error ; for, if unmixed truth had been our greatest good, it would have been our destiny, and
we could not have gone astray in seeking it,
I think.   But all this does not help to answer
your question about the poem you have read."

" No ; but I think some supper would help

us out of several other difficulties," said Mr. K.; "and I move that the cook and his assistants proceed at once to their duty."

Some indistinct word was heard of its being our last supper out; but it was at once unanimously agreed, that any person who should allude, directly or indirectly, to that fact, should be subject to a heavy penalty. The wind freshened as the evening darkened; but there were rosy tints in the sun-set region, which encouraged us to hope that the night would at least not be worse than the previous one had been.

"There must be a studding sail set below here, on the weather side," said the Captain, " or this wind will sweep the smoke and ashes into the *casa* directly."

Some poles were accordingly procured, and set in the ground, and a blanket stretched upon them, which broke the wind off the fire and the lodge, and left us quite at peace for the evening. We were not gay; for the happiness we had anticipated was now a memory, and we discoursed as people always do who are secretly unwilling to confess that there is

less to be expected than has already been
enjoyed.

"It is not easy," said Mr. G., "to bear in
mind, through such a season as this, that the
world really wears to others its work-a-day
garb, and will so soon again put it on for us."

"No," responded Geordie, "and its work-
a-day garb is very hateful to me, because of
the false conditions and relations that make
the life of the millions a period of slavery,
filled with occupations distasteful and disgusting ; and which, being so, cripple the
growth of character, deform its proportions,
and press it through life, shorn, at every stage,
of much of the grace and joyousness that, in
a freer and truer condition, would make it
delightful to possess as our own, and beautiful to contemplate in another. One chafes
and frets at finding one's-self hemmed in on
every side—forced to this, forced to that—
taking up a wearisome occupation this year,
to get bread and a roof; and next year, obtaining the summit of possible freedom, when
one is permitted to engage in something
whereby one remotely or feebly approaches

the accomplishment of some good, to which, if it were possible, the whole of life could be so happily devoted. There is no greatness in slavery, and there can be no labor but by attraction without it. In the world, those only are free whose power is sufficient to enable them to be true to their affections."

"It is an idle use of words," I said, "to assent to the ultimate truth of such statements; and yet, if we consider that, in the sense in which you name slavery, it has, with few exceptions, been the lot of all who have lived and died as we shall, it, perhaps, behoves us to endeavor to seek out the good it has wrought for us. One thing, it must greatly profit us, in our times of discontent, to remember: that no lot is unmixed of evil or good. The worst is, doubtless, a little better to those whose it is, than it appears to us, who, from a higher plane, look down upon it. The deepest moral night is not total absence of blessed impulses; and I believe, in natures most darkened by sin— most impoverished by debasing necessities— most blighted by indulgences, there are oc-

casional flashes of true light, faint though they
be—occasional gleams of glory, let in by love,
by hope, by faith—by some of the ministering
spirits, which, while life is embodied, never
utterly forsake it. The grandeur of a conscious integrity may not be felt; but there
is certainly somewhat of its deathlessness—
somewhat of its beauty revealed in these moments."

" Yes," she replied, " it is true ; and none
know that, dear, better than we who have
followed the spirit through all stages of degradation and suffering, and seen it in every
form of slavery to which sin and untruth could
reduce it; but one so longs to see men becoming strong and good in a freed state, that
one forgets the little things that might be
worse in the opposite condition."

" Is it not true, however," said Mr. G.,
" that we cannot be free alike ? Is it not
improbable that we ever shall be in this life ?
Not merely because of our different capacities, but because of the relations which constitute the very soul of life. Our affections
fasten inseparably in so many directions, they

furnish so many objects of hope and doubt, so many incentives to toils, which, but for them, would never be undertaken, or would be most enslaving and injurious to our whole nature, that, while they remain a part of our constitution, I think the very conditions of the freedom you name, impossible to us as a race—and I confess I see not how organization of labor or of social systems, unless they first strike out the affections of the soul, can render men wholly and permanently free."

"You take an extreme view of the state proposed," replied my friend; "but I do not know that even that necessitates the admission of your doubt; for, in a natural and true condition of the race, or of a portion of it, each individual would be so situated, that his relation to another should be a source of happiness, and of calm certainty of blessing in it. His wants could not bring upon the individual the necessity of slavish toil; for they would be supplied by his free labor in what attracted him; or, if weak and incapacitated himself, by that of the social body. His propensities would lack temptation to call them into excessive action ; his selfishness, the mean stimulus of fear, that nurses its hateful growth."

" I quite agree," said I, " that if the individual were harmonious in his own nature, and truly related in his community, the affections would cease to be, to those who are in themselves capable of freedom, the bond they now are. But I fear we are far, very far, from such a state ; and this favorite theory of yours, I think, we shall have to wait several generations to see the realization of. In our time we do not find the community to whose actual condition it seems suited. But it is very late, and we have to ride home to-morrow."

In the morning, our fruit and shells were packed as judiciously as possible, and, after breakfast, it was announced to us that we had only radishes and butter left for our refreshment on the road. This was rather a startling announcement, but our reliance was on the excellent Captain, whose resources seemed inexhaustible, and who assured us we should find beef at the place where we had left it, that would serve for our dinners.

We mounted and set off about ten o'clock,

the horses in high spirits for home. Randolph and I were renewing our acquaintance in sundry little passages of agreement and difference as to the best path up the hill we had immediately to ascend, when, just as we reached the top, the Dutchman, who also felt his pack somewhat of a stranger, ran across us behind, taking his leading-rope over Randolph's back. I was a little behind the party which the Dutchman circumnavigated (in the ten or fifteen seconds that my horse's heels were flying in the air), and having gained the front, he commenced a dance, the like of which was never seen on circus-boards or elsewhere. My chief means of appreciating his performance, were the peals of laughter from my friends, for it seemed as if Randolph would never again consent to the use of all his feet upon the ground, and while he remained in that state of mind, it seemed necessary for me to attend to him rather than the entertainment. At length the rope slipped from his back, and with half a dozen tremendous snorts of warning, he let himself down into a kind of dance, half of defiance, half of fear, and joined the company.

We were not long in reaching the beach, over which we had another gallop, not tamer but less joyous than that which had so exhilarated us going up. We alighted at Oatnook though our frame had been demolished, partly to look for a brooch which Geordie, in the scattering frame of mind common to her, had left there. We did not find it, however, and mounting, rode briskly on till two o'clock, when a halt for dinner was called, about twelve miles from home. It was at one of those great gateways by which the streams from the mountains pour themselves into the ocean. On either side were towering rocks in detached masses, and immense walls, whose masonry was as perfect as if they had been laid by the hand of man— at the foot of which spread the broad, white beach, clean as the most notable housewife's floor. Geordie and I strolled for shells or other curiosities, but, finding only some vertebræ of a whale, and being tempted by the flashing water as it rolled over the sands, we resolved upon another bath, which was only well over, when we heard shout after shout of dinner! dinner! to which we responded by presenting ourselves in person as hastily as possible, and partaking freely of the delicious beef, which was sated with butter and garnished with radishes.

We reached La Libertad a little after sunset, and I felt thankful, as the fresh evening breeze rustled the rich foliage of the hillside under which our path lay, that the home we returned to was more beautiful than any spot we had seen.

Charlie came out to meet us on Bill, and, in the excitement of showing off his horsemanship, which then, for the third time, perhaps, allowed him to indulge in a gallop, forgot, till we were fairly in-doors, to tell us the great event of our absence—the most wonderful one in the history of the rancho. The old shanty was burned, and all the powder had been blown up, and Tom's clothes were all gone, and Joe's boots—"and the shafts of the wagon, too, mother," said little Eddie, holding my hand tight in his till he could tell me his news. "And, mother, Susan Nipper is hanged in the oak-tree, and Miss Tox has weaned my little chickens, and she went in the tree last night with Major Bagstock."

Indeed, there had been calamities little and great, but we had a joyous evening notwithstanding, and could not have lamented our misfortunes less under any circumstances.

Tom gave a very favorable account of the state of things, and it seeming to us that we had been gone long enough for the potatoes to have got three months growth, he averred that they had.

CHAPTER XXVII.

Notwithstanding the dryness of the season, the late rains, which had fallen more profusely in the coast counties than the inland regions, brought the crops forward very vigorously. It is proper to remark here, that the coast lands of Upper California have great advantages over the arable lands which lie interior to them. The climate, during the dry season, is much more humid than in the inland vallies, and, at some points, if not throughout the entire length of the coast, more water falls during the rainy season than off the seaboard. Hence, in part, its greater fertility. Santa Cruz is especially favored in this respect. The clouds, that are never an unwelcome sight to the farmer, scarcely ever pass us without pouring out liberally of their treasures, and during the summer, heavy fogs often set in toward nightfall, which rarely disperse before eight or nine, A. M., and sometimes give us their friendly shelter till near noon.

Approaching the coast from the interior, at any time during the dry season, the greater life and freshness of the vegetable world are very obvious and grateful to the sense that longs for the old revivification which summer showers used to send upon the earth, in the days when the poplar leaves glistened and danced in them before the door of the country school-house ; what time the sweet-briar gave its perfume to the wind, wandering lazily in at open doors and windows ; and the flowers in the garden, that had been dim, brightened their colors ; and the birds rejoiced aloud on the dripping boughs ; and the foot, languid and weary before, trod the freshened sward as if the fertilizing drops had impregnated the earth with somewhat of a divine life, and drawn it nearer to the Source of all true joy. O, summer showers ! how often have the wearisome months of dust and drouth revived in my mind the poetry with which ye invest forest, field, garden, and lawn, in the more sprightly and varying clime where ye were wont to visit my paths by day and by night.

One must feel here if never before, the earnestness with which a poet—a pastoral one—would exclaim: "O heaven and earth! O God and man! What had I, a simple shepherd, felt in a spring shower?"

The utility and beauty peculiar to such a climate scarcely compensate for what is lost in these smiles of God upon our native lands. The satisfaction of uninterrupted haymaking and harvesting—the entire security of journeying and sleeping, if need be, for months together, under a sky that never weeps, ought, certainly, to pass for something in the account; and, at this stage of our history, when the practical alone is considered, do pass for much, too much, perhaps, since they are counted upon as serving the grand end of all action here. The mercenary spirit is a more despotic tyrant in this land of freemen than czar or sultan could be in a land of slaves.

If we commend any feature of the earth or climate it is less that it animates the spirit with a sense of beauty—that it inspires us with gratitude and love to God as its author—that it kindles in the soul a ray of that heavenly love which clothes the noblest being we look upon with something akin to divinity, and the meanest with somewhat to command our sympathy and nerve our hearts and hands to helpful thoughts and deeds—less for any such reason, or for any less noble of the same character, than that it would enable us to put money in our purse.

Our lotos is the gold which has to be obtained by laborious diligence or hazardous scheming ; but once tasted, like the fabled leaf, it causes forgetfulness of old ties, purposes, motives, restraints, with this essential difference, which, also, is almost a fatal one, that while it buries old brotherhoods, it does not create new ones.

The isolation of the country has not in all respects favored its moral character. For if a noble, unselfish plan or idea, cherished and pursued under difficulties, perhaps, at cost of long accustomed comforts, and of habits that have converted uses into necessities, can ennoble the nature—and who will doubt it ?—then as certainly and equally, will purposes of an opposite character, pursued in like manner, exercise an influence, quite the reverse of good and noble, and exalting, and the more readily, that minds of a common order will more freely entertain and be affected by the latter, than the former. Emigration to California has, up to this time, been no small event in the life of the man or woman who has proposed it to him or herself, and although of the mass, there undoubtedly is a proportion who have had ultimate purposes altogether worthy of humanity, and others who have come for adventure, it is as little to be doubted, that the great body have come as gold-hunters, and have never thought of qualifying their motive by any less selfish.

The gold-hunter has deliberated upon his purpose before leaving his former home ; gradually it has grown into such magnitude that, like a mountain suddenly upheaved before him, it has shut out from his view the objects which before filled his world ; it has hidden friends and relations ; interposed its ungenial self to sever the ties of consanguinity, affection, duty, perhaps of honor ; and, swelling with every tri-

umph, finally launched him upon his momentous undertaking. He has either a long voyage
or a wearisome journey, which may be one of
great hardening as well as hardship, to enter
upon at once ; but every day of either the one
or the other, contributes to the growth and
strengthening of those influences which concen-
trate his thoughts on himself and help him to
forget that he has ever lived for any other.
The influences of the land-journey have generally been most unhappy, often shocking ; hardships of every sort, coarse and scanty food,
exacting toil, naked want ; which in common
natures, especially in men, rouses the deepest
selfishness, irritating necessities, suffering, that
if cared for, would put too far off the attainment
of the grand object, which, by this time, has
grown too pressing to admit of postponement—
all unite in this detestable transit, to make anything like generosity or unselfishness, that may
remain in some hidden corner of the heart,
seem weakness.

The emigrant must be every day renewing
in his mind, if it lack fortifying in that direction, deliberate purposes to be selfish and firm

to a degree that, a few months before, he would have thought criminal, almost diabolical ; so that, when at length the land of hope is reached, he is prepared, if he have a family, to place them, for the sake of getting gold, in situations of exposure, that it would before have shocked him to think of ; or, if he be alone, to enter into schemes and occupations, which, a year before, he would have considered it infamous for any man to engage in. Be it understood that in speaking of the condition of thousands one does not include all. In a hundred families there may be ten or twenty to whom these remarks do not apply. Some have made their journey honorably, humanely, and have not required the efforts of missionaries to Christianize them after their arrival. These were persons whose goodness was too pure and strong to suffer over-turning from bad influences.

I have not yet spoken of what has always seemed to me the most shocking feature in this emigration—its effect on women and children. These are questions of far more importance than any influence it could exercise on men. A demoralized husband and father is certainly a deplorable object ; but a demoralized family—the wife and mother profane, the children entitled to that holy name only by their stature, not in anywise by their innocence or ignorance of the vices which are only less shocking in older lives —these are objects which the partisans for identical rights and occupations might grow wiser and cooler in contemplating.

In all that one sees of this phase of life, in this multifaced land, how clearly is evidenced the superior moral position of woman ! Man may be never so coarse, gross, or selfish, yet, if his fireside be presided over by purity, upright-ness, and integrity in his wife, there is an ever-flowing fountain of good to his children. De-file that, and there is no hope for the elevation of those who surround it. In her home, and fitted by virtue, intelligence, and energy, for its presiding spirit, woman has a power far sur-passing any which man possesses, and which he cannot divide with her. Why should she seek to divide with him that which is as peculiarly his own ?

The lamentable consequences of the de-terioration which women suffer in the journey across the plains are painfully manifest in all the mining towns; but this is not the place or time to dwell at length upon them. I shall elsewhere have occasion to refer to this subject. Meantime, I wish earnestly to do injustice to no class, and, therefore, say that much of what I write I *know* to be true, and state it not in censure, but in sorrow; because the results come almost unconsciously upon those who have little choice in incurring them. They seem to be almost inseparable from the enterprise we are considering—at least from this type of it—and come most surely and broadly upon those who are least prepared to resist their approach.

On the other hand, the emigration by sea is only less deplorable in its direct results, because, chiefly, it requires less endurance and active exertion, which *may* be borne only to the injury of the character. In both, the mind broods over the same purposes—the same ultimate object occupies it, to the exclusion of all others. The universal topic of conversation on all vessels bound to California, is gold. Digging, the size of lumps, the operation of quartz machinery, amalgamators, coarse gold, fine gold, northern mines, southern mines, Yuba, American, North Fork, South Fork, dry diggings, thousands, months, years, pile, these words and phrases are a pretty fair synopsis of the first chapter. The weary months so spent, which happily are shortening with each voyage, produce a sufficient stultification of the better powers to permit the individual, by the time it is over, to apply himself unreservedly to the grand pursuit.

Then the national and individual characteristics come out in *alto-relievo*. The California Yankee is the New England Yankee, with all his peculiar power centupled. All his sharpness is sharpened ; all his 'cuteness is more 'cute. If he belonged to the wooden nutmeg genus in New England, he will manufacture gold beads here ; if he could blow a fife on training days, he will be a professor of music here ; if he have built a pig-sty or kennel at home, he will be a master-builder in California. If he have been six months at a public school, and lumbering the rest of his life, he would become a candidate for the throne, if there were an elective one in the country to be filled ; and, if successful, would whittle out a tolerably smart coronation speech, or, failing, he would go to hear his competitor's, and guess pretty shrewdly how he would *get along*. In the choice of his occupation, he considers its lucrativeness, first, and the *chances* apart from that. These he is always looking out for. He has a wide range of pursuits, places, and employments to choose from. The professions are open to him, if he can read and write ; and every office in his county, if its population is pretty fairly mixed of eastern people. He may keep a monte table, sell strong drink, be treasurer of moneyed associations, or quartz companies , in short, he may be anything that he has the power or the wish to be, but he is always the Yankee. Always under the legitimate occupation is covered something else— some ' *spec*'—from which great results are hoped ; some scheme, or schemes, that will scarcely bear examination by daylight, to fill up the intervals of attending to his regular business, or bear him company to and from his restaurant and drinking saloon. Maturing these, he thrusts his hands deeper into his pockets, is more vigorously attentive to his tobacco, and quite energetic in his enjoyment of the national recreation with the knife. When these symptoms are observable, it behoves Mr. Smith, Mr. Brown, or Mr. White, if they are trading with him, to consider well what they are doing, while they, perhaps, are working their way, with equal industry, into somebody else's pocket.

No land ever lay beneath the sun which so favored the natural speculator, and I have no doubt the genuine Yankee has often astonished himself in it. The world around him he certainly has. But these, which are the chief advantages of the country to him, seem to be thrown away, or to prove embarrassments to other nations.

The Englishman cannot often accommodate himself readily enough to the sinuosities of trade, and to the chances attendant upon it, to insure himself the success which it is reckoned disgraceful not to attain to somehow. If he make a fortune here, it is because he works on a larger scale, or realizes larger regular profits

than at home ; rarely, I believe, by trying any
of the hazards by which fortunes so often
change hands in a few days, or months, among
the Americans.

CHAPTER XXVIII.

WE recognize in California but two types of the republican character, that which I have described and the Missourian. The latter term was first used to represent the entire population of the West; the characteristics of the Hoosier, Sucker, Wolverene, Buckeye, etc., being very generally merged, and the Missourian elected as the type of all. But there appears to have been a prominent class of emigrants, from a region that has become famous throughout our country—Pike county, to wit. It would seem that the people of this celebrated region could not, in their tramontane condition, have mixed very largely with the world ; for they were so little smoothed down in the great human mangle, and shortly became so marked, that Pike county superseded the name of its state, and soon of the whole

West.   To be catalogued as from Pike county, seems to express to all that large class of Americans who are neither Yankees nor Missourians; a little more churlishness, a little more rudeness, a greater reserve when courtesy or hospitality are called for, than I ever found in the western character at home.   Pike county, in short, is not likely to derive from the settlement of California a reputation as the cradle of the graces, the amenities, or the liberalities of life. Nor, indeed, considering the swift degeneracy of more cultivated people, could it be expected. From its log cabin, to the mines of California, would not, at first thought, appear to be any great falling off in material refinement.   But, if the journey of which I have before spoken be taken into account, with the manner of life after it is completed, perhaps we shall be inclined to somewhat more of leniency in our judgment of this much-condemned emigrant.

Arrived in California, he sits down for the first year chiefly in the mines.   Here he purposes to get gold.   At home, like all other men, he had the same object, and he pursued it by raising corn, potatoes, wheat, cattle—which

he took to the nearest market-town for sale.
There his business brought him in contact with
half a dozen, or at least two or three men of
better manners than himself—respectful, courteous, suave, from whom he, at the least, would
not learn to be more rude, uncivil, and stiff, than
he was before. There, also, he would see women better dressed and more refined than those
at home. In short, he would measure himself
and his with those who were better acquainted
with life and its social demands upon the indi
vidual. Thus, the toil and business of successive years, it might be supposed, would improve him a little.

But here he sits down upon the unreclaimed
earth to transfer her treasures directly to his
own pocket. There is exchange neither of
commodity nor courtesy with any. If we consider this, and that he takes the reward of his
labor without so much as thank you, or by
your leave, we shall, perhaps, be prepared to
forgive, in the unfortunate emigrant from that
famed locality, the lack, which else it were
not easy to pardon, of many of the graces and
refinements and *some* of the virtues.

In the whole active life of the country there is now ample space to permit all classes of characters to walk in the most erect attitude of which they are capable, could we but be content therewith—certain conditions that favor the best manifestations of them. The Jew, I think, does honor to his name here. The pressure which elsewhere bows him to the earth is removed. He eschews old clothes, and rarely if ever, so far as my own observation entitles me to speak, attempts to get a greater advantage in trade than his neighbors. There are freedom and prosperity enough in the country to permit men to be honorable, if they will, and enjoy comfort :—if they are not so it is because they choose to be otherwise, and, alas, how great is the number !

Mixed as is the population, the country receives its chief traits from the American mind and energy, which are so speculative, so strongly tinctured with love of risk for the chance of great gain, that one does not wonder that the first tide of gold, flowing down from the mountains, turned every town into a continuous gaming-house. The American is not a working

animal like the Swiss, the German, the Irishman, or the Englishman. He will not sit
down for months together like any of these—
content with their four or five dollars per day,
in return for ten hours' hard labor. It is not
the habit of the nation, and the individuals who
do it never regard it as a settled business, but
are always, while so engaged, looking about for
some better chance—a bakery, or a slaughter-
house, or a few mules for packing, a wagon and
team to drive; a small stock of goods, some
groceries and liquors—anything that will enable him, by laboring a portion of his time, to
divert the gold, which others dig, to his own
pockets. It would be very calamitous to my
ease-loving republican brethren to have the
emigration from the laboring nations checked.

The population of the agricultural districts
is, of course, less marked by the characteristics
I have hinted at, than that of the mining regions. The only *operations*, that distinguish
our farming neighborhoods broadly from similar
communities in the new states east of the
Rocky Mountains, are the jumping of lands,
which title and possession both are often too

feeble to secure to the owner. I have observed that the Western men no longer use the old term to designate this enterprise, but one more in keeping with the swift spirit of the country. A man does not *jump* land in California. He *loaps* it, and then, for the most part, he intends to coin his potatoes, and onions, and barley, and allow himself but three or, at most, five years to make what he would think a very fair result of the labor of a lifetime at home—what, indeed, in many portions of the country, he could not realize by the same labor, so applied, from his twentieth to his sixtieth birthday. If he fails in his expectations, it does not often occur to him that they were unreasonable. He is more likely to guess, calculate, or reckon that he had better try something else, or add something to that—a mill may be, or a share in some trading-house in the next town.

In their native states, the Americans are practically a versatile people. There must be some new word found to express how inexhaustible their resources become in California. As counterpoise, however, to these facilities toward descent, which are more the result of external circumstances than of deep interior capacity for wrong, let us strengthen ourselves by remembering the good gifts and powers that are conjoined with them—the unfaltering energy—the self control—the personal courage, untainted except in certain sections by brutality—the quick sympathy that responds to the appeal of suffering—the resolute, steady, pressing forward toward cultivation and development which is a distinguishing purpose of the American and especially of the Yankee character, and the sublime patriotism which makes the American, whether humble or exalted—wise or ignorant—gentle or rude—under whatsoever skies he may sleep or wake—always and inalienably American.

A national character that embodies these vital attributes, is capable of self redemption any day, and California life, bowing under its load of humiliations and sins, may be likened to the bended shrub upon the summer margin of its streams, which we see borne down by their swollen and muddy winter currents. When the floods shall subside, they will recover their erect position and stand fair in the beauty and strength of health. So will our moral life, when these years of wintry disorder and lawless indulgence shall have passed over us, rise in beauty and harmony from their pressure.

CHAPTER XXIX.

THE history of the rise, growth, destruction, and resuscitation, of the principal towns in California, would, without amplification, fill a larger volume than this is intended to be altogether. I have not reliable means of getting facts of much interest or value relative to any of these, except the metropolis, but it is known that flood or flame or both, have visited them all repeatedly with terrible destruction, and it is characteristic of the wonderful energy and elasticity of the country, that it has sometimes happened, that the ashes of the ruined tenement were not cold under the feet of the trader or artisan, before he had its successor erected of cotton, canvas, or board, and was driving his business again with whatever he had rescued from the destruction. In a few days or weeks the whole burnt region was alive again with the stir of the various callings that had been suspended, and a stranger visiting the city, or an absentee returning after a short absence, would search in vain for any visible evidences of the late calamity. San Francisco, which has in all respects, except for its commercial interests, the most undesirable site in all California, has been six times destroyed by fire, and yet, its growth from the discovery of the gold, up to the present day, has been more like fable than reality. Its total losses by fire are estimated to have been $20,000,000, yet it is now the fourth if not the third city on the continent. Its arrivals and departures, as shown by the marine lists, have increased, since 1847, to thirty, sometimes to fifty, a day; and the number of persons arriving by sea, exceeds that of all the other ports of the United States together, except New York and Boston.

It has two Baptist, two Episcopal, two Presbyterian, three Methodist, and two Roman churches, a San Francisco Bethel, a Chinese Temple without the characteristic architecture,* and two Jewish synagogues. It has

---

* There has since been erected a Temple to Buddha, with all the accompanying interior splendors of that Oriental worship.

five public schools, attended by 791 pupils, with a corps of 11 teachers. There are three theatres, two of large size, capable of seating 2,000 persons, and one of lesser dimensions. The larger are very creditable edifices, quite tasteful in their interior finish, and very respectable in their management, except that they compete with the churches on Sunday evenings, which the gaming-houses no longer do openly.

There is no feature in which the city is so surprisingly changed, as in the reduced number and splendor of these last-named establishments. In '49 and '50, it was no figure of speech to say that the Plaza was illuminated by the glare which shone from its surrounding hells. On two sides of it, they presented an almost continuous front, and the clang of music, generally from good bands, was heard in them without ceasing. I could never before understand that music might really become a diabolical sound.

Those were curious places to look in at of an evening. In the popular ones, the crowd was so dense that you had to thread your way through a mass of people constantly moving and pressing on each other. Every variety of face, clothed with every possible expression, from the most stolid indifference to the keenest excitement, surrounded one in the unceasing hum of those glaring rooms. Every garb, from fine broadcloth and snowy linen, to the dirtiest and coarsest habiliments worn by miners and wagoners, was there intermixed.

In one corner, a coarse-looking female might preside over a roulette-table, and, perhaps, in the central and crowded part of the room a Spanish or Mexican woman would be sitting at monte, with a cigarita in her lips, which she replaced every few moments by a fresh one. In a very few fortunate houses, neat, delicate, and sometimes beautiful French women were every evening to be seen in the orchestra. These houses, to the honor of the coarse crowd be it said, were always filled!

Curious and striking scenes were at times enacted in these places. A rough-looking, bearded man, with slouched hat, from the mines, might enter with one, or may be two, considerable leathern sacks filled with gold.

He would walk up to the heaviest laden table,
and throwing down his burden, boldly say,
" I'll tap your bank." This was explained to
be equivalent to saying, " I will stake the
whole of my treasure against your money."
And in five minutes thousands of dollars
changed hands. I am told that California
gaming is distinguished from the same vice
in any other part of the world, by the calmness of its votaries. I never witnessed such
an incident as I have related ; but have frequently been told by those who have, that
they were astonished at nothing so much as
the perfect coolness with which both the win-
ning and the losing party took his fate. Certainly I never saw cooler faces than were many
of those who, at the instant I was studying
their features, were receiving or paying over
hundreds or thousands of dollars, lost or won
in as little time as it would take to count it ;
and this is very quickly done by measuring
the piles of coin instead of counting each
one.

It was not merely the gaming that gave
character to these pestilent places. In each

there was, of course, a bar; and, if one may
judge from the appearance of the crowd that
haunted them by day as well as by night, their
vices were not altogether nocturnal. Many of
them were the most productive property in
the country; worth more than a placer mine,
however rich; and, belonging to the "first
men"—members of the City Council and of
the honorable professions—were not easily
closed when even the popular nerve began
to be painfully touched by them. The Hon.
Mr. Smith, of the board of Aldermen, had a
host of friends, who would protect his right to
put his property to the most productive use to
himself, let the press, the pulpit, or individuals
say what they might of it.

But relief came, despite the selfishness and
covetousness that, in all times and communities, would enrich themselves on souls if they
could be coined, as greedily as on gold dust:
came from that source which never fails to
mitigate, if it does not root out popular
evils—its own excess. A single soul may now
and then be found, wholly lost to the shame
and weariness of such scenes; but a people,

with Saxon blood in their veins, never. The gaming-houses of San Francisco are now less in number by one-half, if not two-thirds, than they were at the time I speak of; and the crowds who then thronged them are now scattered among the theatres, the churches, and those institutions which I am almost ready to call more sacred—the houses that have since grown up in their midst.

There is no inviolate fireside in California that is not an altar; no honorable woman but is a missionary of virtue, morality, happiness, and peace, to a circle of careworn, troubled, and often, alas, demoralized men. At the opposite end of the scale, in every sense, from the places I have attempted to describe, are the public schools of the metropolis. Public instruction was first commenced in San Francisco early in the year 1850, by a Mr. John C. Pelton, of Massachusetts, and sustained some two months by private exertions, before it was taken in charge by the city. The numbers increased rapidly, till the school became so large that Mr. P. and his wife were unable to give anything like the requisite attention to the pupils, who represented every continent and the islands of the sea, and spoke nearly all the languages of Christendom.

Meantime, a system of Public Instruction was organized by the Legislature of '50–'51, under which state public schools were first opened in 1851. They now number five, varying in their attendance from 600 to 800.* It would be superfluous to dwell on the importance of this branch of the public service, were it not that, from the immense variety of conditions gathered under its influence, it becomes, to those engaged in carrying it on here, not only more complicated and laborious than it is elsewhere, but of the last importance to the state. California will always be the nucleus and home

* This was the number in 1852; there are now (August, 1856) eight public schools, most of them taught in expensive and commodious buildings, erected in '53 and '54. The construction and furnishing of these buildings would do credit to any city in the Union. They are well-lighted, mostly well-ventilated, and well-arranged. There are, at the present time, 2,300 children attending the public schools under the City Board of Education, and 1,200 under the County Superintendent and Commissioners. Over forty teachers are employed in their instruction, which in thoroughness and variety will compare favorably with that of most of our Eastern cities.

of the extreme of democratic tendencies. If America (for with our late accessions of wealth, territory, and power, we may now, without assumption, put ourselves for the whole continent) is republican elsewhere, here she will be democratic. If she be that in her other states, she will something as far beyond it here as the latter condition now is from the former; and one can almost imagine that the day will dawn upon these magnificent shores, when the people shall be choosing, not between a constitutional and absolute government, but whether liberty shall be constitutional or absolute.

The moral and political elements of this state will almost surely make it the theatre of first test for the most radical questions, at the same time that it must, of necessity, embrace in its code of laws many relics of ancient tyranny : witness its recent legislation in reference to the property rights of women, and its death penalty for theft.

If we consider, then, that the first generations to grow up under these institutions come from every state and empire in Christendom, and from many out of it, and embrace every variety of mental condition, of hereditary prejudice, of traditional influence, and every extreme of social and religious bigotry; and that here, for the first time, all these elements are brought upon a common platform, it will be easy to see how arduous, if faithfully and wisely performed, is the duty of the first teachers. One wishes them better sustained than the same class generally is where their function is less difficult.

The press of San Francisco has, in many of its features, been subject to the usual fluctuations of new places. Papers full of life, spirit, and promise to themselves and the country, have been born, and have matured and died, in a few days, or weeks, or months, as the capital —in brains or money—of their projectors could sustain them. The number of these failures has not, I think, been greater than it would have been reasonable to look for; and it is creditable to be able to say of these prints, as of those yet living and flourishing, that if they have sometimes been weak, they have rarely been mean, and never scurrilous.

The character of the whole California press, so far as I have become acquainted with it, has been generally such as to do credit to the state, and honor to the men who have conducted it. There are now (in summer of '53*) sixteen secu-

* The following is a list of all the papers printed in the state near the close of the year 1853 :

1. Yreka Herald, Yreka.
2. Shasta Courier, Shasta.
3. Mountain Echo, Downieville.
4. Express, Marysville.
5. Herald,   do.
6. Nevada Journal, Nevada.
7. Young America,   do.
8. Grass Valley Telegraph, Grass Valley.
9. Placerville Herald, Auburn.
10. El Dorado Republican.
11. Miners' Advocate, Diamond Springs.
12. Calaveras Chronicle, Mokelumne Hill.
13. Sacramento Union, Sacramento.
14.   "   State Journal, do.
15.   "   Banner (Weekly, Religious, Baptist), do.
16. Benicia Vidette, Benicia.
17. Stockton Journal, Stockton.
18. San Joaquin Republican, do.
19. Columbia Gazette, Columbia.
20. Sonora Herald.
21. Santa Clara Register, San José.
22. Los Angeles Star, Los Angeles.
23. San Diego Herald, San Diego.
24. San Francisco Evening Journal, San Francisco.
25. "   "   Weekly Journal,
26. "   "   Commercial Advertiser,
27. "   "   Weekly do.   do.
28. "   "   Herald,

lar papers issued in San Francisco, beside three of a religious character. The latter are respectable in ability, and have thus far been as fair and just as most religious prints elsewhere.

The secular press of San Francisco has been generally fearless, in times of public commotion, in defense of the rights and interests of the country, while its tone has, for the most part, been temperate, firm, and respectful, to the powers and individuals against whom it has arrayed itself.

On the other hand, it must be acknowledged, that a higher position might have been taken by most of the prints, and honor, integrity, and

29. Times and Transcript, San Francisco.
30. Sun,   do.
31. Ledger,   do.
32. Alta California,   do.
33. Golden Era (Sunday paper, literary),   do.
34. Pacific (weekly, religious),   do.
35. Christian Advocate (do., do., Methodist), do.
36. Price Current (weekly, commercial),   do.
37. Cal. Temperance Organ (weekly),   do.
38. Catholic Standard (religious, do.),   do.
39. Echo du Pacifique (Fr. and Span., daily), do.
40. Messager (French),   do.
41. Staats Zeitung (German),   do.
42. Democrat (German),   do.

self-respect in business affairs—and greater regard for decency, restraint, and the claims of
society upon individual virtue been enjoined,
where a very great lack of all has been painfully manifest. Public corruptions and abuses
rarely go unwhipped of a free (and unbought)
press. There is abundant fault-finding generally with those who are in power, to expose any crookedness of policy, any obliquity
of purpose, or official shortcoming or over-
reaching that can be held up to condemnation ;
but it is rare to find newspaper commendation
of personal virtues, of social purity, of self-denial for the good of society ; of integrity in the
tradesman, merchant, lawyer, physician ; of un-
defiled piety added to all these, in the clergyman and professing Christian. Yet if there
were ever a land within the limits of Christendom, where "line upon line, and precept upon
precept" were called for, surely it is here.

In such a land, the press has the power to
stand far in advance of the pulpit in the min-
istration of morality, for tens of thousands,
throughout its length and breadth, will devour
every line in a newspaper, who will not set

foot upon the threshold of a church. An earnest, pure-hearted, courageous man, conducting
a newspaper in the midst of such a society as
California at her best points presents, has a
broad and most important field around him,
wherein, by a thousand indirect, as well as
direct means, he may proclaim the law of life
and temporal salvation to bewildered hundreds
and thousands.

But of this law, duelling is not an exemplification; neither are gaming, nor licentiousness,
nor gigantic speculations, nor stupendous swin-
dlings; and if he practice any of these, the
teacher of morality, either in the press or pulpit, must needs be a vigilant hypocrite not to
fail altogether in his higher calling.

The population of San Francisco has been
more liberally provided with dramatic and musical entertainments than that of any other city
of its size in America. Notwithstanding its
remoteness from the old states, and its isolation
from any thickly-peopled country, it has had,
since the city was a year old, from one to three
theatres open continually, and however their
performances may be marred by the occasional

appearance of a stick where a living man or woman should be, there are generally clever persons enough on the boards to keep the entertainments, at the worst, up to decent mediocrity. But the city is rarely destitute of one or two stars who generally play to full, if not the most appreciative audiences. The abundance of money, and the lack of other entertainments, must cause it for a long time to be a harvestfield to those who have any worth or power on the stage.*

* In the two years between the date of the text, and the present writing, the drama has been nobly served in California, and I am proud to say it, most nobly by one of my own sex. The principal theatre of the state has been under the management of Mrs. Sinclair since its opening in December, 1853. This lady has served the public in her managerial capacity with a generosity and industry rarely equaled. With a just faith in the value of the drama, she has spared no pains or expense to give it, in her theatre, its noblest power. The best boards of our Atlantic cities do not surpass in excellence and variety the entertainments she has provided for the patrons of the Metropolitan.

CHAPTER XXX.

THE chief recreation of our state is the equestrian exercise which we take from our Spanish
predecessors.   It is much practiced by the citizens of San Francisco.   The Mission or Plank
Road representing, perhaps, Third Avenue,
and the Mission itself, Harlem, or some nearer
place of resort.   On Sundays, the latter place
is thronged in patronage of the bull and bear
fights to be witnessed there every Sabbath, and
on most other days, its drinking-shops present
a lively appearance of business which ought to
be very gratifying to their proprietors, since it
is painfully the reverse of this to sober travelers
and persons who love to see industry, order, and
thrift characterize a community.   Yet there is
a thriving and industrious population scattered
thickly over the arable lands in its vicinity,
which are now converted into beautiful gardens
where growth is perpetual, and where "seed-

time and harvest" are every day in the year.
These gardens are the principal productive
lands in the neighborhood of San Francisco.

Passing them, the country for ten or twelve
miles is a succession of barren sand hills inter-
spersed with fertile vallies. The site of the city
is of the same character, but worse, and the absence of soil, the harsh winds, and the long dry
season, discourage hope that its present unsight-
liness will very soon be replaced by cultivation
or beauty of any kind unless it should be
architectural. Up to this time, the San Fran-
ciscans have not shown much appreciation or
love of beauty in this way. Some massive and
very expensive buildings have been erected
since the fires of last spring (1852); but they are
destitute of beauty, sullen, heavy, strong-look-
ing structures—suspicious, chill, and unfriendly
in their aspect, as is the life of many who live
within and around them.*

---

* Since the writing of the above, this feature is also much
changed. There is beginning to prevail an elegant, as well
as costly style of building, and already a few sections of
the business streets are nearly built up with edifices of the
China stone, and bricks tastefully stuccoed.

There is scarcely anything deserving the name of society in San Francisco. In a permanent population of over 40,000, there is not moral cohesion enough to rescue our generous and complete circle from the mass. This is partly owing to the constant changing of so large a proportion of the whole as arrive and depart every week or month, but more, I think, to other causes which it is more painful to reflect upon: to the want of confidence; to the sacrifice of character which is being incessantly made by persons once respected; to the mixed character of the population and to the *parvenuism* which starts its gigantic pretensions at every turn.

This is a wearisome, disgusting and most prominent feature of the whole country—one of the unhappy phases which new Democracy (and old too, perhaps) presents always, but which becomes especially marked in this country of abundant wealth and sudden fortunes. Speaking one day of a pretty row of dwellings that had been erected, the most ornamental and tasteful at that time in the town, an acquaintance asked me " if I knew any of the occupants?" On my replying that I did not, he said one of the mistresses is Mrs. M———. Before she married her present husband, she stopped awhile in a house where I was boarding. One day at dinner, I was late at table, and found her sitting with a lady-friend and one or two others. She was telling her friend that she had been "*dreadfully disappointed*" within a few days. She had heard from an acquaintance at home whom she had been expecting out here, and he was going to England instead. "You see," she said, "he's an Englishman and has been the Queen's best friend afore he come to Meriky, but when the *Ingins* drove her off her throne, she advised him to come to Missouri; and now the Ingins has been beat, and she's got back, so she wrote for him and he's gone."

"My gracious," said the astonished auditor, "I didn't know as there was any Ingins where the Queen is."

"Yes, indeed," replied she who is now mistress of that mansion, "there's plenty on 'em, but they're beat clear out now, and never'll fight agin, I reckon.

I was waiting an hour, one day, in a fine house

in San Francisco, which an Irishman, who had made a large fortune in the country, had built, and was occupying. I asked for a glass of water, and his wife, a sturdy, strong-armed Irishwoman, brought me one as clear as crystal, and very palatable. "Is this delicious water soft?" I asked.

"What do you mean, Ma'am?" she said.

"Is it soft," I asked—"good to wash with?"

"Oh, sure, I think it is thin," was the reply, "but I'm not much of a judge. I don't do any washing."

One could have affirmed that the muscular hand that took my glass at the same moment, had earned many a score of honest dollars in that same despised vocation.

A lady was one day paying me a visit, and in the course of her talk accused me of going too little into society. I replied in my blunt, foolish way, that there was none to go into.

"O, I beg your pardon," said my visitor. "If you have not been out here for some time, you'll find things is greatly *metramorphosist;* there's a circle of the *real ellite* that meets every fortnight at Mrs. So-and-So's and Mrs. So-and-So's, and we have delightful times. You really ought to go. You'd enjoy yourself very much. It's so refreshing to be in *coessecee* with your neighbors in a strange land!"

But pretension is not confined to females. I loaned Combe's Physiology to a gentleman who requested the perusal of it, and he returned it in due time, with the remark, that he didn't consider the *treaty* to be as deep as *Layvayter* was on the same subject; and lighter writings coming under remark in the course of the visit, he replied to a question by Geordie, if he had read the Last of the Mohicans, that he had not, but he had been very much pleased with the First.

It is not easy to dispose of such pretension in so chaotic a social state, and when you find it coupled with a tolerable degree of uprightness, and an obliging disposition, you soon get accustomed to overlook the most ridiculous blunders, you even forget to laugh at them, and look grave and commonplace enough, while people are making themselves absurd to an extent that, under other circumstances, it would be impossible to endure with any show of decorum.

I recollect being introduced to a New-England man, at a sick neighbor's, one evening. The conversation presently turned on the character of the school near by, which did not altogether meet his approbation; but he excused its imperfections on the ground that the settlers were chiefly "western people, and could not be expected to sense the advantages of larnin as much as we, who had been eddicated in the East!"

CHAPTER XXXI.

THERE is very little valuable addition brought
to the mental life, by any trait or influence of
California at this time. It is rare to meet with
a man or woman, who seems at all stirred by
any but the money phase of the country ; and
it is almost literally true, that there is no conversation except upon that subject, and, among
females, upon the adventures of emigration ;
the different routes and their hardships, and the
oppressive sense they suffer from lack of confidence and mutual respect in the communities
that surround them. This feature of California
life is very painful to large numbers of both
sexes, but is especially so to the sensitive and
self-respecting of our own, who reside in the
towns and cities. I have been struck with it,
in the conversations I have had with good women in every walk of life here, except the

favored few, whose lots were cast in homes protected from the approach of suspicion and slander.

There is a universal sense of discomfort, amounting, in many cases, to wretchedness, from distrust and reserve in their own sex, and insulting suspicions in the other. Females, alone, can appreciate the anguish arising from these sources, and to such of them as have here enjoyed the protection, confidence, and respect, which the deserving are seldom denied in older states, they are inconceivable without experience.

A modest young Irish girl, who had been but a few weeks in the country, and had spent those at service in a respectable hotel, in a small town, told me that the conversations she could not avoid hearing through the muslin walls and ceilings of the house, frightened and tormented her. The common expressions when women were spoken of, were that there was not an honest one in the country—that those who professed to be so, were only greater hypocrites or more successful pretenders than the others—that none were entitled to respect, and that among men, only fools and dupes believed in them.   The poor girl, who had been religiously educated, was really good, and had grown to womanhood chiefly under the enlightening and refining influence of the sentiment shown toward females in New England, was terrified at finding herself in such a land, so surrounded, and knew not how to be thankful enough, when a way was opened for her to go into a private family with a mistress, of whose justice and purity she felt no doubt.   It is not difficult to see how scores of weaker and worse trained young females might have traveled from such a position in quite an opposite direction, and so justified, in their own lives, the assertions which had at first caused them so much pain.

Such, I doubt not, has been the first cause which has led astray, in California, many innocent feet.   It is so hard to natures, that have not more than common strength, to live uprightly and purely, when they feel that there is no sympathy with their life, in those who surround them—and, still worse, no faith.   To be always doubted is, to the integrity of common minds, to be as the stone under the fountain that never ceases dropping.

The beautiful proportions of the moral nature will be gradually broken down, as the surface of the stone is hollowed, and its original form in part destroyed by the unceasing friction. And magnificent as is nature here, grand as is the scale of her operations, and lavish as she is of all that can furnish material comfort, or external consolations, there will, I fear, be little in the social and moral life of the country for many years, to invite those whose natures expose them to suffering from these causes. And yet only in the presence of women is to be found the efficient remedy for these great evils. The martyr women of California will one day have an honorable place assigned them, when history shall fill her noblest office and truthfully interpret the motives that lead to noble actions. For they come regardless of the trials and dangers that await them; every steamer sends its precious freight throughout the length and breadth of our borders. The home, holiest and purest nursery of what is good in the heart, springs up everywhere before woman. In town and country, cañon and ravine, on mountain and in valley, the sacred temple rises at the bidding of this true missionary of love and purity. Her presence is the guarantee for the best manifestation of his nature of which man is capable, amid the influences which here surround him; and bad as it often is, we may rest assured that without her it would be inconceivably worse.

There is no country in the world where the highest attributes of the female character are more indispensable to the social weal than in California; for nowhere else have the indomitable energies, the quick desires, and the wide-reaching purposes of the Saxon nature been submitted to so severe a test of their self-regulating power. And it is the pride of American women to feel that their countrymen stand first among the nations of men, in their susceptibility to all that is noble and holy in the character of woman. The loyalty· that other nations pay to kings and queens, to old institutions, and to superiority of caste, is paid by them to woman—to the wife, mother, sister, daughter, friend, or stranger, who is in a position to claim it.

Hence the inestimable value of good and true women in California, whatever be their rank in life; and the mourning that all such must feel over the defection of those whose presence among them is converted to a curse, and whose influence in the chaotic periods of our history followed them as a blight, almost to their very firesides. Yet were those firesides, whether they shone in our dissipated towns, or in the gulches and ravines of the wild upper country, the very centres and nurseries of those better feelings in men, the exercise of which could alone be immediately productive of an improved condition. The woman who presided virtuously over a home in the earlier periods of the gold emigration, is entitled, I think, to look back from the remainder of her life, upon a good work well done; and if, to integrity, she added the charms of gentleness, kindness, and self-restraint, under the exposure and toils which were generally shared by the sex in those days, the greater her self-gratulation may be.

It was the fact that the hard trials and rough experience borne by the women of the west, in crossing the plains, took from their characters and manners much of these qualities, that made it so much to be deprecated. No portion of the republic was, I believe, better represented, in all that concerns the integrity and chastity of women; none worse in the minor morals and graces that give to home its light and charm. A woman in whom you felt an honor as unapproachable as the clouds above her, might suddenly shock you by letting a huge oath escape her lips, or by speaking to her children as an ungentle hostler would to his cattle; and, perhaps, listening undisturbedly to the same style of address in reply.

In that journey, boys and girls took on themselves the cares and toils of men and women, and assumed, unchecked — perhaps unperceived—the manners, consequence, and language of mature years. There were some beautiful exceptions to these remarks, in families where the mother, richly endowed by nature with womanly gentleness, had preserved

it unsullied in herself and children on these
great plains and rough mountain ranges. Two
or three such have fallen within my notice;
one, our nearest neighbor at the mill—a meek,
pious woman, surrounded by a family of beautiful and childlike children—little girls, with
young hearts in their bosoms, and boys, whose
spirits were, like their bodies, elastic, simple,
pure, as childhood should be.

And there is an exquisite and touching story
to be told some day of the unwearied devotion
and faithfulness of another woman, whose name
I am not at liberty to use, though it ought to
be held in honor by all true hearts; who, setting out an invalid from her home in Iowa, became—as her strong husband's will and energies failed under the tremendous sufferings of
that terrible journey—the efficient care-taker
of him and their three sons; yoked and un-
yoked the oxen, gathered fuel, cooked their
food, and divided her scanty share, when their
supplies were short, with those whose very
veins she would have exhausted her own to
fill, had it been necessary or possible.

She drove the teams, hunted wood and

water in men's boots and tattered clothing, and for months performed all the coarser offices that properly belong to the other sex, and reached her journey's end a gentle, soft-spoken woman, with manners as unsoiled by her hard experience, as truly feminine and sweet, as if the refinements and ease of the drawing-room had surrounded her, instead of the dreary horrors and coarse tasks of those dreadful months. One must love such a woman. When I think of her, I can appreciate the feelings which, in early times, exalted characters of such rare beauty to a place in the calendar. Reverence, love, and gratitude ought to flow from the hearts of her family toward her, as richly and freely as odor from the rose, or light from the sun.

The truest devotion is not that which is most heard of; and the deeds of heroism and love—known only to the recipient and doer—that have been silently performed by women on those dreadful journeys, would fill a volume of which our sex might be justly proud. To every field are appointed its appropriate and necessary laborers. Let us be thankful that,

in the silent desert as well as in the corrupt
marts of the world, the heart of woman never
fails to respond to the appeals of suffering—
never refuses healing and consolation to the
wounded in spirit or body.

One is not astonished that great numbers of
women show extreme reluctance toward emigration, notwithstanding that those who are
dearest to them are already in the country;
and, were I able to portray, faithfully, those
features of its life from which the best among
us have suffered most, the picture would, perhaps, turn back even some willing feet. But
this is not the generous view of the subject—
not the woman's, in short. Her life is sacrifice,
and her foot must never shrink from the path
wherein duty to her husband and child call
her to walk. And where toil, exposure to suffering, and moral contamination in California
are the lot of these which she, by her presence, might alleviate or avert, her place is
not the seat of luxury by the fireside of an
eastern home—nor the resorts of the gay, but
here beside them—sympathizing with their successes, soothing their disappointments, lighten-

ing their burdens, and concealing the material discomforts of their lot, by all those little acts which the housewife has at her control, and which, in her higher character as woman, she is prompted to exercise for the well-being and happiness of those she loves.

I would not invite or encourage any of my sex to emigration, without having previously advised them of the pains and perils attendant upon it; but, having done this, I must in faithfulness say to those who leave families here, and who possess sufficient courage, devotion, and firmness to make their presence a blessing instead of a curse to them, that they cannot know how greatly remiss they are in continuing the separation, which may already have worked lasting mischief to some of those who have suffered it. Come to the country which is the home of those you are bound to adhere to and save, when they are ready to receive you. Come strong in the resolution to be true to yourselves and to them, under all trials; to put away pining and discontent, and face your hardest fortune bravely, so that they share it with you; so that you find your presence is not without that saving influence which men everywhere more or less need, but which scarcely the strongest and best among them may be safely deprived of here.

Be thankful if your husband, the father of your children, desires your presence after having passed a year or two amid the wild and lawless excitements of this land. Could those, who are vainly urged and entreated to come, know of the scores, nay, hundreds, who have no word of such invitation addressed to them, whose claims upon the absent seem to be utterly forgotten, they would conceal their reluctance, however they might be unable to quench it, and hasten to their duty, trusting, as they safely might, to find their reward in the performance. There are hundreds of men in the country, whose efforts have been moderately successful, who have urged, entreated, prayed, perhaps scolded, to get those to join them whom they had first, in prudent consideration, or tenderness, left behind them, and finding all in vain have learned to consider themselves alone again, the family ties permanently broken, the marital and paternal obligations dissolved, and them-

selves free. Such facts become, in many instances, the lamentable cause of effects equally
deplorable.

Discouraged, hardened, made reckless of the
most sacred duties, a man so situated can only
be preserved by the rarest purity, self-respect,
and firmness from giving himself up to the lawless habits and vile allurements that surround
him. If he do not become openly debauched,
he finds his former integrity and fidelity to himself and his family superseded by an indifference
to all consideration of them, and a readiness to
wink at habits and indulgences in others, which,
till he felt himself forsaken, he would have regarded and, perhaps, reproved as criminal. I
cannot forbear saying, then, to my countrywomen, that if they have the natures which
can pass unscathed through the furnace seven
times heated, every unselfish consideration,
every sentiment of duty binds them to follow
here, as they would cleave elsewhere, to those
who have the first claim on them. And come
not with the expectation of being surrounded
by luxury and nursed in the comforts and indulgences of an older social condition. Many

of these, very many of them, you will lack for a
long period, some for your whole life, should it
be spent here.   But this consideration does not
absolve you, nor will it heal your wounded
hearts and consciences, when you find those
whose earthly salvation you were bound to
conserve, quite separated from your ways and
influence, quite regardless of their own and
your best good.

To be true to conscience in such a case, requires in many natures self-sacrifice which only
the noblest motives can sustain.   Considerations of the ultimate good that is to be attained
are helpful.   One suffers with so much more
firmness when one feels that good flows from
it—though it be to the antipodes.   Gold-har-
vesting has been always a hazardous and heart-
breaking venture.   Fairly engaged in, it so
absorbs the other and better purposes, that disappointment in it is more painful than the loss
of real good would be when nobler motives
ruled.   But from such a harvest as California
has afforded, good in many forms flows out to
the world.   Forget not this in your afflictions.
If it cost you the peace, happiness and out-

ward dignity of your life, forget not that it is carrying to others, elsewhere, the same blessings it has robbed you of. While it is to be found, men will devote themselves to the search for it, and you cannot justly withhold yourselves from sharing the life it brings them to, however repugnant to your nature it may be.

Nor will the page of your history be the first that records such sacrifices. Time has witnessed many such, and will continue to, while human affairs go on under the laws which thus far have governed them. For it rarely happens that the good which our human desire craves, flows to the first laborers in any new field. Our own age is always less kind and encouraging than the past ones. We see the fruits of the martyrdoms that have been. We feel the pains only of our own.

CHAPTER XXXII.

THE decline in personal, social and civil morality, which has always been a painfully attendant
upon the successful search for the precious met-
als, has not been a less prominent feature of this
first ordeal of the Saxon spirit.   The respect one
feels for the noblest race on earth, does not
mitigate the pain of witnessing its degradation
in the same fields where inferior peoples have
fallen.   One hopes, indeed, for the swift redemption of the noblest ; but with the swiftest,
it will, I fear, be the work of many years, to
toil up to the elevation whence we have descended in a few.

Nor is it to be wondered at if the American,
Saxon though he be, with his naturally speculating mind, and moderate relish for labor, has,
with this experience, become less a laborer and
more a speculator.   Realities both of success

and failure, exceeding the wildest imagination, have been abundant in the history of California. Life in it has been as emphatically a game as any that could be played at the gaming-table ; and that reckless spirit, which is engendered by a constant sense of risk as to all the great interests of life, steels the moral sensibilities so that all conditions and conduct might *a priori* be looked for under it.

Accordingly in the first years of the gold emigration, it seemed as if our people were not the metal for the trial. The furnace threatened to consume them. Scheming, gaming, profanity, licentiousness, and intemperance, reared themselves to such frightful stature that one could not easily see how they were to be laid low again.

I have spoken of the numerous gaming-houses of San Francisco. It was a fair representation of the extent to which the same vice prevailed throughout the country. The inland towns were equally infested ; and every little group of miners had its den of gamesters. Then the profanity, one heard on every hand, was shocking. It seemed really wonderful, how many oaths could be crowded into the commonest conversation without excluding the words that expressed ideas. Men meeting and accosting each other in perfect good-will, exchanging inquiries on subjects to which both were equally indifferent, swore as if unconquerable passion prompted every word. It appalled one to be in hearing, and there was no escape.

For the partition-walls of the best buildings were then only of calico, or paper upon this; and though one could retire from sight, one could not from sound. In the public-houses you went to sleep with terrible oaths haunting your ears, and in the morning they were the first signs of human neighborhood.

Then, too, the drinking of strong liquors was universal, not merely as a courtesy, but as an aid to the nature worn upon daily and hourly by the intense excitement in which men lived. Every place of resort had its bar, which was always thronged. Almost every building proclaimed upon its walls that liquors were sold within; and at every one, groups of idle men were to be seen at all hours; not broken-down ruins in the garb of paupers, such as we should

chiefly see in other countries at such places,
but vigorous, hale persons, many elegantly, and
all comfortably clad, with abounding life and
energy in their countenances and movements,
and the flush of first dissipation on their features.

"What will become of us if we go on so?"
was the question constantly asked by the sober
and more thoughtful.   We shall become a nation of drunkards!   But there was too much
excitement of other kinds for this fear to be
realized.   Drunkenness can scarcely become
the general vice of a people who are incited by as
wild hopes and unimaginable successes as were
the Californians of those days.   Men do not de-
generate to so beastly a condition under such
sharpening excitements.   There is far more
likelihood that they will become unscrupulous
in business, and forget their consciences in
other things than in this.   And the history of
the country, thus far, proves this as truth.   Intemperance has certainly greatly diminished
among us, and though drinking-houses are still
far too numerous for the respectability or
welfare of the people, the resort to them is

greatly fallen off in number and quality—a most cheering indication of the progress of the country.

At the period to which I refer in these remarks, the trade—the whole commercial business—of the country seemed to be little else than a game of chance. There was no scale of profits, no regulation of sale by cost. The price demanded was whatever the vendor thought he could get; and it was not uncommon to hear two persons, who had purchased the same article, on the same day, state the most enormous difference in the price paid.

One small incident in my own experience will serve to show how insecure an amusement shopping was at that time. I wished to purchase that small household utensil called a spring-balance. At home, a single one would have cost seventy-five cents, or at most a dollar. After many inquiries, I was directed to the only place in the city where it was believed they were to be had; and, on going in, was shown several that were such as I wanted. Having selected one, I drew out my purse, which was just then better filled with gold

coins than it has often been since. The shop-
man looked at it, as he was wrapping my purchase in a bit of paper; and when I asked the
price, he coolly told me it was forty dollars!

I was so astounded, that I went speechless
into the street, huddling the two or three coins
I had poured into my hand back to their place
of security. An hour brought me round to the
same house again, in search of something else.
When I entered, the individual who had attempted the gross imposition presented himself,
with unabashed smile, and after answering my
other inquiries, told me, that if I really wanted
the balance, I should have it for thirty dollars.
I, of course, declined.

It is scarcely likely that so gross an outrage
would have been attempted in the case of a
man, unless he had been a very tempting subject; but there was continual practice of a like
kind in every branch of trade. And I have
heard numerous anecdotes, illustrating a kindred spirit in the different departments of the
public service.

Public functionaries, in those days, seemed
as far from immaculate as private fortune-

hunters were; and if the secrets of their proceedings, in many instances, could be printed,
it is quite probable that we should find in them
the most incredible page of our unparalleled
history. One fact, which was related to me
by an eye-witness, is so illustrative of the spirit
of the time in which it occurred (1849), that I
must relate it, even at the possible risk of af-
fronting some of the actors in it. As they are
all, however, wholly unknown to me, I trust
they will receive kindly the assurance I offer
them, that it is from no personal motive that I
speak of this little circumstance in their history,
but only to show, as faithfully as I may, how
large was the liberty enjoyed then, and how
shrewdly some profited by it.

A judicial functionary in a responsible station, was believed to look rather too sharply
after the effects of men dying within his jurisdiction. It was known that several persons
had died possessed of considerable amounts of
gold; but it could never be heard of afterward.
An order was generally sent to the persons having charge of the sick man, by which his effects
were sealed up and placed in official custody,

to be kept until his heirs should call for them, when it generally happened that the sum accounted for was a mere trifle, or that the whole had quite disappeared. In one instance, when several thousand dollars' worth of gold were called for by the heirs of a deceased miner, the demand was answered by the statement that the judge had removed twice since he had taken charge of the treasure, and the trunk containing it must have been lost!

These facts coming to the knowledge of the public, stirred the indignation of a small number of men, who made themselves so troublesome in their scrutiny, that his honor determined to dispose of them by silencing their leader. An anonymous complaint was lodged in his office against this individual, praying his arrest, and an anonymous warrant issued thereon; but, as no officer would proceed to execute it under such questionable circumstances, a party of his honor's friends and partisans, of the tribe called Hounds, volunteered for that service, and brought the unoffending citizen into court.

Here he was informed that his judge and the

complainant were one and the same person; for that officer frankly informed him that he had complained against him, as a private citizen, and should proceed to try him as a magistrate.

The affair got wind, and a crowd collected in and about the office where the trial was in progress, which attracted the attention of a gigantic Missourian, who was passing. He inquired what was going on in thar', and got, in a dozen energetic words, from some indignant member of the crowd, the gist of the whole matter. Whereupon, coolly elbowing his way in, he advanced near to the prisoner. He listened a few moments, and, becoming satisfied that he had not been misinformed, he laid his broad hand on the shoulder of the astonished man, and said: "Hyur, you come away with me."

The court and audience were astounded and silenced for a moment by such audacity, but the judge, re-collecting his shivered dignity, and settling his spectacles afresh upon his nose, said, with awful sternness: "Sir, by what authority do you interrupt the proceedings of this court?"

The giant administrator of practical justice turned his eye coolly upon his honor for a moment, and then advancing close to him, good-naturedly swung his clenched fist under the sacred nose, and, with fearful brevity, replied, " by the authority of that." The next moment rescuer and rescued walked quietly out of court, leaving it to vindicate its wounded dignity in the way that might seem to itself best.

Such were some of the scenes enacted in the early history of the country. In this instance, courage and power came to the aid of justice. It is to be feared they were often arrayed against it. It is a fact, however, in which we may feel a reasonable pride, that there was very little crime against the laws of the state until after our population received its unwholesome accessions from the British colonies. Town and country alike enjoyed exemption from the presence of gross offenders against the human laws.

In the mines, treasure, to any amount, was constantly left accessible, within and without the tents and shanties of the owners. Theft was almost unknown throughout the country;

a fact which goes far to vindicate human nature from the charge of spontaneous proneness to low crimes; and though it may with truth be said, that the population at that time was, almost unmixed, of persons who had not before been criminal, yet, I believe the same exposure of property could not safely be made even among a more virtuous population in a poorer country. After the colonial immigration commenced, all this rapidly changed. The securities demanded elsewhere became necessary; and, as usual, these did not prevent crime; did not deter from the commission of even a frightful amount of it. There came first occasional administrations of Lynch law in the mines, and after the reign—truly. one of terror to rogues—of the Vigilance Committees in the towns, it appeared, from the manner in which those fearful scenes were conducted, that the excitement in which men daily lived, gave them calmness and cool self-control in those emergencies, when people, whose every-day life is quiet, lose them. Scenes of this kind have taken place in the mining regions, and been scarcely heard of beyond the little community that enacted them, which, had they occurred in London, or New York, would have roused the people through the length and breadth of the land.

A gentleman told me that news was one day accidentally brought to the locality where he was mining, that a man who had committed a robbery in a neighboring camp, or diggings, some two miles away, had been arrested, and was to be hanged. It created no excitement; drew nobody from their employment; but, being himself somewhat curious in such things, he walked over to the spot, and found several miners gathered near some trees, talking very quietly in little groups. Not knowing any one, and wishing to have the criminal pointed out to him, he inquired of a person who was standing a little apart, which was the man they were about to hang; to which he replied, without the slightest change of countenance: "I believe it's me, sir!" Half an hour after, he was suspended from a bough of a tree, and the little community dispersed to their respective suppers, without the smallest demonstration.

There have been a great many such administrations of popular justice (?), and I believe that their righteousness has rarely been questioned. These people's courts have, at least, been far more efficient and prompt in the desperate conditions of society than the duly authorized judiciary of the state. Juries have been empanneled on the spot; witnesses examined; and proof made, in almost all cases, stronger than would be required in the legal tribunals; and, if the accused were found guilty, his doom was pronounced, and swiftly executed, in a cool, altogether unique manner; and the people, in an hour or two, fell quietly back upon their picks, pans, and toms, as if nothing had happened out of the daily routine of their lives. *

* It is fearful to think how many persons meet death in this country by accident or design, of whom nothing is ever known here, or in the far-off land, where their return is awaited. With what indifference we read those little paragraphs which appear almost daily in our prints, setting forth that the body of an unknown man was found yesterday, on the road to some mining settlement, or in the suburbs of some of the cities or towns; or, that the coroner held an inquest on a body found in the water, or concealed in the bushes, with a stab in the breast, or a bullet mark in the head. It would not exceed the truth, I think, to say that

The administrations of Lynch law were generally regarded by the people with much greater favor than the proceedings of the courts in criminal matters. In many of them rogues were so seldom convicted, that trial seemed to be rather a protection than an exposure. Especially was this the case after the active inauguration of the Vigilance Committee of 1851—a measure purely self-defensive on the part of the people. These committees consisted of the best part of the population of the towns where they were organized; men of substance and character, who, disgusted with the farcical and corrupt administration of legal justice, and, trembling for their possessions,

throughout our state there are, at least, three such deaths for every two days in the year, and we, in time, get some intimation of the anguish they cause, from the numerous advertisements, calling for information of persons, that appear in the prints of the state ; a father or mother resorting to that last hope of the afflicted ; a wife pining for tidings that will never reach her ; a sister grieving for the companion of her childhood, and the friend of her later years. Alas, alas ! how many houses are saddened with such sorrow ; how many lives, that were otherwise sunny and bright, are darkened by the shadows that fall upon them from this land of gold ?

their families, and their lives, saw no safety but in the vigorous system of self-defense which they adopted.

It is not impossible but they may have erred in some of the many cases which they acted upon ; but do not the proper tribunals the same, even when their action is purest and soundest ? Their measures were characterized neither by passion nor fear, but cool determination to protect the dearest interests of society, and put an end to the shocking villainies that rendered California, for the time, the most insecure country for life and property in Christendom. And to their promptness and resolution is it indebted for the purifying it received in '51 and '52. The exodus of rogues in those years has made our beautiful country habitable and comparatively safe again, for a period, at least.

San Francisco, especially, was made a place of terror to them at that time. They fled in all directions, seaward and landward, from her limits. And since that time Australia has invited back to her own gold-fields many of the children of her unwilling adoption ; so that there now seems little reason to apprehend that we or our children shall ever witness the return of such days. There are also more cheering evidences of positive good to us.

14*

CHAPTER XXXIII.

In the accessions the state is constantly receiving to its female population, and better classes of its male inhabitants, in the multiplication of its homes, its churches, its schools, its temperance and other benevolent organizations; in its more settled basis of trade; in its institutions, tender and protracted though their infancy may be, for the cultivation of science and literature; in its more respectable judicature; in its less shameful legislation, may be seen the dawn of hope over its hitherto darkened history.

For it is idle to talk of our rapid growth in population and wealth; our phœnix-like cities, and numerous lesser towns, wherein enterprise and intelligence have so often demonstrated their indestructible elasticity, as evidences of the greatness to which a Christian and refined people ought to aspire. It is not wealth, it is not numerous and large cities, not harbors crowded with shipping from every mart on the globe, not grand agricultural operations, nor mining, by which the nations are to be enriched, that will constitute a truly great state.

We demand that a man, or a people, claiming greatness in these days, should present some other evidence of their right to do so than is to be found in well-filled coffers, in mere intelligence, or power to execute its conceptions. Some recognition more or less clear there is now among most men, that these do not well support such a claim; that there belongs to genuine greatness a moral quality, which conceives of truer purposes in human existence than the accumulation of wealth, the increase of power, or the investing our external life with material splendors. And this lesson, it seems to me, the grand and kindly aspects of the natural world in California are powerfully calculated to second in the progressive, unpolluted mind.

Previous to the gold-emigration, California was the home of peace and rest. Where was ever a people so steeped in contentment, as that which was found here? The labors of the devoted Jesuit missionaries had planted the cross beneath these lovely skies, long years before they came hither. The Indians were already converted, to their hands, from lawless enemies to useful and perfectly manageable servants. A magnificent country, with variety of soils and a climate uniformly salubrious, lay open to their choice ; and well did they repay the lavish kindness with which nature invited them to be happy.

How they luxuriated in the ease of their abundance ! How they reposed on the generous soil whose redundant energies sprang to their coarse husbandry with a profusion scarcely equaled in any other clime habitable by the white race ! With what a pleasing, but unlaborious joy we may imagine them hailing the rare arrivals of the trading-vessels that visited their coast ! Their herds multiplied without care, and their frijoles and grains, once sown, required no diurnal renewing. Crops sufficient for their plentiful subsistence— and what wanted they more ?—came spontaneously the first, second, and sometimes the third year, after the seed had been sown. Their horses were fleet, and so numerous, that it was no extravagance to destroy them whenever caprice, pleasure, or convenience (and they rarely knew more earnest motives) dictated. Their greatest luxury was ease: ambition was unknown to them as a people. They were born, they matured, and died, in an undisturbed round of animal enjoyments.

Their quarrels were not mercenary, for they were surrounded by plenty, and a hospitable table awaited them in every house, from one end of the land to the other.

But now, how are all these aspects of their life changed! Nature still is fair and liberal, as she was wont to be; but her broad acres, instead of reposing in the peace of past ages, are vexed with all the toil of modern husbandry. The solitude of the plains, where only the low and tramp of herds broke the silence, is replaced by the noise of vehicles and of groups of footmen and horsemen, moving in various directions so earnestly, that we feel, in looking upon them, that gain is the object, and hope the spur of their movements.

It is no longer the flying zarapa that we see, the huge, dull spurs, made of enormous diameter, that no effort need be made to prick the steed; the great, easy stirrup, in which the foot rested as upon a cushion; no longer the untrimmed mane and flowing tail, indicating the sinecureship enjoyed by the groom; but smart riders, trimmed to press forward against wind and weather; horses carrying no superfluous graces to impede their motions, and showing, by their shining coats and sleek condition, that labor has been expended on them.

On the long, silent rivers are heard the rushing of steamers, and the shout of commercial transit. The recesses of the stern mountains, where, three years ago, a human foot had never left its trace, now resound to the clang of machinery, the stroke of the miner's pick and shovel, and the incessant click from hundreds of busy hands.

Armies of men labor in them, sustained through successive disappointments and fearful sufferings, by the hope which first drew them together. Among those incongruous battalia, are represented the homes and hopes of the world. Benighted Africa, despotic Asia, restless Europe, complacent America, sit down side by side in these treasure-houses of nature.

Will they gather nothing but our gold there? Will they ever return to those distant homes, the men that left them one, two, or three years ago? Will the shackles they have thrown off be ever permanently resumed?

Not so. California is the world's nursery of freedom. The centuries that have brooded over her since the treasure was first poured into her bosom, have witnessed no event so significant to the nations as its development under a free government. It marks an era to which, in future years, the new men of nations grown hoary in despotism, will point as the time when the masses began to gather the earth's treasures and make them their own.

The lessons in political and religious freedom learned here, will be remembered and repeated beneath the palm-trees of India—in the tea-fields of China—among the frozen snows of Russia—in the saloons of the proudest cities of Europe, where dotard monarchy yet hugs his shivering members together—in the cloudless islands of the ocean. They will travel to remote hamlets, and to rural firesides; and the wondrous beauty of the clime whence they were carried, and its boundless wealth, shall clothe the narrator's tongue with magic power to stir the hearts of his listeners. He shall tell of the grandeur and bounty of the land of gold, and his auditors shall then first feel that the wealth which a people develops and commands, benefits and blesses it, and not alone its rich, its noble, or its rulers.

What hopes are awakening in these years! What noble alliances of purpose and circumstance! What generous disclosures of nature! What persistency, on the whole, in man toward a high destiny!

He prints, he reads, he communicates by lightning; he traverses the broadest ocean in a few days, and the globe in a few weeks. He executes his labor, not by hands, but endows metal and steam with intelligence to clothe as well as transport him; and, having thus far undertaken the deliverance of his brother—the

" born thrall" of want and ignorance—he demands that he shall no longer suffer the one nor the other.

The islands and continents of the Pacific—latest conquests of man's knowledge and enterprise — last redeemed from the midnight abyss of time—shall bring their treasures to redeem the millions, and their light shall spread abroad, and the millions shall receive both the treasure and the light. The march will be onward with triumph into the ages.

How spotless should be the banner borne in advance of it. It should bear no narrower motto than universal brotherhood. So does nature teach her lessons on these golden shores. In her smiles, in her bounty, is nothing stinted — nothing exclusive. Broad, genial, maternal, she nurses man to the noblest ends of self-development and fraternal helpfulness. Should we exclude the oppressed and meaner races from her bounty? Perish the selfish heart that cannot more truly interpret her.

CHAPTER XXXIV.

CALIFORNIA will not always be the theatre
of unrest, of reckless hazard, and unscrupulous speculation, that it has been since 1848.
There is too much genuineness in the American character, too much true enlightenment of
the people, to permit a final failure in the balance, however it may go to the beam in the
first years of our experiment. The redeeming
influences of our toil and its rewards, neither
we nor our children may see; but they will
come not the less certainly because of the delay. Time alone can develope the true character of events and movements, that send vigor
and strength to the lowest roots of the gigantic forest tree. The fertilizing agent must
spread broad and strike deep before its effects
will prove its excellence in the finer flower
and nobler fruit. In the first days, they may

even droop and suffer; but the very disturb-
ance of the soil in which the roots have begun
to slumber, will renew their vigor. America
is young and strong; and, though her rapid
growth may have swelled her proper pride
into something akin to self-conceit, she has
moral health to bring her to a giant maturity
among the nations. Her civilization, springing
from Saxon energy, Protestant Christianity,
and social, political, and religious liberty, has
in it elements of durability never before com-
bined. It may be trusted to resist the currents that have strewn the centuries with the
wrecked hopes of humanity.

The eagerness of her people, and their con-
sequent superficialness—their offensive irrever-
ence and gross defiance of right, in adhering to
the institution of slavery, whose very existence
among them up to this day, is a terrible evidence, either of their incapacity to understand
the ultimate principles of freedom, or of selfish determination to trample on them when it
suits themselves to do so—are the discouraging
features of the national aspect. They will be
obliterated. One, and that the worst, is des-

tined to swift decay.   The very violence of its struggles declares its wounds to be mortal.

The California phase of America has been, in many respects, its most forbidding one.   But it must be remembered that the mother nation is not responsible for the character of the suitors to her daughter.

" The reason," said a clear-headed, honest man to me, one day, " why California is the worst country in the world, is, that here you have all types of rascality.   The villainies of one people may be studied and fenced off in part, but not those of scores in an admixture like ours."

Inestimable to California is the blessing of the later discovery of gold in Australia.   The foul population from those regions, which had rushed like carrion birds to our shores, and in a few months made its pestilent presence felt throughout the land, is now again drawn homeward, and we may trust that the greater security they will feel under social and civil institutions with which they are familiar, than they could enjoy under ours, will conduce, with the mineral wealth of their country, to keep them there. At the same time, let us, in all honor and self-respect, hope that our own countrymen going thither, will not avail themselves of the bad reputation of the country they are in, to disgrace their own.

CHAPTER XXXV.

However willing readers might be, that a book on California should be silent on the mines, it is impossible for a writer to feel that his work can be dismissed without an attempt at least to examine, in some of their multifarious phases, these great distinctive features of the land.   It would be impracticable for a lady to become possessed of statistical knowledge respecting these wonderful regions that would be accurate and reliable enough to possess any great value; but the visits I have paid to the mining regions have sufficed to inform me, pretty correctly, of the character of life in them; of the features of the mining country, and of the different methods of obtaining the gold.

I must give them a few pages, which, if they do not edify, shall at least not weary a reasonable patience.

It is now, I believe, generally supposed that the mountain ranges and the regions visited by streams coming from them are auriferous throughout California. Gold-bearing quartz has been found from the Sierra Nevada to the Golden Gate. And I think I shall not exaggerate in saying, that free gold or some of its concomitants has been taken from every water-course, ravine, gulch, and cañon, that has been examined in the state.

But the country, which is properly the mining region up to this date, lies, for the most part, east of the second range of mountains from the seaboard, and extends from north to south, over a space of some six hundred miles, reaching to Oregon, and probably embracing the entire latitude of our state.

This immense tract embraces every variety of scenery. Mountains crowned with a perpetual diadem of frost; vast plains; fertile vallies; enormous ravines, which the sunlight only penetrates a few hours each day; streams which dwindle to a mere belt in the long summer drought, and, in the rainy months, swell to raging, deadly floods; prairies clad with indigenous grains and grasses, and flushed, during the season of verdure, with innumerable flowers, and giant forests, which the floods of ages have matured—dark, solemn, grand—may all be seen in a single day's travel. There are vast regions yet unexplored, but already curious and wonderful spectacles have been found here, which bid fair to rival the world's older shows.

Natural bridges spanning chasms of fearful depth, and giant waterfalls leaping into them, are the legible language in which nature declares the power she has exercised in past ages on this wonderful theatre. The wealth which has slumbered in these sublime solitudes, now at last set free, will in a few years bring the Pacific coast of the continent into successful rivalry with the oldest empires of commerce; but to the nobler faculties that push scientific inquiry, that urge the keener pursuit of secrets which have hitherto baffled the acutest, that continually say to the phenomena of nature "why and wherefore," there is also abundant stimulus and bountiful food.

The naturalist finds spread out here, larger and more varied fields than have ever before been opened to him on the Western continent. Geology, Mineralogy, Botany, Conchology, Icthyology,* Zoölogy, are each magnificently illustrated in the seas and shores, mountains and vallies of California, and when their light shall havè been shed upon her various products, and shall have illuminated her secret places, California will be found to have contributed equally to the higher as well as the baser wealth of the nations.

* The Bay of San Francisco, has furnished the first viviparous fish ever seen. It was discovered and reported by Dr. W. H. Gibbons in 1854.

15

CHAPTER XXXVI.

IN entering the mining country, one of the first features of it that arrested my attention was, that there appeared to have been a vast deal of labor wasted in turning over ground that had yielded nothing. I was often, for the first several miles, as we rode along beneath the summer sun, saying mentally, poor fellows, how many a weary day has been spent here, without reward, and I enjoyed afterwards not a little amusement (which was also mental) at my own simplicity, when I was reminded that these very diggings had, perhaps, abounded in gold, which might at that moment be circulating in Wall street, at the Royal Exchange or on the Bourse.

I did not remember that the earth would not resume her original aspect, after the loss of her treasure, and that my grandchildren might walk over the ground I was then upon, before it should cease to be vexed with the gold-hunters' implements.   In some parts, immense banks of earth were thrown up awaiting the fall of rain, when the miners would throng their respective claims, and pans, rockers, etc., be put in requisition to complete the labor they had begun.

The different methods of obtaining the gold, are not, perhaps, so familiar to persons who have never visited the country, that a brief description of them will be wearisome.   It is found in a great variety of combinations and juxtapositions.   The commonly-received theory, I believe, is, that it was originally locked up in the quartz rock, but that earthquakes, volcanoes, and other such jail deliveries, have, from time to time, while they prevailed, set portions of it free, which have been borne during the lapse of countless ages, by floods and streams, to the various positions in which the men of the nineteenth century find them.

By far the greater part of it still remains imprisoned, and the most imposing feature of the mining operations is the freeing this by machinery.   The ponderous engines for crush-

ing quartz, with the clang of their huge stamp-
ers resounding night and day among the stately forests and towering mountains, where, but
three years before, the silence had scarcely
been broken, since their tremendous upheav-
ing, struck me as one of the most impressive
and significant sights of this age.

Those stern fortresses in which nature seemed to have secured forever her great treasure
from the knowledge and power of man, are
daily surrendering their wealth, and the hot
besiegers press eagerly up from every quarter
of the globe, for a share in the spoils of this
bloodless but effective war. Ages must elapse
before it is suspended—as many, perhaps, as
have preceded its beginning.

CHAPTER XXXVII.

THE implements used in river mining were originally the pan and rocker.* These have now been superseded by the tom, the long tom, and sluice—the last being the most effective instrument now in use. The tom is a sort of box, eighteen to twenty-four inches wide; varying in length from twelve to twenty feet, and employing, according to the nature of the earth, four or six men. It is open at the top, terminating in a sort of shallow basin, lined with perforated tin, zinc, or sheet-iron, under which is placed a second trough or box, which receives the gold and fine dirt upon a bottom, crossed by many ledges, over which the water

---

* Since this writing, the large hose has been introduced, by which heavy columns of water are discharged with immense force into the localities where gold is found. It is an immense improvement upon any former method of washing earth. This is called the hydraulic process.

carries the dirt and gravel, while the heavier gold is deposited against them.

The sluice, which is now leveling hills and exalting vallies, is a box or trough, from one and a half to two feet wide, and sixty to seventy long, crossed in its entire length by ledges rising three quarters of an inch, or an inch above the bottom. The fine gravel and sand in the river beds are thrown into this, and a sufficient portion of the stream kept running through it, by means of spouts or hose-pipes, to carry off the coarser stuff, and leave the gold free to sink to the bottom, where the ledges arrest it. Fifteen or twenty men may be employed at one, according to its size.

This plan is now adopted, also, for washing rich earth. Water is conducted by canals or flumes through large tracts of country, remote from its natural channels and hills, gulches, ravines, and cañons are sluiced for their precious deposits. At Nevada, one of the richest mining regions in the state, a whole mountain of decomposed quartz is thus being washed down.

In some localities the auriferous vein descends, to a great depth as at Nevada, where shafts are sunk on the respective claims, to depths varying from fifty to more than a hundred feet. These are called coyote diggings, from their resemblance to the manner in which that animal burrows. When they had reached a considerable depth, they were mostly abandoned, though the yield often continued the same, because of the expense of raising and washing the dirt. Since the introduction of sluicing, however, the working of the hill has recommenced, and at the present day, there is every probability that much of it will be ultimately run through the sluice.

It is curious to see, in these regions, how nature is forced out of her lawful ways. Some of the largest mountain streams of California are now lifted from their beds for miles, and the earth, over which they have rolled since the edict " Thus far and no farther" was spoken to them, is being searched and researched, washed and rewashed, one year after another.

As you approach them, the noise of the toms and of the swift current rushing through the narrow artificial channels into which it is forced, the hum of voices and the clink of spades among the gravel, rise up from the deep chasms to the very tops of the mountains that almost overhang them. The great height and steepness of these border-hills on many of the streams, make one of the grandest features of California scenery. Some of them are two, three, and four miles high, and they rise at angles varying from 45° to 60°. You scramble down them, in the best way you can. Sometimes you feel as if your horse were about to turn a summerset, but you push back as forcibly as possible, by way of helping him to preserve the centre of gravity, and, with an occasional halt and then a rush—a detour to the right and another to the left—a fearful looking forward, and an anxious glance backward, you finally reach the bottom, and, drawing a free breath, once more look about you, and ascertain that, deep down as you are, there have been plenty before you; that Mary Avery keeps a boarding-house for miners on your right, and that Patrick Doyle has the best of liquors and wines for your refreshment in his shanty or tent, on your left; that John Smith, honest man, is a carpenter and no swindler, as he has so often been represented to be in the wicked world you have left up yonder; that he is ready to furnish the busy community about him, indiscriminately with "rockers, long toms, or coffins,"* as their condition or convenience may require; that the National, or the United States, or the American hotel is kept in that rough one-story hut, which, as you pass, discloses dismal rents in its cotton walls and ceilings, and allures the thirsty wayfarer by a display of a bar, bristling with bottles—and that at the El Dorado or Pavilion are billiards and bowling, and, also, of course, the more spicy and earnest games in which men are wont to try their chances for fortune or ruin.

Twice, or may be thrice, as your horse loiters through the dusty street, you see a little garden spot, wherein a few cabbages, laden with dust, plead silently for water, and half a dozen rows of choked potatoes remonstrate against their hard lot. At the door of this

* A literal copy of a carpenter's sign in one of the mining towns.

shanty, you, perhaps, see a child, which looks much like the plants; for its mother cannot keep it clean, and she, perhaps, sits within, or may be by her husband's rocker in the bared bed of the river, working it while he shovels the earth. If it be at midday, the sun pours his light and heat into this gorge so fiercely that you scorch beneath his rays, and envy the men working in the cool stream or upon the damp gravel.

The heat will soon drive them to the shade for a couple of hours and then all will be still for the time, save the gurgling of water and the hum of voices occasionally raised above the drowsy noontide tone. Between two and three o'clock the miners straggle out again, the shoveling recommences, lazily at first, by two or three, who are soon joined by a score or two, and the familiar sounds return. The traders and publicans stand at their doors or lounge upon a bench just within; your horse is brought round looking sleepy and tired, you mount, ride through the stream, and push him up the opposite hill with a deal of toil and dust, and when you have gained the dry and sunny plain, wish you could again feel around you, if only for a moment, the dampness and coolness of the " Bar."

But you turn around to look back while your horse breathes ; the warm atmosphere about you moves gently, as if some languid giant had expired a square mile of it from a monster pair of lungs—the motion is very grateful though the heat is little relieved by it, and when you again face the plain, you gallop off lazily, wondering calmly whether Mary Avery, Patrick Doyle, John Smith & Co., realize their condition, or pass all their days in the dreamy mood which seems to you to steep their " location," and everybody in it.

For the first few miles, the country is smooth about you, and you would think nothing more hopeless than the search for gold anywhere on those dry red plains. Presently you see, ahead, banks of it freshly thrown up, and approaching, you find a specimen of the dry diggings, awaiting the fall of rain, perhaps, or being prepared for that auspicious season.

By the roadside is a "hotel," where, if you stop for an hour to rest, or see what is doing,

you will find a landlady bustling about the
kitchen in an atmosphere that shames the feats
of Mons. Chabert.   In the dining-room a table
is laid, which, with everything upon it, seems to
be a fixture—plates of pickles, saucers of oil,
which were butter at Cape Horn, dishes of
dried fruits, pies of the same, bread, sugar, salt,
cheese, and castors, lie scattered along over
fifteen or twenty feet of table-cloth, and seem
utterly to forbid the idea that you could ever
taste food unless it came from an ice-house.
The walls of the room are lined four deep with
sleeping shelves, before which depends, from
ceiling to floor, a scarlet, blue, or print curtain.
You drop upon the first chair, and having declined dinner begin your observations, first by
noting that the landlady is a young woman,
quick, tidy, and self-respecting, with a reserve
in her countenance which shows that she has
lived among people whom she has been obliged
to repel.

Presently her husband steps in from the bar-
room to confer privately with her, and you observe, as they stand near each other, that his
face is inferior to hers, if not in the quantity of

character then in the quality of it. He, perhaps, partakes a little too freely of his own
wares, or, if not, he is so accustomed to serve
those who do and to look with indifference upon the consequences, that he has a hard, don't-
talk-to-me sort of look, which holds your eye
till he returns to his post. This is a room
which is at once a bar-room and a store, perhaps, also, a post-office and a gambling-saloon.
You place yourself in a position to command a
view of this apartment, which is occupied for
the moment by a group of Kanakas, who purchase a few pounds of meat, a little soap, a
paper of a brown mixture called coffee, a small
sack of flour, and a gallon of liquor, and depart. They are succeeded by one, or perhaps
three thin featured Yankees, who, looking
coolly about them, inquire first the price of an
article they have as little intention of buying
as if it were the Urim and Thummim of Aaron
himself. The question answered, they try the
flour by touch, taste the sugar, examine the
butter, drink, renew their tobacco-quids, purchase two or three parcels and move off.

Casting your eyes out of a window, looking

in the opposite direction, you see a pair of sad-
eyed Chinamen approaching.　Their first quest
is the rice barrel, and their wants are soon supplied, for their English is limited to bits, dollars,
pounds, and shoes.　After them comes a sturdy,
square-built Englishman, with a short pipe, for
which he desires a supply of tobacco, a few
pounds of hard bread, some cheese, bacon, and
beer, or in default of the last article, some bran-
dy or gin.　He is succeeded by a German, and
he by three or four chattering Frenchmen, and
they by Sonorians, Chileans, Spaniards, Missourians, and Irishmen, " sure ;" and so on, until,
in the course of your hour's rest, you have seen
representatives from a dozen different nations,
and each of the four quarters of the globe—a
succession which the wilds of no country but
California can present, and what is even more
wonderful, each of your parties is equally at
home.

It is as if they had been born within an
hour's walk of the spot on which you see
them.

They are not foreigners—strangers living on
the land and extracting its treasure for a small

per cent. left them by the lord thereof. They are citizens, if they so choose—all but the proscribed Asiatics—themselves part and parcel of the ruling power, and, strangers though they may be to the American character, a few weeks' residence gives them a confidence in the people and its institutions, which quite frees them from any apprehension or timidity which they could not fail to feel under a less liberal government.

CHAPTER XXXVIII.

In these dry diggings, a shovel, pick and pan are the implements required. The pans are of common tin, and are now chiefly used in prospecting the earth. A panful is taken to the water, and washed, and from the amount it yields, the richness of the earth is estimated. The yield varies from one cent to ten dollars, and, sometimes, even more, per pan. Happy are they who find the latter residuum. On every return to camp, which is, if possible, near some water-course, a panful is tested, and thus, the miner keeps himself advised of the quality of his diggings.

My own experience in mining is confined to this variety. I washed one panful of earth, under a burning noon-day sun, in a cloth riding-habit, and must frankly confess, that the small particle of gold, which lies this day safely

folded in a bit of tissue paper, though it is
visible to the naked eye, did not in the least
excite the desire to continue the search.

A large portion of the gold which has so far
been taken out of the earth in California, has
been gathered in these dry diggings. To extract their treasures, no capital is required but
perseverance and industry ; and the thousands
of men who have singly applied themselves to
it since 1848, have aided throughout the world,
more powerfully than any cotemporary laboring class, the growth of that republican sentiment whose rugged justice threatens the throne
and smiles upon the hovel. Success to them,
not only in their gold quest, but may true manhood, with all its honor, purity, and faithfulness, be among them, and abide with them,
whether success or failure await them in it.

How inadequate to their results seem often
the events of life ! When the apple fell before
the meditative gaze of Newton, and the chan-
delier of the Roman cathedral, vibrating from
its lofty ceiling, suggested the discovery of the
immortal Florentine, how little even those saga-
cious and far-reaching minds could foresee of

the extended results which should flow to man from their notice of these common facts.

So, when in June, in the year 1848, in a narrow valley, between huge mountains, in the wilds of California, a country then known only by name to the civilized world, a laboring man picked from the bank of a river, wherein he was digging a mill-race, a piece of yellow, shining metal; and, after turning it many times over in his hand, "guessed" it was gold, and showed it to his companions, who united in his opinion, and turned from their labor to search for more, how little could they—or wiser, had they been there—prophecy of the results of their discovery?

As facts, they almost stagger the cool judgment which witnesses their existence : the wildest imagination could not have foretold them.

Standing by that swift, rushing stream, whose power they were then first about to render subservient to man, amid the deep solitude of the great mountains, whose summits propped the cloudless lift that smiled upon them, how calm were their days! The constancy of the natural world took from their lives every feature of hazard, every tint of excitement. We may imagine that, for an hour, this event seemed as unimportant as any that had preceded it in their lives; but, searching for more of this "stuff," they soon found it so plentiful in the bed of the stream and its banks, that it seemed altogether the most desirable question they could then have answered, whether this was, indeed, gold, or only something that resembled it.

There was a man in the country whose dictum they could trust, and it was thought advisable to start a messenger to him with some specimens. Behold him, then, the first California gold-carrier, mounted on flying, ungroomed horse, zarapa floating on the wind, huge stirrups jingling, cigar-smoke trailing in his dusty wake, dashing off to Sutter's Fort. He arrives, seeks his oracle, takes him aside (for the Fort is populous with Indians, laborers, trappers, travelers, tradesmen, and others, either serving its proprietor or recipients of his bountiful hospitality), and, showing his "specimens," awaits the momentous answer. It is soon given.

" This is gold. Is there more where you found these lumps?"

"Plenty, sir, I reckon."

Next day a party set out for the mill. The search was commenced in earnest. In the immediate locality of the first discoveries more was found. News was sent to the Bay. Men roused themselves from their sleepy trading, mounted horses, or took such small boats as had been in use on the rivers before, and set out for the mines. The first excited adventurers came down with laden pockets and crazed brains; sailors left their vessels; lazy Spaniards their ranchos; merchants their stores; clerks their desks. The news flew over the country, and went to sea in vessels that could fortunately get away; and thus commenced that gathering which has since revolutionized—physically as well as politically—one of the most beautiful and attractive lands on which the sun shines, and opened an era in history which, considered in all its tendencies, inspires the progressive mind with more rational hope for man, than any that has preceded it.

This is the pleasant side of the picture, and

I have got far away from the starting point, to which I return, to say a few words more on the mines—on one, especially, of their saddest features. I mean the condition of children and youth, growing up in them. Surely, nothing in the worst conditions of the young, in our large cities, could be more deplorable than much of what I saw in the mining towns. In the lesser ones, there are not, generally, churches; and religious meetings are held, if at all, once or twice a month, by appointment.

The Sabbath is a day of revelry and dissipation. A majority of the miners repair to the towns to make purchases for the ensuing week. Then those who are disposed to indulgence take full license. Drunkenness, carousing, profanity, are frightfully prevalent. The children participate in all the vices of their elders. I saw boys, from six upward, swaggering through the streets, begirt with scarlet sash, in exuberant collar and bosom, segar in mouth, uttering huge oaths, and occasionally treating men and boys at the bars. A mother with whom I was talking, saw from my window her son, a young hopeful of ten, walk into a rum-shop opposite, and call up two or three men and large boys to drink. I called her attention to the fact, not knowing that she had a son.

"Yes," she said, sadly, "that is my boy."

"And is it possible that you cannot prevent him?"

"No; he washes his own gold, and gets from three to five dollars a week; and he will spend that for what he pleases."

"But, can you not put him in child's clothes, and keep him from that dreadful, premature mannishness?"

"No," said the poor soul, "I cannot. There are so many boys in town that do what you see him do, that it is impossible to stop one; and the fact is, that up here our boys grow old very fast, anyhow. There is no school* to send them

* Since the time here referred to, schools have been established in every county in the state, and, although many small communities are yet without them, the great mass of the population is as well provided in this respect as that of any other state or nation of people. The common-schools of California are established upon a basis calculated to insure in them the greatest efficiency and perfection attainable.

to, and no church, and it's useless trying to make good boys of them, when they see men behave so badly, and hear so much swearing and bad language."

It is lamentable, indeed, to witness the exposure to the worst influences and examples that children suffer throughout the country, but nowhere so generally and inescapably as in the mines. Doubtless, remedies will be rapidly provided, as the settlements grow older; but it requires a great stretch of vision to foresee a time when one could willingly sit down in a California mining town to rear a family. For it is not so much considerations of moral welfare that engage these communities as fluming, canalling, sluicing, damming, washing, etc.

There are now in the state numerous water-companies, with heavy capitals, whose purpose is to convey water from rivers, springs, etc., by artificial means, through regions that are naturally destitute. In a very few years, there will, no doubt, be an immense capital invested in works of this sort—in tunnels and other means of approaching and taking possession of the locked-up treasure. The amount of labor which these works have already absorbed, is greater than has been expended, since their first discovery, in opening half the mines of South America. The mechanic arts, generally, have kept pace with the improved methods of mining. Flour and lumber mills of the best description have been erected in or near the cities and towns, and many of the latter in the forest regions; the best agricultural implements are now to be had, and all the more common and necessary descriptions of mechanical labor can be procured in the cities and older towns. Artisans of all nations may be found in San Francisco, from the Chinese tailor to the Parisian artiste—from the sturdy blacksmith to the Swiss watchmaker.

The country abounds in the best kinds of timber, in many parts, in good stone, and coal is believed to be abundant, though as yet it has not been actually found, in any quantity, south of Oregon.*

* Coal, it is said, has been since discovered at no great distance from Marysville. The vein has been examined at different points through a distance of some eighteen miles,

The climate and soil admit the growth of many tropical productions, and bring to fullest perfection the fruits of the temperate zones. For cereals California is unequaled. It is the opinion of many intelligent Chinese, that tea would do well in some of the inland, hilly regions, and it is confidently expected that California will in time grow at least her own cotton. Flax is spontaneous in some parts, and wool, of the coarse sort, may be very abundantly produced, almost without expense.

For the rest, we need have little fear for the growth and prosperity of a state which, before the close of its third year, had exported between two and three hundred millions of gold.*

A country which can sustain such a drain upon its wealth, and in the same years build and re-build towns and cities, construct public works, and enlarge its mechanical, agricultural, and

and found to be very excellent in quality and abundant in quantity.

* The export, in 1850, is estimated to have been about $26,500,000 ; in 1851, about $68,000,000 ; in 1852, about $90,000,000 ; in 1853, about $108,000,000 ; in 1854, about $102,000,000 ; in 1855, about $106,000,000.

commercial interests, as California has, can never be allowed to plead inability for any of her short-comings. She *can* do anything a state is called upon to do for the welfare of all classes of her citizens. And she has done much. A public-school system has been organized, and partially put in operation; a state prison commenced, a lunatic asylum, a state hospital; the people have built churches, organized charitable associations, supported private schools, founded libraries, and other institutions for the general improvement, and are moving vigorously on in similar efforts. In what they have done, they have shown what they can do. God speed them!

CHAPTER XXXIX.

CALIFORNIA is well represented, in many of
its features, by its metropolis. The rapid
growth, the incongruous character, the extremes
of condition, the inextinguishable energy, the
material luxury, and the spiritual coarseness—
the pretension and the ignorance which are
observable in San Francisco, characterize the
state.   The city is an epitome of the state.
But it has also its individual features, unlike
those of any other city on the continent, if not
on the globe.

As a maritime city, it has no peer. In her
sixth year, her merchant navy includes, on almost any day, more magnificent vessels than
are to be found in any other harbor on the continent, New York excepted. No American ship
can be considered as fairly entered on the commercial race-ground, that has not tried her

speed to San Francisco, nor any builder's triumph complete until she has awarded him her
verdict. And no harbor affords a finer picture
than ours on a beautiful morning—the tall
clipper masts piercing the radiant blue skies;
the huge, sullen steamers lying in black silence
at the wharves; half a dozen vessels dropping
down to the Golden Gate, their white sails
bearing them slowly on, as do the half-folded
wings of a great sea-bird about to rise from his
liquid bed.

Small boats are glancing about the still
waters in all directions, in which every variety
of color, countenance, and costume are to be
seen—the half-wild, picturesque-looking Malay,
the long-tailed Chinaman, the compact, shaven
Swede, the sturdy Briton, and the nonchalant
Yankee, lord and host of all, whose imperturb-
able face, as he looks about on his numerous
guests, says to them, " This California is a great
' location,' and, I calculate, about the smartest
people in the world have got hold of it."

Great store-houses border the water's edge,
which is now more than a mile further out
than it was in '49. A Bethel church lies be-

side one of the wharves; innumerable hotels, cafés, restaurants, and indispensable drinking-shops, rise on either hand; then succeed cloth-ing-shops, presided over by those much-abused but elastic and persistent tradesmen, the Jews; then commission and heavy-looking wholesale establishments, offices, retail stores, fruit and candy stands, newspaper offices, the Plaza Chinese California, the churches, and you are in town, near the foot of the sand-hills, which, in a year or two, will be removed into the bay, not by the exercise of faith, but of men, horses, and the steam paddy.

CHAPTER XL.

THUS, I have endeavored to give a sketch, which, with more ability, might have been a picture of the wonderful country to which, for the last five years, the eyes of the civilized world have been turned with new hope, and in which, during that short period, there have been ages of suffering.

I have not designed to conceal any inviting or repulsive feature; and, if on one page I have related a history of success that has nearly turned the brain, or described some of the advantages or charms which nature has lavished on this favored land; and, on the next have presented some of the obstacles and fearful trials that have been encountered in the settlement of it, let not the reader fancy that the author has contradicted herself. It is rather the country, and the life of it, which are full of contradictions. To-day is black, to-morrow white. In January you are enabled to play your game so prosperously, that you would scarcely thank one who should offer to insure to you, gratis, its successful issue; in April every chance is against you, and you feel impatient of the folly or ignorance of the man who talks to you of success. In June your hopes revive; in August they decline. In October you scarcely know where or how to start; and, by the setting in of the new year, you have, perhaps, laid broad the foundation of life-long prosperity.

Thus, life wears on, constant in nothing but its fluctuations;* and, although every year

---

* One of the most painful results of this excitement, is a frightful amount of insanity, and of desperation, so closely bordering upon it, that the jurist ought often to be replaced in function by the expert. The incessant strain upon the mental powers; the constant torture of the affections, either through the absence of their objects, or, what is far keener, their unworthy conduct when present; the disappointment of hopes; the prostration of plans, conceived and partially executed, with infinite labor; the absence of repose, and of those restoring influences of home and society, which elsewhere soothe the irritability, and mitigate the weariness, of the commercial and speculating life; all these influences,

diminishes, in a measure, the force of these destructive influences, they yet have strength enough to cause a feeling of insecurity that haunts most persons by night and by day; banishing freedom from their gaieties; earnestness from their devotions; and single-heartedness from every act not directed to the accomplishment of the grand scheme of fortune. For if, according to the great analyzer, the modern hell of the world is " not to succeed," it is the concentrated, intensified hell of California.

Failure here seems to cut off hope. To return to old homes and friends with a story of failure, passes mortal courage; for, it is one of the influences of the country to destroy confidence in friendship; in natural affection; in human sympathy. They enter so little into our daily experience, that we forget their existence, or finally disbelieve it altogether.

one foresees, must inevitably result in the frequent dethronement of reason. Only the benignity of nature; only the miraculous climate, restoring, in the sleep of every night, the energies that, exhausted during the day, could save such a country, inhabited by such a people, from becoming a vast mad-house.

I erred in saying that our life was constant in nothing but its fluctuations. There is one other painful feature of it, which remains to this day, but little mitigated by the increase of population, and the other changes that have taken place in it; I mean the lack of social confidence and friendly intercourse. It is the one first and last complaint from all conditions and classes. What was truly said respecting this in 1851, required little modification in 1854, and is only less generally true in 1856. The want of mutual confidence and respect keeps people apart. Acquaintance often fails to obliterate the lines which self-respect, or suspicion have laid down, and people meet each other with a reserve, which continually hardens them, till their sympathies perish, and they are only talking-machines to each other.

But I have, perhaps, said enough on this subject; more than hundreds, who live butterfly lives among us, will admit as true, and sufficient to give those who may think of coming, a just idea of the condition they are proposing to themselves. A more generous social life would soften many of the sterner features of our lot;

check the fearful destruction of character that is going on at all times among us; and tend to the preservation, not of business honor only, but of faithfulness to the ties of affection, and the obligations of duty, now so often and shamelessly forgotten.

CHAPTER XLI.

THE gigantic enterprise which has brought California, before the completion of its sixth year, to its present growth, will stand long unparalleled in the history of the world. But the admiration it challenges is frozen, at the contemplation of the moral turpitude which has walked hand in hand with it, in many of its most brilliant achievements. The enormous frauds, forgeries, and briberies, that have been charged, attempted, and perpetrated, would startle one familiar with the criminal records of the world. Never were such tremendous schemes conceived. Never did perpetration so little tarnish the character. Never were failures so generally and broadly rebuked, as evidence of weakness or stupidity. Never were such damning accusations made with so little injury, either to accused or accuser. The active life of the country opens a frightfully easy descent from integrity. There is first, decline in the minor moralities. Against this, many very good natures may be quite unguarded. Trifling infringements of the commandment, " Thou shalt not covet," are easy in a country where to get is the law and the gospel of every man who would thrive, and where little unlawful acquisitions, that one would shrink from in another country, seem quite in the natural way.

The old restraints are too stiff to fit easily or gracefully, where so great adaptation is exhibited. Natures not intimately penetrated with the sacredness of the law of right, take short steps over its limits, feeling that the sentiment of the community will not thereby be outraged. The more eager and ambitious reach a little further, feeling all the while the presence of a spirit that insures to them toleration. And finally, those who are capable of operating upon a grand scale, take the large territory that lies between open disgrace and strict integrity, ready at any moment to flee to the latter, when the stake shall become sufficiently heavy.

We may suppose that Messrs. Meiggs, Woods and many others, lingered long on this debatable ground before going over. They did not become swindlers on the day of failure. The strife of speculation—the haste to be rich, which winks at any, and all exposure of the rights and possessions of others, whereby you propose great gain to yourself—would first encourage them to equivocal dishonesty, and a short apprenticeship there, under the wild chaotic conditions of the country, would suffice to prepare them for a career. The soul sickens at the criminal catalogue of these short five years.

I go back less than one from this day, and recall three cases so notorious, that I shall injure no party by referring to them. The famous case in the Senate of 1853–4, is the oldest of them. A charge of bribery was made by one of its own members, against a distinguished banker ; was tried at a cost of some two or three weeks' time of the entire body—supported and refuted by a great deal of testimony, and finally disposed of, by acquitting the accused, and *passing a complimentary vote to the accuser !*

On the eve of an election, a city paper charges an alderman with offering one of his colleagues a bribe of five thousand dollars, for his influence in securing the election of a certain firm to a lucrative office in the gift of the council.　There is a very little ambiguity in fixing the charge; but the accused does not see fit to avail himself of it.　He comes out in a card, literally flaming with virtuous indignation.　His horror at such an accusation knows no bounds.　He blusters, rails, and flatly and solemnly denies that it has a shadow of truth in it.　Whereupon, Mr. Editor goes to the incorruptible and says, in effect: "Sir, this charge, which was made indirectly upon your authority, is denied; are you prepared to sustain it?"　There are some difficulties in the way, perhaps a little delicacy due to the freedom of intercourse between official brethren; but whatever their nature, they are removed, and next morning the charge is directly made in the accuser's own name, and supported by such detail of occasion and circumstance as insure credence.

Now the accused, if wronged, had ample

ground for demanding redress, and an antagonist more substantial than a newspaper. Did
he do what an innocent man would have done?
Judge ye who are such. He sat quietly down
under his implied guilt. His indignation eva-
porated in silence.

What penalties were visited upon him for so
foul an act? He, indeed, lost his re-election,
(which was quite as likely to have happened
if his villainy had not been disclosed) but not
his position in the business or social life he had
before shared, and there are not wanting numbers of respectable persons who scout the
weakness of the man who refused the bribe.

The moral tone of our communities is " balm
and healing" to such wounds as this gentleman
received.

If Mr. Meiggs, after two or three years of
gentlemanly travel, should feel a preference for
this country, he might return if with sufficient
fortune to support a princely style, and find
himself the hero of envious crowds. It is
mournful to consider how we ignore all distinc-
tions in worthiness, and receive and sustain
rogues and villains with a welcome regulated

solely by their wealth and lavishness.   Wealth
secures to its possessors one reception, whether
worthy or unworthy, while poverty, whatever
its worth and intelligence, stands perpetually
rebuked and repelled.   Hence the game of life
is played more hazardously with us than elsewhere.   The imp who sits opposed to the
absorbed player, has no aspect of sympathetic
seriousness; no tender compassion lurks in his
features, for he recognizes there before him no
elevated purpose. No far-off noble end is in view
for which willing sacrifice is offered of present
gains and enjoyments.

Eagerness, the grand American characteristic,
is here developed to a fourfold power.   Life is
robbed of the calm majestic dignity in which
it rests upon issues appointed of God—in
which it abides results that are hoped for or
dreaded, not with the consuming terror that
awaits the last heave of the earthquake, or the
final blast of the destroying tornado, but with
the spirit that could rejoice in rewards, or bear
up patiently and nobly against undeserved
calamities.   Present good is the desire, present
attainment the determination that rules the

thought and action. It need scarcely be suggested, how rapidly nobility and aspiration die out of characters thus controlled.

Yet, let us trust, that despite these and all other untoward influences, California will finally prove to have been good, and not evil, unto us. Surely, the nation, which is in so many respects the nurse and examplar of what is noble in the race, will not fail, through lack of faithfulness to itself, to convert to true blessings the gifts which nature has so unsparingly bestowed upon it.

Let us encourage ourselves by anticipating the better period of our history, when our beloved state shall no longer be the hunting-ground of the striving nations—when the chances of fortune, and consequently of ruin, are less numerous—when business life takes on a more settled aspect, when our population shall have lost somewhat of the emigrant mixed character, and when, in the eloquent language Bushnell, society shall have struck its roots into Californian soil.

Then the benign summer heavens will smile upon hearts tranquil enough to expand beneath them into charity and love—free enough to be penetrated by the exquisite harmony of the material world—then the glorious hills and teeming vales will be dotted with homes wherein plenty reigns, with her younger sister content. A country so clothed with majesty, so bathed in perpetual sunshine, so fanned by heaven's own breath of health, so munificently endowed with mineral wealth and productive energies, so grandly stretched along the border of that continent whose physical greatness and civil stature are beheld even now in her youth with awe—the gateway—the one point of egress and ingress. through which the tottering civilization of the Old World and the vigorous, curbless genius of the New, must clasp unequal hands, must have a hopeful destiny before her. Surely there is not lacking stimulus to the noblest ambition of her citizens; to their loftiest aspirations for the commonwealth.

But let them remember that the foundations of a state are not best laid on the moral ruin of its citizens; that decayed integrity and broken credit, however brilliant the achievements that have led to them, are at best but indifferent

pillars to the republican edifice ; and that ve-
nality cannot better consist with true civil and
political greatness, than can organic disease
with perfect animal development. It is the
gangrene ever surely eating its way to the
sources of vitality.

> " What constitutes a state?
> Not high-raised battlement or labored mound,
>   Thick wall or moated gate ;
> Not cities proud with spires and turrets crown'd,
>   Not bays and broad-armed ports,
> Whereon, laughing at the storm, rich navies ride ;
>   Not starr'd and spangled courts,
> Where low-born baseness wafts perfume to pride.
>   No ! men, high-minded men,
> With powers as far above dull brutes endued
>   In forest, brake, or den,
> As beasts excel cold rocks and brambles rude—
> *   *   *   *   *   *
>   Men, who their duties know,
> But know their rights,
>   And knowing, dare maintain.
> These constitute a state."

APPENDIX.

NARRATIVE OF THE EMIGRATION OF THE DONNER PARTY TO CALIFORNIA, IN 1846.

I HAVE spoken but briefly within these pages of woman in California, and have, withal, been less direct and fearless on this topic than is my wont, on a subject I have so near at heart. The effort made by myself in '49, to facilitate the emigration of females, failed through an illness which disabled me from seeing or corresponding with those who wished to join me, until within a very few weeks of my departure —a period quite too short to admit of preparations for so momentous a movement.

I have elsewhere expressed the thankfulness of heart, and the cause of it, with which I have often since reflected upon that failure ; but I wish not to be understood as thereby admitting what I do not believe—that the defection of my own sex here is more deplorably general than that of the other. Except as women are more nearly allied to the sources of good than men are, and that, therefore, any general dereliction from moral purity in them is more disastrous to the weal of the community, there is nothing from which we need shrink, in the comparison of our sex in California, with the sterner and more boastful one.

The disgusting skepticism, one everywhere hears among men on this subject, is, doubtless, evidence of a moral condition of those condemned, which all good persons must lament; but it proves, also, that those who bear that testimony, make themselves familiar with the worst side of our social life rather than the best. And in testifying to a result which no true man or woman can think upon without anguish of heart, they ignore, with a sublime assurance, any instrumentality of their own in producing it. Ask Judge A——, or Hon. Mr. B——, or Dr. C——, or any untitled gentleman of the same school, what is the cause of the laxity they assert among women, and they will coolly answer, perhaps, by enumerating many, among which their own bad conduct is entirely omitted. They do not see that phase of the phenomenon in which they are themselves a feature. Here it is :

"I am going home on the next steamer," said a lady one day to a friend. "The Judge bought my ticket to-day."

"Dear me !" was the reply, "and you have been here but four months. Why do you return so soon ?"

"Because, to speak frankly, it is of no use for me to remain. I have been long enough here to be convinced that I can do no good by staying ; and I only make myself miserable by being away from my children."

"But your husband; he has some claim on you, surely."

"I would not deny his claim," said the poor wife, with tearful eyes, "if he ever asserted it. But I contribute nothing to his happiness. All day he is engaged in court. I do not complain of that ; but I scarcely ever see him till one or two o'clock in the morning—sometimes not at all for three or four days. I do nothing for him but take care of his wardrobe; and the expense of my support here for three months is equal to that of a year at home, where I can have the care of my children, and at least enjoy the happiness of serving them."

This lady was beautiful, amiable, accomplished. Had she been a gayer woman, and less devoted mother, doubtless some of the numerous persons who admired her, would have succeeded, in some degree, in gaining her confidence; and then, had she erred, whether gravely or not, she alone would have stood condemned—the part her depraved husband had in preparing the way for her unhappiness being quite forgotten or overlooked.

The true worth and real integrity of men and women was never more severely tried, on a broad scale, than it has been in California; and it might be expected that those who sink with greatest facility themselves, would make the loudest outcry about the general downfall, forgetful of the tremendous tests to which many of those who had sunk with them have been submitted. All good women here have felt the keenest chagrin and anguish at conduct in their sisters, which would justify, in some measure, the generally light respect entertained for the sex; but, while women are reckoned only human, and, by many of their judges, something less than that, one finds it difficult to discern the justice of the general condemnation and distrust with which the sex is visited for the defection of a portion only of its members.

Grant that woman is superior to man in those attributes of humanity that assimilate it to its Father; that her fall is consequently a more painful moral phenomenon; that a false life, derelict from noble self-respect and divine purity, is more monstrous in her than in him, as doing greater violence to her loftier nature, and we have the basis of a severer judgment for her offenses.   Such a judgment, humanity, in all conditions and ages, has visited upon fallen woman—curiously and absurdly enough denying, at the same time, the only ground upon which it could, with any justice, be pronounced.   Human weakness has never, in any thing beside, been guilty of so cruel and universal a wrong as that it has practiced toward women in this respect—of the two offenders,

savagely condemning the one, it pronounced
inferior and subordinate, to the keenest punishment, to be remitted only when the sufferer
passed beyond its reach—while the superior
should escape even censure. One is encouraged
by the growing indications of truer perceptions
in this momentous question. A just estimate
of the noblest moral life and function, apart
from physical, intellectual, and money power,
and a corresponding award of freedom of action, will, I am convinced, insure to woman
her full rights, and an ample stage for the
exercise of them; which, I equally believe,
will be found to be quite other than the bar,
the forum, or the caucus chamber. But systems of great magnitude, gone widely astray
through ages, require ages for return and adjustment; and my friends who would become
lawyers, senators, governors, or presidents, may
have ample time to try themselves in these
capacities, and, perhaps, to fit their grand-
daughters for the same, before woman will
be fully acknowledged (and respected and
employed accordingly), as standing nearer to
God than her lordly brother does.

I confess myself unable to see why the many defections among the reputable of my sex in this state (and be it understood that I do not speak in these pages of that destroying army of another class who have invaded every portion of it) should be considered so fatally derogate of the dignity and worth of the whole. Thousands of men have not only forfeited character, but abandoned all pretension to it; and tens of thousands have stained themselves by deeds, at the contemplation of which they would have shuddered before coming here; yet no reputable man, emigrating, would consent that he should be adjudged as thereby compromising himself. He would very rationally demand that only his own acts and life should be taken in evidence against him. And have not we an equal claim to the same justice?

I would appeal to the firmness and self-respect of every pure woman in our state, to struggle against the shrinking and humiliation that oppress her when she moves in public, and to assert, by the calm, confident, modest bearing which she would have preserved in the land she came from, her consciousness of fully deserving here all the respect she ever enjoyed there. Whatever opinion is expressed by men, be sure that there are good and true women about you, who, if you have trials, will perceive them, and feel a joy and triumph in seeing you come unscathed through them. Do not believe for a moment, when temptation comes, that there is no sympathizing soul near to rejoice in the firmness with which you deafen your ears to its seductive tones—in the grand respect for your nature, inviolate, undimmed by corrupt purpose or deed, which lifts you to the region where no cloud can follow you, and "no less high desire" than the noblest you are capable of, can come. If you are unhappily deprived of the expressed sympathy of good women, forget not still, how admirable in all eyes is true womanly purity : forget not, that after the hour of temptation you have to meet your own heart in judgment, and, more fearful still, His Spirit who, by the very laws of your being, declares the high position in His creation which he has made you to fill.

The self-sacrifice to which women, in all conditions, are called, presupposes the better nature which would prompt them to make it; and California is an exemplification of this on a scale to which the history of ages offers no parallel.   There was no salvation for the country but from her presence in it, and the necessity to come was in very, very many instances, the cruelest she could be called on to obey. Thousands have reached the land through incredible hardships and scenes shocking to every sensibility; and thousands more, without these trials, have landed on our shores, unconscious that in doing so they were literally laying themselves upon a rack.

And if the weakness which has been cultivated and nurtured at home, failed to become strength and self-reliance in the new and fearful trials that awaited them, who should exercise harsh and unrelenting judgment toward them?   Shame and ruin have been not only the precursors, but the consequents of anguish to many a wretched woman among us; but truth, which compels this acknowledgment, glories also in placing side by side with it the noblest proofs of all that we claim for our sex—illustrations of sublime self-sacrifice, of heroic fortitude, of calm endurance such as may have been equaled but never surpassed in its history. The annals of the overland emigration are especially rich in these histories, kindling, despite the detestable demonstrations about us, a love and reverence for humanity, which refreshes and strengthens the soul.

One of these is related in the following pages. I have gathered its material from several individuals of both sexes, who were members of the unfortunate party; and I believe that in almost every particular it is deserving of entire credit. This party emigrated before the discovery of the gold, and consisted chiefly of persons led by the love of adventure and confidence in the charms of the clime they sought.

They set out from St. Joseph's, Missouri, in May of the year 1846.

California was then in a state bordering on revolution; and among the male members of this party were several persons who, doubtless, believed that among its half-civilized population, positions and advantages might be won, which they could never hope to enjoy at home. In any case, they were destined to a land unequaled in beauty, and in its magnificent generosity of soil and climate. And, though a long journey lay before them, they were confident, at the worst they could foresee, of a result that would satisfy, in a large measure, the hopes they entertained, and they were fearless of dangers by the way. They numbered from eighty to ninety, and comprised many families, with children of all ages, from a few months upward. They set out in spirits corresponding with the sunshine and breezes which accompanied them. The men were earnest — the young people gay — the mothers only, a little doubtful, when they considered the precious lives they had in charge, and the possible dangers that might have to be encountered before they should see them all safely housed in the distant land of their destination. Their journey was uninterrupted by any but the occurrences common to such travel—the delays to rest weary cattle or recover lost ones—the necessity to repair a broken wagon, or adjust some of the many affairs that on such a journey constantly lack adjustment.

There was then no thoroughfare on the great plains that lay stretched between them and the setting sun. Their solitude was rarely broken by the passage of a trading or trapping party, or a band of Indian hunters, moving to and fro, in search of game, or bearing homeward the trophies of the chase already past. But the emigrant fires burned at evening, and their light shone cheerfully into the silent darkness that walled them in. When supper was over, the young people gathered around one of the fires, and there were music and dancing, or social, cheerful chats, after the adventures of the day.

There was a family consisting of twelve members: a father, mother, nine children, and a son-in-law, husband of the eldest daughter. The father was a man in middle life; healthy, hopeful, adventurous; with strong affections, that were generous enough to receive a powerful stimulus from the presence of his large, active, and promising family. They had been born in one of the most beautiful regions of Illinois. The youngest, at the time of starting, was a babe, of four or six months. The eldest unmarried, a daughter of eighteen. The young women rode on horseback, or in the wagons, as suited their convenience or fancy. They were excited by the novel features of the country over which they passed, and the anticipations with which they looked forward to that region which had, in their minds, but a vague, half-real existence; and seemed, to the more imaginative of them, more like the happy hunting-ground, of which the Indian dreams in his untutored reveries, than a part of the common-place, work-a-day world.

They crossed the Missouri on the 20th of May, and, on the 3rd of July, reached Fort Laramie. Here they found a party of Sioux Indians; warriors going out to give battle to their old enemies, the Snakes. The Sioux were then the most powerful race of the great prairies; and our emigrants, partly, I suppose, from a desire to conciliate them, partly, because of their abundance, gave them a dinner at the Fort, on the 4th. They were grand-looking men, the warriors, well-made, power-ful, and lithe, grave and courteous, dignified, solemn, and majestic. The hospitalities over, they parted, with friendly remembrances on one side, and wishes on the other. The emi-grants moved on, and were overtaken by the same party on the afternoon of the 6th. The recollection of bread and salt did not restrain the commoner sort from attempting to steal various articles that seemed desirable to them. They heeded no remonstrance from the whites, nor even from their chief, till the latter person-age, with a majestic determination to rule, shot down two of the robber's horses. They wished to buy one of the young ladies, who was riding a little in rear of the company, with her bro-ther, and made two or three handsome offers for her, which, being declined by the bro-ther, one laid hold of her horse's bridle, and attempted to lead her off a prize, but he drop-ped the rein when her protector leveled his gun, and rejoined his company. Such little inci-dents, happening rarely, served to enliven their travel, which now began to grow a little tedious.

They reached Fort Bridger in the latter part of August, and there heard much commendation bestowed upon the new route, via Salt Lake, by which Mr. Hastings had preceded them a few weeks. It was said to be shorter than the old one, by Fort Hall, and quite practicable. They debated, and delayed, and finally divided. A small company had proceeded, on the new route, from the fort, a few days before them, whom they overtook, and joined on the sixth day. Their whole number was now eighty-three, or, as some say, eighty-five; and this was the company fated to those appalling trials, under which so many perished, and so many more failed in all human senses. Terrors and sufferings, so great and protracted, seldom try the nature of men and women; but, rarely as they come, they find few among those whom they visit furnished to the occasion. In the trials of this kind, of which we have narratives, women have rarely been participators. Here the numbers were nearly equal; and the result is one of which every woman who reverences her sex may be justly proud.

At the time when they joined the advance company, it was lying still, awaiting the return of a small party that had been sent out to improve the road, and, if possible, overtake Hastings, who was supposed to be but a few days before them. They hoped to secure his guidance into the valley of Bear river. They were disappointed in this, and, after the loss of many days, finally journeyed on. Could the fearful consequences of this delay have been apprehended, it would not have been submitted to. But the disposition of common characters to be controlled by anything but their own intelligent determination, prevailed over the dread of the women, and the impatience of the men. Days went by, till they amounted to weeks. The fair summer had drawn to a close, and autumn had tinted with matchless pencil the herbage and foliage of the great mountain barrier that divided them from their land of promise, before their feet, now growing weary and slow, touched its eastern base. I extract from a narrative furnished me by the kindness of Mr. John Breen, who was of the party, and, at that time, about fourteen.

He says: "We traveled several days, without much difficulty, till we left Weaver river. Here our work commenced, for we had a new road to make through a heavily-timbered country, with no other guide than the sun. One day's travel from the river, the road became so bad that it was necessary to let the wagons lie still for two or three days at a time to prepare a way for them. Over much of the ground it was impossible to pass with the wagons till a great deal of labor had been done. In one place all the men in the company worked hard for two weeks, and only advanced thirty miles. We, at last, came within one mile of Salt Lake Valley, when we were compelled to pass over a hill so steep that from ten to twelve yoke of oxen were necessary to draw each wagon to the summit. From this height we beheld the Great Salt Lake, and the extensive plains by which it is surrounded. It gave us great courage; for we thought we were going to have good roads through a fertile country; but the saline atmosphere, and the long drives, without water, rendered our route through that valley particularly harassing. When we reached what was called the desert, we had a drive of seventy or eighty miles, without grass, or water, over a plain covered with salt. Here our real hardships commenced; cattle giving out, or straying away, mad with thirst. One man (Mr. R.) lost all his oxen but one yoke, and was, consequently, compelled to leave all his wagons but one; into which he put a large family and their provisions, which, of course, made traveling very tedious. Several people came very near perishing on this desert for water; but, it was very remarkable that the women stood it better than the men. After we got across, we laid by one or two days to recruit; but, when we were ready to start, Mr. R.'s last yoke of cattle were missing; so, all hands turned out, and made a general search for six days, but we found no trace of them. In fact, it was impossible to find cattle on those plains, as the mirage, when the sun shone, would make every object the size of a man's hat look as large as an ox, at the distance of a mile or more; so one could ramble all day from one of these delusions to another, till he became almost heart-broken from disappointment, and famished from thirst. While we laid here, two men were sent on, on horseback, to California, to get provisions, and return to meet us on the Humboldt."

Thus their provisions were getting low. This, the loss of their cattle, and the reduced condition of those that were left, weighed upon their spirits, and impeded their progress. There had been no death in the party until they reached Salt Lake Valley. They had a consumptive invalid, who had been steadily declining through all their rough experience, and one afternoon, the wagon in which he was carried was observed to fall behind the others. Inquiry was made. He was not much worse, it was said, but after the party had encamped at evening the wagon came up bringing his corpse. He had neither wife, nor child, nor near friend. He had set out an invalid in search of health, and happily had expired before the terrible days came that were now drawing fast on. Next morning a rude coffin was constructed of boards taken from one of the wagons, and the body committed to the earth, according to the rites and ceremonies of that mysterious, and world-wide brotherhood tow hich he belonged.

Those who had before been comparatively infferent to their delays, began, by this time, to be earnest. "The more so," Mr. Breen says, "that on the morning of their leaving the long encampment at the desert, there appeared a considerable fall of snow on the neighboring hills. The apprehension of delay from this cause, and of scarcity, made the mothers tremble. But they knew that to give way was to make unavoidable that which they dreaded, and they put the best possible face on to meet their discouragements. The men were irritable and impatient. A dispute arose one day after dinner, between two of them, respecting the driving of a wagon up a very difficult hill. Hot words were followed, almost instantly, by blows—one with a knife, or dagger, which proved fatal in about twenty minutes. The man was buried next morning. Feeling respecting the affair ran high, and the survivor very soon left the company, alone, his family being constrained to remain in it, by the previous loss of their cattle, on the desert. How keen must have been that parting—from a wife and four or five children!

"They reached Truckee river without any incident of an extraordinary character except the disappearance of a German, whose immediate party lagged behind awhile, and when they at length came up, could, or would give, but a vague account of him. It was said that he had strayed away in search of cattle and they supposed he might have been killed or lost. The press of care had now become too great, from the necessity to get forward, to permit the loss of any time, or even the manifestation of any interest in the fate of one who was a stranger, by blood and tongue, to most of his fellow-travelers. At the last encampment on Truckee river, another life was lost, by the accidental discharge of a pistol. Two men, brothers-in-law, had been handling their arms by the camp fire in the morning. Wood to replenish it was called for, when one said to the other, 'hold my pistol while I go for some.' In the transfer, by some means it went off, and the contents lodged in the body of the unfortunate man, who lived only two hours. Death did not startle them now. They were too much engrossed by their own necessities to heed his presence, further than naked decency required. They had buried their first dead in a coffin and shroud, with masonic ceremonies, their second with only a shroud and a board beneath and above him. The last man was buried literally dust to dust, nothing to separate his clay from that of the great parent who opened her bosom to receive him."

They journeyed on, hoping that at the worst they should be met by relief, but as the mothers have told me, with inexpressible anxieties at heart already. "On Truckee river," says Mr. Breen, "the weather was already very cold, and the heavy clouds hanging over the mountains to the west were strong indications of an approaching winter. This of course alarmed several people, while others paid no attention to it. My father's family, among the former, used every effort to cross the mountains if possible before the snow should become too deep. We traveled up the river a few days, when we met the excellent Stanton, returning with five

or six mules, packed with flour and meat. Capt.
John A. Sutter had given him the mules and
provisions, for the mere promise of compensation, an act for which he deserves the love of
every soul of that suffering company.   He will
always be remembered by me, with gratitude
and reverence, for that generous act.   And
Mr. Stanton, who sacrificed his life to assist his
companions—for he had no family or relations
in the company—should be held in honored remembrance by every one who can appreciate
a noble act.   The clouds on the mountains
looked very threatening, but he naturally looked at the bright side of things, and assured us
there was no danger, little thinking that the
the next summer's sun would bleach his un-
buried bones, not far from that spot."

It had snowed at the last burial on this river,
and they traveled up its banks amid wintry
desolation, made a hundredfold more desolate
by the frowning presence of the stern gigantic
mountains, by the feeble condition of their cattle, which the snow deprived of sustenance, by
their scanty stores and already overtasked powers of endurance.   They reached Truckee Lake

on the fourth of November. It was cold, and on its banks the snow already lay to the depth of a few inches. They encamped for the night, availing themselves of a couple of huts which had been erected there the winter previous by a few belated emigrants or trappers. They hoped to push on in the morning. Their exhausted and starving animals were offered some boughs. By this time their wagons were nearly empty of their burdens, but they were, even thus light, an overmatch for the feeble cattle.

Mr. Breen says of this day's work and that which followed it : " In the morning it was very cold, with about an inch of snow on the ground. This made us hurry our cattle still more, if possible, than before. We traveled on, and, at last, the clouds cleared, leaving the towering peaks in full view, covered as far as the eye could reach with snow. This sight made us almost despair of ever entering the long-sought valley of the Sacramento ; but we pushed on as fast as our failing cattle could haul our almost empty wagons. At last we reached the foot of the main ridge, near Truckee Lake. It was sundown.

The weather was clear in the early part of the night; but a large circle around the moon indicated, as we rightly supposed, an approaching storm. Daylight came only to confirm our worst fears. The snow was falling fast on that terrible summit over which we yet had to make our way. Notwithstanding, we set out early to make an effort to cross. We traveled one or two miles—the snow increasing in depth all the way. At last, it was up to the axle of the wagons. We now concluded to leave them, pack some blankets on the oxen, and push forward; but by the time we got the oxen packed, it was impossible to advance; first, because of the depth of the snow, and next, because we could not find the road; so we hitched to the wagons and returned to the valley again, where we found it raining in torrents. We took possession of a cabin and built a fire in it, but the pine-boughs were a poor shelter from the rain, so we turned our cattle at large, and laid down under our wagon-covers to pass the night. It cleared off in the night, and this gave us hopes; we were so little acquainted with the country as to believe that the rain in the valley was rain on the

mountain also, and that it would beat down the
snow so that we might possibly go over. In
this we were fatally mistaken. We set out
next morning to make a last struggle, but did
not advance more than two miles before the
road became so completely blocked that we
were compelled to retrace our steps in despair.
When we reached the valley, we commenced
repairing the house; we killed our cattle and
covered it with their hides.'

The courage to make such great exertion was
not evinced by the whole party. Many remained in the valley awaiting almost with indifference its result. One of the leading spirits in
these efforts was the mother of our narrator,
who had, indeed, a world to struggle for—a sick
husband and seven children, the youngest a
nursing babe, the oldest but fourteen years.

They were an Irish family, who had been
well-to-do before leaving their last home in
Iowa, and they had still a large number of cattle, and as many other resources as any other
in the company. The father, in these terrible
days, was nearly or quite disabled, from an attack of a distressing ailment which he had suf-

fered for several days before reaching their encampment, so that the responsibility of saving the family devolved chiefly on the mother. And the unshrinking firmness, resolution and self-devotion with which she served them, in that fearful season, deserve commemoration beside the noblest deeds of humanity. Conceive with what palpitating anxiety she watched every struggle of the faithful beasts ; with what heart-sinking she saw them utterly fail, thus dooming her tender babe, and young children, and feeble husband to trials of which human fear could not depict the appalling character and duration.

They sat down at the huts helpless—compelled to abide the issues that might await them. Their stores were nearly exhausted. Bread had quite disappeared—a little tea, coffee, and sugar were all they had left, except the flesh of their miserable beasts. The relief stores were very soon consumed by a community of seventy or seventy-five cold and hungry people, and as removal was impossible to any but the ablest, it was soon decided that the most hardy and capable should at once set off

on foot, to complete their journey, taking with
them only enough to support life for six days,
by the end of which period, if ever, they thought
they should reach Bear Valley. They set out,
reached the tops of the mountain with infinite
difficulty, and then, finding it impossible to ascertain what precise direction to take, waited
on the snow two days and nights, for the man
Stanton who had come out with the stores, and
was to go in with them. His mules had strayed away, and he was reluctant to set off to go
to their owner without them. So the foot party was obliged to return to camp, where, for
the time, they might all be considered as settled. Trees had been felled for the walls of
cabins, which were covered with the hides of
their oxen and horses. There were three camps
in the space of about three quarters of a mile,
and another seven miles away further down the
shores of the lake. In these the whole party
were in some manner sheltered from the rigor
and storms of that unfriendly region, and they
had need be well sheltered, for on the night
after the return of the party lasts poken of
from the summit, a snow-storm set in which

continued almost without intermission for ten days.

Whose hand will ever adequately record the discouragements of those days? the sickening apprehensions, the yearnings over the helpless and unconscious ones, the destroying fluctuations between hopes that only dawned upon the crushed spirit to be succeeded by fears of palpable midnight blackness! At length the storm was over. The dreary gray clouds, which had lowered so mercilessly upon the devoted party, trooped away, and the blue sky smiled coldly and finely down upon them, as a haughty spirit triumphant does upon its subdued victim. The adventurers made ready and started again on snow-shoes, it being impossible now to move in any other manner.

Every day of the storm had reduced the provisions fearfully, and now no relief could be relied on till fresh tidings of their dreadful situation were taken into the settlements. They set out on the 16th of December. They had been forty-two days at the cabins—an age of terror, anxiety, and dread—but up to the time of their departure, actual starvation had not taken place. They numbered fifteen—ten males and five females. The faithful Stanton, and the two Indians who had been sent with him by Gen. Sutter, were of the party. Under their guidance, hope was entertained that they might reach Bear·Valley in five or six days, and they took with them enough of the poor dried beef to allow each person, thrice a day, a bit of the size of two fingers. There was the father, before spoken of, and his two eldest daughters —the married one accompanied by her husband; —an unfortunate young mother, who had been obliged to leave an infant behind her, and two other females. A Mexican, who had joined the emigrants at Fort Laramie, was of the number; the remainder were all men who had come through from the states. They took each upon his or her own person all on which the preservation of life depended in the fearful journey before them—coffee, a kettle to boil it in; beef, of their poor sort, barely enough to nourish their emaciated bodies sufficiently to support life; matches; a flint-gun; a small axe, and a blanket each. Their snow-shoes were made of their ox-bows and green hide interlaced.

They were about two feet in length, by one in breadth. Thus they were equipped. There were but two or three who did not leave behind them father, mother, wife or child, or brother or sister. The country before them was a dreary waste of cold white. Frequently, only the tops of the trees were visible above the snow, its depth varying from a few feet to sixty.

All the long day—and it was long to them, though the sun was warming the southern tropic—they urged their fainting, wasted bodies onward, and, at nightfall, gathering a few boughs, they lighted a fire, boiled their morsel of coffee, and drank it with the little scrap of beef they could afford for the evening meal. They then wrapped their blankets about them and slept upon the snow till the morning light recalled them to their weary travel. On the morning of their fifth day out, poor Stanton sat late by the camp-fire. The party had set off, all but Miss G., and as she turned to follow her father and sister, she asked him if he would soon come. He replied that he should, and she left him smoking. He never left the desolate fireside. His remains were found there by the next party who passed.

They pressed on. There was too little of life in them to wonder or fear at anything. They were alone with starvation, and would have been roused and even cheered by the sight of any living being ferocious or docile. Their helplessness and despair were fearfully increased by the loss of their guide. The Indians did not know the country when undisguised, and its chilling mantle would have deceived eyes the most familiar with it. They were now making the small allowance of one day serve for two ; but even this could avail them nothing. Their whole store would not have satisfied the moderate appetite of one person for a meal. So, on the evening of the seventh day, when they had given up all expectation of seeing their guide, and would scarcely have lifted a hand or foot to escape from death, a violent rain set in. There was then no possibility of kindling a fire to warm their shivering frames. The pitiless flood drenched, in a short time, their tattered garments. They laid their aching bones upon the oozing snow, and wore away a night which inflicted the agonies of a hundred deaths upon them. The morning came, and still the flood fell. They roused themselves to move on a little, if it were possible, despite the storm ; but they had lost their course, and the sun no longer befriended them. It was proposed to return to the cabins, following their own tracks, but the Indians would not consent, and Miss G. resolutely determined to follow them. There was nothing possible, there, but starvation. The fate before them could not be worse, and might be better. Miss G.'s resolution encouraged her companions. They went on all day without a morsel of food, the rain pouring continuously. At night it ceased. Some were confused in their perceptions, some delirious, some raving. Those who were still strong enough to realize their condition, might well now despair. The women bore up better than the men. One of them had about her a cape or mantle stuffed with raw cotton, and, upon a minute examination of it, she found, between the shoulders, about an inch square of the inner surface dry. The lining was cut, and enough taken out to catch the spark from the flint. They had lost or left their axe, but were able to make a fire, after much difficulty, of a few gathered boughs. They sat down around it. There was nothing else to be done. Preparing, distributing, or eating even the wretched morsel that had kept them alive to this time, no longer occupied them. They had no speech but the ravings of their delirious companions, no hope but that of death.

Scarcely had they begun to feel the warmth which faintly revived their decaying sensibilities, when the angry clouds began to descend upon them in snow. It fell with a silent, blinding, merciless steadiness. It came as the messenger of that power whom they no longer dreaded—death. The father, whose two daughters were of the company, was the first released. The chilling rain had pierced his emaciated frame, and subdued the energy which had resisted courageously all that had gone before. He had much to struggle for. His wife and seven children were at the cabins, and he had pressed forward, feeling in that effort the only hope of saving them. But now, all power to serve them was gone, and, perfectly conscious of their own and his condition, he laid down under the relentless storm to die. In that desolate hour of death, he called his youngest daughter to his side, and bade her cherish and husband every chance of life, in the fearful days which he knew awaited them. They were still far from habitation or help, except such as God gave them, and their own courageous hearts. She must revolt at nothing that would keep life in her till she could reach some help for those whom they both loved. He clearly fore-shadowed the terrible necessity to which, within a few hours, he saw they must come, and died, leaving his injunction upon her, to yield to it as resolutely as she had done every-thing else that had been required of her, since their sufferings began.

His death scarcely moved those to whom it was most important. To the others, it, perhaps, furnished a hope—a fearful and terrible one certainly, yet still a hope. But another victim was fast preparing; and scarcely had the white mantle of the storm been softly and silently spread over the stiffening limbs that had just ceased to struggle, when another soul took its flight—the poor Mexican lad who had joined them at the fort. They had been forty-eight hours without tasting food. The storm increased. They were in imminent danger of perishing of cold, and the weight of the accumulating snow upon their persons. They wisely took the only measure of defense that was left them against the storm. They spread a blanket, and seating themselves upon it in a circle, stretched another over their heads, thus raising a community of warmth, which greatly assisted their slow vitality. Occasionally they had to raise the blanket, pushing up from beneath, to throw off the accumulating snow.

Under its shelter what horrors were endured and apprehended! Some, who raved, seized upon the persons of those near them—a hand or arm—mistaking it for food, which they were eager to devour. Others sat in the stupor of despair, the idiocy of inanition, or silent, sullen rebellion against the fate which clasped them as in arms of iron. During the night they ate of the flesh of those who had died. That first dreadful repast! The heavens frowning above; the earth glaring beneath; the night air moaning over the great waste, whose silence seemed to snap and rend the very chords of sensation and life in the lightened brains of those who partook. It roused them more effectually than anything had for days. It stirred their utmost remaining capacities for appreciating the horrors of their situation. But the voracious digestive function was more faithful to their need than the revolted will, which, though conquered, stood aloof. The sustenance they took assimilated rapidly and healthfully. They were better and stronger in a few hours.

The storm continued two days. At the end of that time they moved on. But two more died before they set out from this " camp of death." While there, the Indians heard words which, though spoken in a language unknown to them, alarmed them. They left the party by stealth—ran away.

They now went forward without any guide but the setting sun. They took with them what they hoped would subsist them till they should reach human habitation ; but when the last morsel was consumed, there was still the same white waste about them. Then the first provi-

dential relief came. A skeleton deer came in
their way and was shot—for they had clung to
their gun when every other implement had
been cast away in weariness or despair. The
wretched animal was starved, like themselves,
upon the desert of snow, and its slight carcass
was consumed to the last inch of hide—every
atom that could be eaten. They descended till
they reached bare ground. Their snow-shoes
were no longer necessary, and the strings and
bits of hide were eaten. And yet there were
no indications that they were approaching relief. Suddenly they came, one day, upon the
two fugitive Indians, resting. Poor fellows!
they had had nothing to eat since they had fled
from the camp of death on that terrible night.
They had traveled on, feeble and hungry, but
hopeful; for they knew that abundance was
before them, and that it was really not far off,
could they but struggle forward.

They never saw their bountiful home again.
The starving emigrants, who could not slay
each other, thought with less scruple of the
fate of these. They had left the wintry mountains so far behind, that it seemed quite certain

before the sustenance should be exhausted, which was thus providentially thrown in their way, relief would come from some source.

It was expected that parties would be out to meet them from the nearest settlement; and so, indeed, there were—but they did not fall in with the wanderers, and the first indication of human neighborhood to them was a rancherie, of Digger Indians, who gave them of their stores—acorns, seeds, etc. They sent them forward, when they had a little refreshed themselves, with a guide, to the next rancherie, whence another conducted them to the next, and so on, till they reached Bear Valley. In it an emigrant had settled the year previous, and there were shelter and food for them. Before they reached it, they were met by a party who had come out to them with mules and provisions. They were then within a day's travel of the rancho, where they arrived after nightfall. Miss G. and one of her companions assured me that the cheer of a royal palace could never so satisfy them as did that of this rude home. The friendly light shining, not, as they afterward observed, from a window, but through gaps in the walls, far into the dreary darkness that had walled them in so long, seemed to promise them, while yet afar off, princely comfort and abundance.

They entered it on the evening of the thirty-second day from the cabins! They had set out, fifteen in number; they were now seven—haggard, tattered, with naked feet, frozen and bleeding, emaciated, wild countenances, unnatural voices, and incoherent speech, they entered the hospitable dwelling where they had been expected and prepared for—two men and five women!!

No more starvation, no more horror before them! Did they consider it then? No; they sat down, housed and fed, and simply rejoiced in the blessed sense of warmth and plenty and repose. Few experiences can be richer in satisfaction than theirs of the first few hours, before memory began her painful work—before the stunned sensibilities revived to feel their own wounds—before the subdued intellect reasserted itself—before, indeed, the life which was not animal reclaimed its power.

How perfect the rest to the exhausted nature.

The party whose sufferings I have attempted to record, left at the cabins in the mountains about sixty souls. Nearly half of them were children, from a few months old, upward. When this party left, there were no provisions in their camps but the poor beef of the wasted cattle they had slaughtered, and this was so scarce that it was very sparingly used—the question with the thoughtful and faithful minds of that unfortunate community being, How little is it possible for me to support life on? The relief party had made them fully aware of the almost impossibility of transporting provision to them over the deep snow. Animal strength was out of the question, and men could bear but little beyond what was necessary for their own support in the journey to and fro. There could no others leave the cabins without a guide; the feeble and the young it was thought impossible to start with till the snow that lay in their way should have, at least partially, disappeared. Thus they were to husband every atom of sustenance. A few inches of hide supported a family an entire day. Nursing mothers could no longer nourish their infants. Some were happily released before the days of sorest hunger came.

Their cabins were deep down in the snow after the heavy storms came, and it had to be shoveled from the roof, and cut in stairs from the doorways, to afford communication with the upper world. In each of the three cabins that were near each other, as, indeed, in all, there were women and children, and kindly offices and sympathies were exchanged, as their needs varied.

There was little visiting, except when death entered one or more of those memorable homes. He was never preceded by disease; gaunter and feebler grew his victims daily, the strongest and ablest first. Men who loved none that were near—who felt themselves doing battle alone with the terrible foes that hemmed them in, were the first to surrender. Some half-grown youths and children perished, but no women—especially no mothers—for a considerable period. These went, where the deepest

misery was, ministers of mercy and tenderness
to the suffering—too earnest to mitigate the
pains of others to be altogether consumed by
their own;

"Love's divine self-abnegation"

raised them above the naked animal necessities
which destroyed those not thus supported.
With the true instinct which such a tremendous situation would unclothe of all con-
ventional or false leanings, they were, in being
always sought, acknowledged as the most merciful, the most tender, the most efficient.
Starving men appealed to them. Women who
had children perishing, called for help on women who also had children to suffer. In the
middle cabin of the three I have described as
being near together, lived the Irish family I
have spoken of. They had reached that place
with all their animals, and consequently were
among those best prepared to meet the terrible
emergencies before them. Their store of beef
was piled in a corner of their little apartment,
and upon the other side of a partition, which
did not quite divide the house, there was a profane, coarse, blasphemous German, or Dutch-

man. His revolting language had terrified and shocked the good Catholic mother often, before they reached this spot, and now it made her tremble to hear his imprecations. He was entirely destitute, with a wife and two children, one of whom, fortunately, died early in the days of starvation. He had wisely established himself near the largest stores and liberal hearts—his unblushing selfishness having proved, before that time, that he would not lack what was essential to support life while his neighbors had it.

There the indefatigable, self-denying mother and wife watched over her family, nursed, tended, fed, clothed, and kept them alive from the sixth or seventh of November till about the middle of February. What a record would the history of those three months make ! One feature of it, not to be forgotten, was the constant expectation of relief. They lived, as it were, a subterranean life. The people who came would first be heard above ; and the silence that surrounded them, no living thing approaching, was seldom broken without. Those who were of their community, came silently and went silently; and their ears had soon become so familiar to the accustomed noises, that they knew each one. But the painful tension of the organs, to catch a tone that should foretell release from their dreadful lot! A shifting of the wind, so that it brought from the angles of their snow embankment an unfamiliar tone, would make their hearts beat more quickly. They went to sleep with this hope, and woke with it. It attended them in the preparation and taking of every miserable meal, and in all the weary hours between those events; and though they talked many times as if it had utterly forsaken them, yet it never did for a moment. But for it few of those who survived to better days would have outlived those dreadful ones.

Mr. Breen says: "About this time an incident occurred which greatly surprised us all. One evening, as I was gazing around, I saw an Indian coming from the mountain. He came to the house and said something which we could not understand. He had a small pack on his back, consisting of a fur blanket, and about two dozen of what is called California soap-root, which, by some means, could be made good to eat. He appeared very friendly, gave us two or three of the roots, and went on his way. Where he was going I could never imagine. He walked upon snow-shoes, the strings of which were made of bark. He went east; and as the snow was very deep for many miles on all sides, I do not know how he passed the nights." One can believe that he would do as well in this respect as the poor starved men and women who had left the cabins.

Once day a man came down the snow-steps of Mrs. Breen's cabin, and fell at full length within the doorway. He was quickly raised, and some broth, made of beef and hide, without salt (that necessary article having been forgotten in the wagons at the top of the mountains, which were now entirely buried in snow), put into his lifeless lips. It revived him so that he spoke. He was a hired driver. His life was of value to no one. Those who would have divided their morsel with him, were in a land of plenty. She said that when a new call was made upon her slender store, and she thought of her children. she felt she could not withhold what she had. God had given and preserved it to her, and she trusted firmly in Him to save them when all should be gone.

Thus she fed the fellow, her next neighbor, whose wickedness made her tremble lest it should provoke the judgment of God, and whose dreadful conduct afterwards showed a nature not human but altogether monstrous and fearful; and thus she shared with perishing women and children the store that had been spared to them. Her pious faith, her warm heart, and her energetic nature fitted her for her lot. In her the sublime promise, "As thy day, so shall thy strength be," was literally fulfilled. Her husband had been ill on their arrival, and he had barely recovered strength to move ; but, seconding her humane purposes, he dispensed their meat to those who had none ; and the houseless and starving never went from them altogether unfed. Their hut became the resort of the utterly destitute—those who had no share either in heart or hearth. Eleven of the wretched ones expired in it, and more who fed there live to this day.

"O! dear Mrs. Breen," said one of her neighbors, coming quickly in one morning, "my dear boy is dying. Will you not give me some food for him?"

"Indeed then I will, dear," was the ready answer. "Take some of the beef."

The poor mother had often had some before. She took it, and, fast as her wasted limbs would carry her, hurried back to her cabin. She first tasted a few morsels raw, to give her *heart;* but this time her speed was vain. The poor emaciated boy, though he tasted what she brought, was too far gone to revive; and in a short time she sent a messenger up to ask her good neighbor to come down with one of her sons, and assist in burying him in the snow! What a burial was that! Performed by two starving women, and a lad scarcely more alive than the one he was assisting to bury!

The man who had fallen in their door, died with them. Children, whose parents were gone before them, either to the grave or on the journey, were taken in and fed, and tended. It was wonderful how, with her nursing babe, with the care that was necessary in preparing and dividing the little food she dared to give them each day, with the constant calls upon her humanity and strength to attend to those whose lot was more deplorable than her own, she bore up under all—encouraged everybody, and constantly gave out, as it were, life to the sinking, hope to the despairing, courage and faith to the doubting. They needed it all and more, for the long-hoped relief came not. Day after day went past, and they wasted, and death crept closer and closer to them.

Mr. Breen says : " About this time, Mrs. Reed put afoot, as brave an undertaking as was ever recorded of woman. It was to travel with a man and another woman across the mountains and send relief to her family (her husband was gone before, and she had four children in the camp).   But her heroic undertaking failed. After traveling several days she was obliged to return, and the greatest wonder is how they were ever able to retrace their steps, as the snow fell several feet while they were gone. The man who accompanied her died a few days after their return, then another man, then a child, and, in a few days, a woman, the mother of several children. Death had become so common an event, that it was looked upon as a matter of course, and we all expected to go soon."

With what joy and hope a relief party was hailed that arrived about the last of January. It brought but slender supplies, and the individuals composing it were to return immediately with as many of the sufferers as could set out with them. This party had been sent out chiefly, or in part, through Mr. Reed's efforts, and his family were among twenty-one who left the cabins to travel over the snow, on the first of February. The children were to be assisted forward by the strong men; but after a mile or more up the mountain, the difficulty proved too great in the case of the two younger, and they were taken back to Mrs. Breen's cabin to await their further chances there. The rest of the party pressed on.

I know but little of that transit; some perished by the way, and all were reduced to the utmost extremity before they reached the settlements. Mr. Reed's wife and children reached him after a separation of four months. What a meeting must that have been! The wasted persons, the haggard countenances, the tattered clothing, and, then, the painful thought of those who were yet behind. Could they also be saved? Two of Mrs. Breen's sons were in this party, the ablest and eldest. She received the little ones who were returned to her, and fed and cared for them with her own, and she told me that in giving them their scanty meals, she could never divide a larger portion to her own than to the strangers. Their constant nourishment was the dry hide boiled without salt (she had a little pepper) and a very little beef with it. The hide was burned to remove the hair, scraped, and, when boiled, made a gelatinous broth, far more nutritious than the poor beef would have made without it. But this could not last them much longer. Already one cabin had been unroofed and thus rendered untenantable.

Among those who perished was not the wretch who lived under the same roof with the Breen family. He yet lived to consume the sustenance that would have sustained a worthier life. His wife and surviving child had come in with the last party, and there is a sort of satisfaction in knowing that base and brutal as the man-cannibal was, the wife was not altogether lacking in traits that allied her to him. For the only act told of a woman in this whole dreadful history, that was unworthy of her sex, was of this one. It is said that on their way in, after they were a day or two from the cabins, her child appeared to be dying, and she herself seemed unable to travel. She was advised to return. It was much easier traveling back than advancing, because the road was well beaten, and she was in no danger of encountering anything, for the waste of snow was an utter solitude.

She refused; and with the word, tossed her helpless, sinking babe from her, saying: "Why should she go back with a half dead child!" The development of her husband's atrocity, which afterwards took place, would have made it painful to think of her as linked to him had she been altogether so noble and self-sacrificing as those of her sex who shared her lot.

About the thirteenth of February, a relief

party arrived. Mr. Reed conducted it. They had *cached* provisions on the road, and reached the cabins with only a small quantity of wheaten meal, made at Sutter's Fort. They left a morsel at each of the camps, and went below to the solitary one where death had been busy, indeed, and hunger had driven humanity to its last resort—preying upon the dead.

They left at this camp only a mother and her three children. Everybody else had perished, and the distraught mother refused to leave her wretched habitation because of the treasure of money and goods it contained, insisting that government should find means of transporting her family and effects safely to the country whither she was bound.

There was no time to be lost. Every day imperiled lives. So the second day after the arrival of Mr. Reed's party, twenty-one souls set out ; many of them were children, and two infants who had been nursing till the maternal fountain had been dried. The wheaten-meal had been baked into biscuit for the journey, and the provident Mrs. Breen had reserved through all, a few strips of their poor beef dried, four

pounds of coffee, and a small paper of tea.
The latter article, with a lump of loaf sugar,
weighing about a pound, she carried at her
waist.

When they set out they left at the cabins a
father near to death, a mother and three children; at the lone cabin two children, two and
four years, and the grandmother of one of
them, and the dreadful German at the upper
cabins.

The man was alone in the hut, he occupied;
the woman and the two children in a neighboring one.

The moving party camped the first night at
the top of the mountain, a place bleak and cold
enough to bodies well fed and clothed, but
dreadfully chilling and wretched to the feeble
starving creatures who had, with difficulty,
reached it from the comparative shelter and
warmth of their habitation below. Here a
very scanty supper was made of the biscuit; a
few spoonfuls of meal, thrown into some snow-
water, made a little gruel for the infants, and
after a night of aching wretchedness which can
well be imagined, they rose early, and taking a

few morsels, each, of the bread, journeyed on
Mrs. B. was not fortunate enough to taste her beef
or coffee, which she had, at starting, committed
to the keeping of one of the men.   Sometimes,
when she sat in the long nights watching her
perishing family by the camp-fire, she saw those
on the opposite side of the logs preparing and
drinking the latter ; but with that feeling which
will be readily understood by many natures,
and those not of the worst, she could not ask
for a drop of it.

On the third day out, they met a party going
to the cabins—the fathers of the two children,
to bring them on.   And I may as well state
here, that when these men arrived, they found
their two young children dead ; also the grandmother who was with them, and the husband
at the lower camp.   Evidences of the most
atrocious conduct on the part of the German
were too palpable to be mistaken; and on entering his hut, the father of one of the murdered children seized an axe with the purpose of
cleaving him to the earth ; but in the act of
upraising it, he said he suddenly remembered to
what dreadful straits they had all been reduced,

and it fell at his side. They left this wretch,* who was well able to travel, and the insane mother, at the lower camp (taking with them the three children), the only living beings in those homes of desolation and death, and journeying as rapidly as possible, overtook the party they had passed, before they were far on the way.

On the afternoon of the day they joined them, a snow-storm set in very violently, and increased to blinding thickness before the evening was far advanced. They encamped early, and the men of the relief party gathered and set brush in the snow, and threw up a bank against it, to break the storm off the fire and those who surrounded it. Mrs. B. told me that she had her husband and five children together, lying

---

* Not to have to return to this monster again, I may as well state, that the next party who went out in the spring, found him still there alone, and in a box in his cabin, the body of the unfortunate woman who had been left in the camp below, chopped up ! When accused of her murder, he denied it stoutly, and said she had died; but a pailful of blood, found beneath his bed, gave the lie to his words. He had murdered the woman, plundered her cabin, and was at last compelled, after reaching California, to give up a part of his stolen treasure.

with their feet to the fire, and their heads under shelter of the snow breast-work ; and she sat by them, with only moccasins on her feet, and a blanket drawn over her shoulders and head, within which, and a shawl she constantly wore, she nursed her poor baby on her knees. Her milk had been gone many days, and the child was so emaciated and lifeless, that she scarcely expected at any time, on opening the covering, to find it alive. The other lay with her babe and three or four older children, at the other side of the fire, where were, also, most of the rest of the party. The storm was very violent all night ; and she watched through it, dozing occasionally for a few moments, and then rousing herself, to brush the snow and flying sparks from the covering of the sleepers.

Toward morning, she heard one of the young girls opposite call to her mother to cover her. The call was repeated several times impatiently, when she spoke to the child, reminding her of the exhaustion and fatigue her mother suffered in nursing and carrying the baby ; and bidding her cover herself and let her mother rest. Presently she heard the mother speak, in a quite unnatural tone, and she called to one of the men near her to go and speak to her. He arose after a few minutes, and found the poor sufferer almost past speaking. He took her infant; and after shaking the snow from her blanket, covered her as well as might be, and left her. Shortly after, Mrs. B. observed her to turn herself slightly, and throw one arm feebly up, as if to go asleep. She waited a little while, and seeing her remain quite still, she walked around to her. She was already cold in death. Her poor, starving child wailed and moaned piteously in the arms of its young sister; but the mother's heart could no more warm or nourish it.

This was the first death in this party. The storm continued through two days and great part of two nights, and the whole party were obliged to lie awaiting its close. As the third morning advanced, it abated; and the men, feeling how nearly impossible it would be for the young and feeble to move on over the deep fresh-fallen snow, and the certainty of death to all, if they remained waiting, proposed going on rapidly, taking Mr. Reed's two children, and hurrying out help to those who were obliged to stay behind. The provisions that had been brought out to this point had been consumed; so that those who remained, remained to certain death, unless relief came speedily. They departed, promising, in this respect, everything that was possible, and leaving poor Mrs. B., the only active, responsible adult, beside her feeble husband, to care for those ten starving children. A higher trust sustained her, or she had sunk in that appalling hour. The sky was yet draped in sad-colored clouds, which hung over them most of the day. They had no food —nothing to eat, save a few seeds, tied in bits of cloth, that had been brought along by some one, and a part of the precious lump of sugar. There were also a very few spoonfuls of the tea remaining in the bottle. They sat and lay by the fire most of the day, with what heavy hearts who shall ever know? The husband, the wife, their five children—the three just left motherless, and two or three others—the remnants of families that had perished.

They were upon about thirty feet of snow, beside a fire made by falling several trees together from opposite directions. The stark mother lay there before them — a ghastlier sight in the sunshine that succeeded the storm, than when the dark clouds overhung them. They had no words of cheer to speak to each other — no courage or hope to share, but those which pointed to a life where hunger and cold could never come, and their benumbed faculties were scarcely able to seize upon a consolation so remote from the thoughts and wants that absorbed their whole being.

A situation like this, will not awaken in common natures religious trust. Under such protracted suffering, the animal outgrows the spiritual in frightful disproportion ; yet the mother's sublime faith, which had brought her thus far through her agonies with a heart still warm toward those who shared them, did not fail her now. She spoke gently to one and another — asked her husband to repeat the litany and the children to join her in the responses, and endeavored to fix their minds upon the time when relief would probably come. For nature taught her as unerringly and more simply than philosophy could have done, that the only hope of sustaining them was to set before them a termination to their sufferings.

What days and nights were those which went by while they waited. Life waning visibly in those about her; not a morsel of food to offer them; her own infant, and that little one that had been cherished and saved through all by the mother now lying dead; wasting hourly into the more perfect image of death; her husband, worn to a skeleton, indifferent to his own fate or any one's else. It needed the fullest measure of exalted faith, of womanly tenderness and self-sacrifice, to sustain one through such a season. She watched by night as well as by day. She gathered wood to keep them warm. She boiled her handful of tea and dispensed it to them; and when she found one sunken and speechless, she broke with her teeth a morsel of the precious sugar and put it in his lips. She fed her babe freely on snow-water, and, scanty as was the wardrobe she had, she managed to get fresh clothing next its skin two or three times a week.

Where, one asks in wonder and reverence, did she find strength and courage for all this? She sat all night by her family, her elbows on her knees, brooding the meek little victim that lay there; watching those who slept, and occasionally dozing, with a fearful consciousness of their terrible condition always upon her. The sense of peril never slumbered. Many times during the night she went to the sleepers to ascertain if they all still breathed. She put her hand under their blankets and held it before the mouth. In this way she assured herself that they were yet alive; but once her blood curdled to find, on approaching her hand to the lips of one of her own children, there was no warm breath upon it. She tried to open the mouth, and found the jaws set. She roused her husband.

" O, Patrick, man, rise and help me; James is dying!"

" Let him die," said the miserable father; " he will be better off than any of us."

She was terribly shocked by this reply. In her own expressive language, her heart stood still when she heard it. She was bewildered, and knew not where to set her weary hands to work; but she recovered in a few moments, and began to chafe the chest and hands of the perishing boy. She broke a bit of sugar, and with considerable effort forced it between his teeth with a few drops of snow-water. She saw him swallow; then a slight convulsive motion stirred his features; he stretched his limbs feebly, and in a moment more opened his eyes and looked upon her. How fervent were her thanks to the great Father, whom she forgot not, night nor day.

Thus she went on. The tea-leaves were eaten, the seeds were chewed, the sugar all dispensed. One child of the mother, who lay upon the snow, perished — not the youngest. An older sister had that in charge, and it still lived, though not a particle of anything but snow-water had passed its clammy lips for near a week.

The days were bright, and, compared with the nights, comfortable. Occasionally, when the sun shone, their voices were heard, though generally they sat or laid in a kind of stupor, from which she often found it alarmingly diffi-

cult to rouse them; but when the gray evening twilight drew its deepening curtain over
the cold, glittering heavens and the icy waste,
and when the famishing bodies had been covered from the frost that pinched them with
but little less keenness than the unrelenting
hunger, the solitude seemed to rend her very
brain. Her own powers faltered—her head
seemed to distend enormously, and grow to a
vast cavern, in which a thunderous silence
reverberated — ceasing at intervals, when it
appeared to have gone out into the borders of
that great ringing space.

But she said her prayers many times over in
the darkness as well as the light, and always
with renewed trust in Him who had not yet
forsaken her, and thus sat out her weary
watch. After the turning of the night, she
always sat watching for the morning-star,
which seemed, every time she saw it rise clear
in the cold eastern sky, to renew to her the
promise, "As thy day is, so shall thy strength
be."

Their fire had melted the snow to a considerable depth, and they were lying upon the

bank above it. Thus they had less of its heat than they needed, and found some difficulty in getting the fuel she gathered, placed so that it could burn. One morning, after she had hailed her messenger of promise, and the light had increased so as to render objects visible in the distance, she looked, as usual, over the white expanse that lay to the south-west, to see if any dark moving specks were visible upon its surface. Only the tree-tops, which she had scanned so often as to be quite familiar with their appearances, were to be seen, and with a heavy heart she brought herself back from that distant hope, to consider what was immediately about her.

The fire had sunk so far away, that they had felt but little of its warmth the last two nights, and casting her eyes down into the snow-pit, where it sent forth only a dull glow, she thought she saw the welcome face of beloved mother earth. It was such a reviving sight, after their long freezing separation from it! She immediately roused her eldest son, and with a great deal of difficulty, and repeated words of cheering and encouragement, brought him to understand, that she wished him to descend by one of the tree-tops which had fallen in, so as to make a sort of ladder, and see if they could reach the naked earth and if it were possible for them all to go down. She trembled with fear at the vacant silence in which he at first gazed at her, but at length, after she had told him a great many times, he said " yes, mother," and went.

He reached the bottom safely, and presently spoke to her. There was naked dry earth under his feet ; it was warm, and he wished her to come down. She laid her baby beside some of the sleepers and descended. Immediately she determined upon taking them all down.

How good, so she thought, as she ascended the boughs, was the God whom she trusted !

By persuasion, by entreaty, by encouragement, and with her own aid, she got them all into this snug shelter. At this removal another child was found dead. He was one of the three that had been brought from his mother in the lower cabin. He had a young sister who had set out in comparatively good condition, but was now emaciated and stupefied The warmth of the fire revived and enlivened her, and when she missed her brother and learned that he was dead, she begged Mr. B. to go up and cut a piece off him, for her to eat.

"O child," exclaimed the horror-stricken woman, "sure you would not eat your own brother."

"O yes, I will. Do, Mr. Breen, I am so hungry, and we ate father and uncle at the cabin!"

The man dared not resist her entreaty; for he thought, If she should die when her life might be saved by it, the responsibility would be on me! He ascended to the terrible task. His wife, frozen with horror, hid her face in her hands and could not look up. She was conscious of his return, and of something going on about the fire; but she could not bring herself to uncover her eyes till all had subsided again into silence. Her husband remarked, that perhaps they were wrong in rejecting a means of sustaining life, of which others had availed themselves; but she put away the suggestion so fearfully, that it was never renewed nor acted upon by any of her family.

But they were now, indeed, reaching the out most verge of life. A little more battle with the grim enemies that had pursued them so relentlessly, twenty-four or at most forty-eight hours of such warfare and all would be ended. They wished it was over; those who were capable of wishing anything. The infants still breathed, but were so wasted that they could only be moved by raising them bodily on the hands. It seemed as if even their light weight would have dragged the limbs from their bodies. Occasionally through the day, she ascended the tree to look out. It was an incident now, and seemed to kindle more life than when it only required a turn of the head or a glance of the eye to tell that there was no living thing near them. She could no longer walk on the snow, but she had still strength enough to crawl from tree to tree, and gather a few boughs, which she threw along before her to the pit and then tumbled in to renew the fire.

The children, who had refreshed their failing powers with the food that others refused, were soon in a better condition, and so her burden was somewhat lightened, and her fear lessened.

But those, whose life was her life, were yet failing. The eighth day was past. She watched for the star of mercy. On the ninth morning, clear and bright it stood over against her beseeching gaze, set in the light liquid blue that overflows the pathway of the springing day. She prayed earnestly as she gazed; for she knew there were but few hours of life in those dearest to her. If human aid came not that day, some eyes, that would soon look imploringly into hers, would be closed in death, before that star should rise again. Would she herself, with all her endurance and resisting love, live to see it? Were they at length to perish? Great God, should it be permitted that they, who had been preserved through so much, should die at last so miserably?

Her eyes were dim, and her sight wavering from inanition. She could not distinguish trees from men on the snow; but, had they been near, she could have heard them; for her ear had grown so sensitive, that the slightest unaccustomed noise arrested her attention.

She went below with a heavier heart than ever before. She had not a word of hope to

answer to the languid inquiring countenances
that were turned to her face, and she was conscious that it told the story of her despair, yet
she strove with some half insane words to suggest, that somebody would surely come to them
that day. Another would be too late, and the
pity of men's hearts and the mercy of God
would surely bring them.

The pallor of death seemed already to be
stealing over the sunken countenances that
surrounded her, and weak as she was, she could
remain below but a few minutes together. She
felt she could have died, had she let go her resolution, at any time within the last forty-
eight hours. They repeated the litany—the
responses came so feebly that they were scarcely
audible, and the protracted utterance seemed
wearisome ; but at last it was over, and they
rested in silence.

The sun mounted high and higher in the
heavens, and when the day was three or four
hours old, she placed her trembling feet again
upon the ladder to look out once more. The
corpses of the dead lay always before her as
she reached the top—the mother and her son,

and the little boy, whose remains she could not even glance at, since they had been mutilated. The blanket that covered him could not shut out the horror of the sight! The rays of the sun fell on her with a friendly warmth; but she could not look into the light that flooded the white expanse. Her eyes lacked strength and steadiness. She rested herself against a tree, and endeavored to gather her wandering faculties. In vain. The enfeebled will could no longer hold rule over them. She had broken, perceptious fragments of visions, contradictory and mixed, former with the latter times. Recollections of plenty, and rural peace, came up from her clear, tranquil childhood which seemed to have been another state of existence; flashes of her latter life—its comfort and abundance— gleams of maternal pride in her children, who had been growing up about her, to ease and independence.

She lived through all the phases which her simple life had ever worn, in the few moments of repose after the dizzy effort of ascending. As the thin blood left her whirling brain, and returned to its shrunken channels, she grew more clearly conscious of the terrible present, and remembered the weary quest upon which she came. It was not the memory of thought, it was that of love—the old tugging at the heart that had never relaxed long enough to say, "Now I am done; I can bear no more." The miserable ones, down there: for them her warring life came back; at thought of them, she turned her face listlessly the way it had so often gazed, but this time something caused it to flush as if the blood, thin and cold as it was, would burst its vessels. What was it? Nothing that she saw; for her eyes were quite dimmed by the sudden access of excitement. It was the sound of voices. By a superhuman effort she kept herself from falling. Was it reality or delusion? She must, at least, live to know the truth. It came again and again. She grew calmer as she became more assured, and the first distinct words she heard uttered were, "there is Mrs. Breen, alive yet, anyhow!"

There were three men advancing toward her. She knew that now there would be no more starving. Death was repelled for this time from the precious little flock he had so long threatened, and she might offer up thanksgiving unchecked by the dreads and fears that had so long frozen her.

A little food was soon dispensed, and shortly after a little more, and soon a third meal. It was astonishing to see the almost instantaneous revivification that took place. Some had voracious appetites, and had to be imperatively restrained. In the other parties, lives had been lost by overeating at first. Here, that danger was carefully guarded against, and by morning they were all, except the poor infants, so much refreshed and strengthened, that it seemed possible to set out: indeed, it was an imperative necessity to move, as the supplies that had been brought were very slender, and were already materially reduced. They had snow-shoes, and sank deep—almost to the body at every step. O, it was weary traveling! but hope and fear both urged them forward, despite their extreme feebleness. The poor mother bore her baby, and the little orphan was taken by turns.

One source of exquisite suffering, was the dreadful condition of their feet. They had been so often frosted, that, in several cases, every trace of the integuments had disappeared, and the unsheathed, lacerated flesh left its bloody mark at every step on the snow. This was torture to the poor mother's heart. But she had to urge her little ones onward, painful though it was to them and herself. Their road often lay along the slopes of hills, where a single false step would have precipitated them fifty or a hundred feet; but feeble as they were, they went on without accident, sometimes two, sometimes five miles, a day, till they reached Mule Springs, whither government supplies had been sent, and were then awaiting them, together with animals, and whatever was necessary for the further safe transport of the disabled. There Mrs. B. learned of the safe arrival of her sons who had preceded her, and of the fate that had befallen others, and there she found new cause of thanksgiving for the unspeakable love that had sustained them through all the sufferings and perils which it froze her very heart to look back upon after they had escaped them.

CONCLUSION.

THE sublime endurance which I have here attempted to portray, as well as that dis covered by females in innumerable other in stances where hardships and danger have had to be borne, are now confessed by all acquainted with these movements. And one is surprised to hear, even among intelligent persons, all causes but the true one assigned for so significant a fact It is said that men perish first because they have all the care, but the same argument would prove that women—mothers, have none at all, or the least of any class, for they are the last to perish, or they survive all. This is too absurd to deserve a moment's notice.

It is not negative circumstances or quali ties of character, that can confer the power of which I speak. It springs from the noblest human attributes—it is their highest exercise It is love—the most devoted and self-oblivious

—love, such as only woman's heart is capable of—love, that is nowise allied to intellect— neither limited nor expanded by it—love, such as outlived Gethsemane and triumphed over Calvary. Give to a nature, largely endowed with this divine quality, a motive, and it will prove itself possessed of fortitude as noble as its love. Thus have many delicate women, who at home were invalids, exhibited on these dreadful journeys such powers, such miraculous endurance, such indifference to personal suffering, such fertility of resource, in serving others, as have seemed incredible when related. The littleness, the petty weaknesses, and querulous selfishness which women often show under the ordinary fatigues and annoyances of travel, are, in all characters of real worth, replaced, when times of danger and suffering come, by the noblest courage and self-sacrifice. Sensible, honest, and brave men, who have crossed the plains, agree that they would greatly prefer, for courage and resolution, a company of women to one of men, unless the latter were picked and proved beforehand.

I must be permitted a single remark on the

condition of my sex in this anomalous country before closing my last page. It is to express my full persuasion, that the distrust shown toward women here, is in a far greater degree a consequence of the corruptness of the other sex, than of ours. Men whose consciousness accuses them, if not of crime, at least of fearful proclivity to it, believe that they are not alone in experiencing this. They go further and judge others, whom they see tried in similar ways, to be worse than themselves; for if they have, perchance, resisted temptation a little, they are apt to believe that their neighbor, under the same circumstances, has yielded—it is so comforting to many persons, to think worse of the condition of those about them than of their own. And men of common intelligence and perception of character, often think women weak in the very directions wherein those whom they judge know themselves to be strongest, and thus it happens that in chaotic communities, the harshest judgments may be exercised toward large numbers who are least deserving it. Every thoughtful observer of new society can testify to this truth; and painful as it is, to think on the ruin that has overtaken such numbers in this land, there is strength in the knowledge that human nature never, in any other age or clime, resisted more potent or pervading temptations. Honor and love to the souls that have proved their integrity here! They should never more be doubted.

SUPPLEMENTARY CHAPTER.

THE PRESENT CRISIS IN CALIFORNIA.

SINCE the latest of the preceding pages were written—a period of several months—California has developed a higher phase of her history than we have hitherto seen. Destined, from her physical and civil condition, to rapid development and great fluctuations in her internal affairs, the present crisis in her history has not surprised any intelligent person who has spent the last three or four years within her borders. But the case is different to many of our eastern friends, who cannot, from the point of observation they occupy, nor from any experience they have ever had, truly estimate the causes of the events of the last four months in California. They are consequently less able to appreciate their true character and probable consequences.

It will be necessary, in endeavoring to state the present case fairly, to refer to the past in so far as will serve to show that the real friends of order in California do not adopt or defend the extraordinary measures of this crisis, but for reasons equally extraordinary, and as imperative as they are uncommon. Comment upon the incongruous character of the population of that state is needless. It is already well understood that, from the year 1848, there has been steadily gathering upon its shores such a body of people as were never before assembled anywhere on the face of the globe— so mixed of all the elements and conditions that make up humanity. Considering this fact, and the purpose which drew them there, together with the collateral influences of the life after arrival in the country, it was not to be expected that the early years of the state could be passed without agitations. Extraordinary causes were in operation, and corresponding effects must appear and be disposed of in some manner.

I have alluded, in the foregoing pages, to the Vigilance Committees of California, and their wholesome action in the years '50 and and '51. At that time the state contained a dangerous admixture of outlaws from many parts of the civilized world, but chiefly from the neighboring British colonies in Australia, and from the older states of the republic. There was also a large body of industrious people, not criminal, with families, lives, and property, which often they seemed to hold by sufferance of the bad. There were, then, nowhere in the state, it may be said, any proper means for securing a sound administration of the criminal laws. There was not a safe prison within its limits. A widely-scattered population, occupying a country which offered every sort of natural security to the fugitive—game for subsistence, a climate in which shelter was superfluous three-fourths of the year, fleet horses in abundance, and impenetrable retreats and hiding-places—could not, it will readily be believed, feel itself efficiently protected by any but the promptest measures. In many neighborhoods, there was often literally no way to dispose of a criminal or dangerous man, but either to put him to death, without the slow and uncertain intervention of legal process, or set him at large to repeat his crimes.

Accordingly, as I have said, there were in those years, in the mining and country regions, frequent administrations of Lynch law, where no organizations, such as I have named, were gone into for that purpose. But in the cities, where like measures were equally demanded for safety, these apparent ebullitions of popular indignation were too insecure, as well as too undignified; and when—as in San Francisco in '51—crime, in the form of incendiarism, murder, burglary, and robbery, multiplied frightfully with each passing month, and the law, from whatever cause, was powerless to check it, surely it will not be urged by any reasonable person, however great may be his love of order, that the people were wrong to take self-protection into their own hands. Society had run far ahead of any prescribed methods of self-preservation — it must take such as it could command. It did so promptly when it begun; but with such entire absence of passion or excitement, and with such careful regard to justice and necessity, that

it lost none of its self-respect, and none of the
confidence of those who could truly understand
its emergencies, and the manner in which they
had been disposed of.

The proceedings of those early Vigilant Committees were characterized by a most admirable
temperance and moderation, which, however,
never partook of timidity. To every act of
theirs, the people responded with one voice,
"It is well done."

In August, 1851, the Vigilance Committee
of San Francisco took from the city prison two
men named McKenzie and Whitaker, and hanged them in front of the rooms occupied by that
body. These men were notorious criminals.
Both confessed to crimes which would have
brought upon them the same penalty elsewhere; and they had been in the courts so
long, that it was justly feared that, if left to
them, they would finally escape, as many of
their companions in crime had, and live to repeat the offenses which had made them a terror to peaceable citizens. This act was warmly
approved throughout the state. At the time
of its occurrence, I was visiting the mines, and

I had the amplest means of knowing how the laborious and honest people among that class regarded it. It was, I believe, the last, or the last that attracted public notice, of a series of executions and banishments which made San Francisco and the whole state comparatively safe and quiet for a time.

The class of people, then dealt with, were, for the most part, low criminals—generally professedly such—murderers, notorious or dishonorable gamblers, incendiaries, robbers, or inveterate thieves.

The state was well and seasonably rid of them. It had, then, no safe means of confining them, could they have been duly tried and convicted in the courts; and it was utterly incompatible with the safety of its good citizens to suffer them to be at liberty within its borders.

When this work was well done, there was a long period of tranquillity. Civil and criminal laws were enacted; a judiciary system organized, and put in operation throughout the state; elections were regularly held; and, to all appearance, the machinery of civil and political life was fully and successfully set in motion. Most persons thought the troubled days were past, and indeed, for a time, there seemed no good reason to apprehend a return of them. But one bad and alarming feature was always observable—the election of the worst men to office. I know it may be said that this is true of other states, as well as of California, and it is painful to have to confess it. But there is a broad distinction between such results in the older states and in this—a distinction which has two phases—one, viz., that such choices were much more dangerous there than elsewhere, because men in office were practically unchecked in their deeds— almost unrestrained in their imaginations of wrong. The truth of these assertions is shown in the fact that, notwithstanding the enormous malfeasances known to have been committed, notwithstanding that the state is disgraced by a catalogue of official abuses and crimes, at which every good citizen stands aghast, when they are recounted to him, there is not yet recorded one sentence of punishment upon an official offender ; not a single verdict awarding to a doer of such deeds the disgrace which he merits. I will not stop to comment upon the shocking laxity which this not only indicated but fostered. When such men could be chosen to office, and do such deeds, undisgraced, where were the people to find their standard of character?

But, there was another, and, if possible, worse side to this political fact. This was, the positive and notorious foulness of the characters often chosen to fill public stations. It is often said of the candidates in our popular elections in other states, that we lose sight of fitness in chosing them, and it is too often true; but in California it has been frequently seen that gross, positive, disgraceful unfitness was the surest means of success. Of two candidates, one of whom would not elsewhere be admitted to the society of respectable persons, or recognized by a gentleman in the street, who was ignorant as well as vicious; and the other, intellectually capable, cultivated, and of known integrity, the chances were, as ten to one, in favor of the former. There seemed often a systematic, deliberate choosing of the worst

material offered ; which is ever a fatal omen for
the accomplishment of right work. This was
more especially true of the cities, and of the
counties containing considerable towns. It
has happened at different times in all parts of
the state. I am not deeply enough skilled in
the mysteries of political life to be able to
speak with certainty of the real origin of this
humiliating, but undeniable fact. I am unwilling to think that it originated wholly in the
indifference of the good citizens to such results.
It seems more reasonable to suppose that it
might first have been due in part to this cause,
and in part, sometimes, to frauds perpetrated
by a class of men who have since become
well known in California. But, whatever its
primary cause, the fact is indisputable. At
this hour the ranks of officials of all degrees,
throughout the state, furnish abundant painful
evidence that it is so. From Oregon to Lower
California, and from the Sierra Nevada to the
shore of the Pacific ocean, there are men, this
day, holding offices of trust and dignity, whose
moral life (I speak advisedly) would disgrace
the lowest resorts of the most degraded beings

in human form ; and others, whose intellectual
incapacity and want of cultivation would be a
hindrance in the commonest mechanic shops of
New England, and the northern and middle
states.

Such a state of things, be the direct cause
what it might, could not long exist without
producing manifest and fearful disorder. Practically, intelligence and integrity are at a dis-
count among any people which puts its worst
material to the noblest and most important
uses. An architect would be condemned at
once who should lay decayed timber for his
main beams; and so, a people stands, to all in-
tents and purposes, condemned to disorder,
misrule and dire confusion, who will make its
highest judicial officers of men whose single
lives unite, in an unparalleled glory of degradation, the fearful trinity of dice, drunkenness,
and debauchery, or choose, as one of its highest
representatives, a man whose nature assimilates
him to criminals ; whose deeds, previous to his
elevation, gave all, who would take heed, fair
warning of the wrong and shame that have followed that disgraceful event.

But our supreme judges and members of Congress are fair indices on those high elevations, visible to the whole country, of what is continually happening on the lower planes of public life. Be the station high or humble, the incumbent is infinitely more likely to disgrace than honor it. In one county and town, which I happen to know the history of, the town constable, who was kept in that office for four successive years by annual elections, was a Botany Bay convict, known to be such; and he had been, once at least, publicly whipped there where he was elected, for petty theft, while California was a Mexican province. While in office, he was once indicted for perjury, and escaped by that universal remedy for such attacks—non-agreement of the jury—and *even after that was reëlected*. One of the county judges, though well qualified for his place in point of native ability and cultivation, was a drunkard and debauchee. His manner of life, during the whole of his official term, was an insult to every good and self-respecting person in the community; and on leaving the country, he left behind him one or two unfortunate children, whom he acknowledged as his, to the care of their depraved, vicious, beastly mother, with whom he had lived openly and unrebuked during his official career. By the time it expired, many of those who had helped to place him in office were heartily tired, and demanded a change of some sort. They got it. His successor is, I believe, an honest man. He would not take a bribe, I think, nor disgrace himself or his family by any immoral act; but in a written opinion, which he rashly ventured on giving, in a case that was brought before him, on an appeal, he says, after giving the title of the cause, in characters which no keenness in the art of deciphering has ever yet rendered truly :

" In the abov intitled caws the summons are defected etc. ;" and arriving at the fourth division of his subject matter, he says: " The coaret ered in adgouring the caus on motion of the constable, and afterwards trying the caws. It is tharefoure orderd that the gudgement be reverst and a new trial ordered ;" but on being advised that the ordering of a new trial set aside his own decision on the judgment of the lower court, he wisely determined to efface it, and so the original document remains to the entertainment of all beholders, exciting their wonder in an equal degree by its chirography, its varied orthography, and its wonderful construction. It has a value in this connection, however, apart from these; it shows us that there was another tribunal in the country, in an equal state of illumination, since it first " *adgorned*" this cause, made famous for evermore by its treatment, and *afterwards* tried it. O that some one might be found competent to the treatment of these modern Dogberrys, to write them down, and the scores who are like them in the country, as they deserve to be.

I should not do justice to my argument did I not state, that on both occasions, when these men were elected, the profligate as well as the incompetent, there were candidates very well qualified as to ability, and of good character and standing. I cannot undertake to say why those should have been chosen and these left, unless the answer made by one of the voters of the country, when the question was put to him, may throw some light upon the election of the last man.

"It was his three daughters that elected him," said this man.

The questioner looked surprised, perhaps, incredulous.

"It is true," he reiterated, "you can see for yourself; there are a great many single men in the country, and the judge's daughters are fine girls, though they are ignorant. I am a single man myself and I voted for him, though I never expect to ask one of them to marry me, and should certainly have voted for the other man if the daughters had been out of the question."

So absurdly do people, here, more than anywhere else, I believe, suffer themselves to be influenced in grave acts. Not many bad elections are due to such innocent causes as three virtuous and good daughters; but, from one cause and another, enough of them had taken place, and enough corruption of character, through this and other influences, had been exhibited, two years ago, to warn those, who would take the trouble, to think seriously upon public affairs. Grant that, primarily, the people, absorbed in their personal interests, were selfishly, and even

criminally neglectful of their duty at the ballot-box. Grant that they suffered bad men to
be elected to office, without considering the
means how, or reflecting upon the fatal consequences of such acts repeated through years.
Grant that dangerous and criminal men escaped
punishment, sometimes through the neglect
or unwillingness of competent and honest persons to sit as jurors. Grant that thus, in spite
of able and faithful judges (and California has
had, and still has, some such), the courts, instead
of being the terror of criminals, are become their
protection and refuge. Grant, in short, that
the wiser and better portion of the people
had shamefully neglected their duties as freemen
and faithful defenders of their own rights, and
that, consequently, the baser sort had introduced
corruptions which were sweeping over the
country and carrying it to ruin. What then!
shall the master of a vessel, who has unwisely
neglected his duty, and suffered his charge to
fall into incompetent and dishonest hands,
therefore madly hold himself still, and let her
be driven upon the rocks and dashed to pieces.
Shall he not rather, if the usurper of his au-

thority will not freely surrender when he claims it, take it from him by any sort of violence, so that he may get the ability to steer in a safer direction, and save life and wealth thereby?

There is one invariable law, wisely established, to reign, forever, throughout the kingdoms where moral wrong can come, that, happily for us, governs all such cases; every evil, grown to a certain degree of excess, procures the application of its own remedy. Abuses in any department cannot pass a certain point without provoking an active antagonism, which, if it do not uproot them, efficiently checks, for the time, their further growth.

Public affairs, in all departments, civil and criminal, political and commercial, had, as I have said, more than a year ago become corrupt enough to challenge the scrutiny and provoke the earnest opposition of many good persons to their proceeding further in the same ways. It began to be evident that something must be done. Dreadful abuses prevailed everywhere, but more especially in the cities, and most of all in San Francisco, which is, in some respects, to the state at large, what the heart is to the body and limbs.

San Francisco, for about three years, I think, has been under a rule that has been called an economical rule. Comparisons have often been instituted to show how much more economically the city government was administered than it had ever been before, and yet property-holders there were literally groaning under a taxation which they declared they could not support without ruin to themselves. The taxes were levied and paid, but the citizens saw nowhere, but in their empty purses, the evidences of such payment. There were few improvements, none that would bear mention in the way of accounting for the disbursement of the enormous sums of money collected—the condition of the streets was disgraceful and dangerous; the public school teachers and police officers were unpaid for such long periods, that they were subjected to heavy loss and inconvenience, and, at last, received often but a nominal compensation in scrip, which they were obliged to dispose of at 40, 50, 70, or 80 cents on the dollar, as might happen; yet, with all the boasted economy and retrench-

ment, the administration of the city government of San Francisco, for the year 1855, cost
$1,400,000. The state of Michigan, for the same
year's expenses, paid out of her treasury
$350,000.

It was well understood that many of the officers, who were concerned in this onerous administration of affairs, had not been elected by the
people ; for election-frauds were, by this time,
fully believed in, though their extent and fre-
quency were little dreamed of by the people
generally.

The papers complained, sometimes sharply
and bitterly; but the denunciation was too
general to avail in correcting abuses. There
seemed, now, to be demanded some fearless
champion for right, who would not shrink from
suiting his mode of attack to the conditions he
was to assail ; who would not hesitate to designate individuals, when it was necessary to do
so, and to describe their deeds without circum-
locution. Such a man presented himself to the
people in Mr. King, and he established, as the
organ of his peculiar censorship, the *Evening
Bulletin*. It was a pungent, spirited, fearless

print, not always written in the best taste, for
Mr. King was not a literary man, nor, in that
sense, a scholar; but he was more valuable in
that emergency than almost any such accomplished person could have been; for he taxed
himself with no concern about style or effect,
except the one effect of hitting his mark. And
this he did effectually. Between the differences of opinion which are entertained, respecting Mr. King's career, I do not feel disposed to
arbitrate. He was a peculiar man, and he
undertook a peculiar work. If he sometimes
offended taste, and at others, as I think he did,
on some rare occasions, forgot the justice and
fairness which generally characterized his treatment of persons and institutions, it should be
borne in mind, by way of extenuating these
faults, that he had assumed a very hard position, in which it would have been next to impossible for any man to have altogether avoided
mistakes and some exhibitions of bitterness.
He did the community, of which he was a member, genuine service; and it has abundantly
testified its high appreciation, both of his life
and death. The citizens of the state have

raised, by contribution, about $30,000 for his family; and a considerable fund is already collected toward a monument to his memory.

Mr. King's editorial career was a brief one. It commenced, I believe, in October, '55, and was terminated on the 14th of May, '56. It was a short period, but one of incessant action and most arduous and diffi cult labor. It is easier to criticise, I think, than it would have been for the best of us to have improved it.

Mr. King was shot on the 14th of May by a man named Casey, formerly a criminal before the law, and yet unreformed. He had arrived, by the currents of California life, to a position in public affairs in San Francisco; was a member of its Board of Supervisors, and held almost unlimited sway over the political caucuses and nominating conventions of his party. He sold nominations to the highest bidder, taking money from all; he furnished judges, shoulder-strikers, and stuffers, on election days; he procured, for a consideration, the passage of fraudulent bills through the board of which he was a member, and in many other ways wronged the people to an extent that called loudly for exposure

of his true character, that he might be dis-
armed of the power he abused. Mr. King,
having provided himself with evidence which
could not be disputed, attacked this man, by
stating the general tenor of his previous history, and asserting that he had been convicted
of a felony in the State of New York, and
punished by imprisonment in the state prison,
at Sing-Sing. It is unnecessary to particular-
ize the subsequent steps of the affair, up to the
shooting of Mr. King. The ball that wounded
him seemed to have struck every man in the
state. There was a universal outcry from the
mountains to the sea, over all the state, and
an irrepressible, enthusiastic approval of the
steps taken by the people of San Francisco
immediately after it.

The Vigilance Committee, which had never
been disbanded since its organization in 1850,
but had lain silent and motionless, was put in
active organization at once, and increased to
thousands for hundreds in a few days. Casey,
who had taken good care to have himself arrested immediately after the shooting, was
taken to the city prison, where a strong guard

of citizens was placed at once, and kept on duty night and day, until the 18th, when, about noon, the Committee, through its appointed officers—who were attended by a force of several military companies—proceeded to the prison, and demanded of the Sheriff the surrender of his prisoner. The quietness, energy, and determination of the movement would have made resistance madness, had it been possible to offer any; but it was not, and Casey was taken to the Committee rooms, on Sacramento street, and locked up. The Committee then returned, and demanded the surrender of Chas. Cora, a gambler, who had, a few weeks before, shot Mr. Richardson, U. S. Marshal for the northern district of California. This demand, also, was acceded to, as, indeed, it could not be resisted; and, on the day of Mr. King's burial—the 22d of May—they were both executed by hanging, in front of the rooms of the Committee.

These measures were not taken without a good deal of excitement which spread throughout the state. The press warmly sustained the Committee. In San Francisco there were but two exceptions—The Herald and Sun—and it may be seen how strong and unanimous the public feeling was, from the fact, that the Herald, in its third issue, after condemning the proceedings of that body, had suffered such a reduction of its subscription list, and advertising patronage, that it appeared on a sheet of half its former size, at which it yet remains. The body of the merchants, auctioneers and other business men, withdrew from it at once. The clergy, to their praise be it spoken, discussed and approved, in their pulpits, the measures the people were taking, and from nearly all classes in public and private life, throughout the state, there came one strong expression of approbation, and hope that the Committee would continue its labors till the grievous wrongs were righted—the plague spots removed.

The Committee increased in numbers daily. Hundreds thronged to join it, because it was clearly seen that it had a righteous work in hand, and was able to do it well. Careful, temperate, order-loving men, saw nothing to dread in its proceedings, and so, freely subscribed to its constitution,* and paid their money to sustain it.

* CONSTITUTION OF THE COMMITTEE OF VIGILANCE, SAN FRANCISCO. *Adopted* May 15th, 1856.—Whereas, it has become apparent to the citizens of San Francisco, that there is no security for life and property, either under the regulations of society as it at present exists, or under the laws as now administered, and that by the association together of bad characters, our ballot-boxes have been stolen, and others substituted, or stuffed with votes that were never polled, and thereby our elections nullified, our dearest rights violated, and no other method left by which the will of the people can be manifested :

Therefore, the citizens whose names are hereunto attached, do unite themselves into an association for maintenance of the peace and good order of society, the prevention and punishment of crime, the preservation of our lives and property, and to insure that our ballot-boxes shall hereafter express the actual and unforged will of the majority of our citizens ; and we do bind ourselves each unto the other, by a solemn oath, to do and perform every just and lawful act for the maintenance of law and order, and to sustain the laws when faithfully and properly administered. But we are determined that no thief, burglar, incendiary, assassin, ballot-box stuffer, or other disturber of the peace, shall escape punishment, either by the quibbles of the law, the insecurity of prisons, the carelessness or corruption of the police, or a laxity of those who pretend to administer justice. And to secure the object of this association, we do hereby agree :

1. That the name and style of this association shall be the Committee of Vigilance, for the protection of the ballot-box, the lives, liberty and property of the citizens and residents of the city of San Francisco.

It provided itself with arms and ammunition ; it drilled its forces, fortified its head-quarters, constructed cells for prisoners, and furnished

2. That there shall be rooms for the deliberations of the Committee, at which there shall be some one or more members of the Committee appointed for that purpose, in constant attendance, at all hours of the day and night, to receive the report of any member of the association, or of any other person or persons whatsoever, of any act of violence done to the person or property of any citizen of San Francisco ; and if, in the judgment of the member or members of the Committee present, it be such an act as justifies or demands the interference of this Committee, either in aiding in the execution of the laws, or the prompt and summary punishment of the offender, the Committee shall be at once assembled for the purpose of taking such action as a majority of them, when assembled, shall determine upon.

3. That it shall be the duty of any member or members of the Committee on duty at the Committee Rooms, whenever a general assemblage of the Committee is deemed necessary, to cause a call to be made in such a manner as shall be found advisable.

4. That whereas, an Executive Committee has been chosen by the General Committee, it shall be the duty of the said Executive Committee to deliberate and act upon all important questions, and decide upon the measures necessary to carry out the objects for which this association was formed.

5. That whereas, this Committee has been organized into sub-divisions, the Executive Committee shall have power to call, when they shall so determine, upon a Board of Delegates, to consist of three representatives from each Division, to confer with them upon matters of vital importance.

other apartments for its various necessities. It
arrested rogues and dangerous men, who were
at large, tried and disposed of their cases

6. That all matters of details and government shall be em-
braced in a code of By-Laws.

7. That the action of this body shall be entirely and rigor-
ously free from all consideration of, or participation in, the
merits or demerits, or opinion or acts, of any and all sects,
political parties, or sectional divisions in the community ; and
every class of orderly citizens of whatever sect, party or na-
tivity, may become members of this body.   No discussion of
political, sectional, or sectarian subjects shall be allowed in
the Rooms of the Association.

8. That no person accused before this body shall be punished, until after fair and impartial trial and conviction.

9. That whenever the General Committee have assembled for deliberation, the decision of the majority upon any
question, that may be submitted to them by the Executive
Committee, shall be binding upon the whole : Provided, nevertheless, that when the delegates are deliberating upon the
punishment to be awarded to any criminals, no vote inflict-
ing the death penalty shall be binding unless passed by two-
thirds of those present and entitled to vote.

10. That all good citizens shall be eligible for admission to
this body, under such regulations as may be prescribed by a
Committee on Qualifications ; and if any unworthy person
gain admission, they shall, on due proof, be expelled : And
believing ourselves to be executors of the will of the majority
of our citizens, we pledge our sacred honor to defend and
sustain each other in carrying out the determined action
of this Committee at the hazard of our lives and our fortunes.

promptly.*   The bad men it took in hand, began to feel that their palmy days were gone.
One notorious man, known as Yankee Sullivan,
committed suicide while awaiting their decision on his case, and thus rid them of any further responsibility in relieving the community
of his presence, which, according to his own con-
fessions, had been most destructive to its rights
and interests.   Beside the catalogue of his early
crimes, which included theft, robbery, and
murder ; he acknowledged that he had been
engaged in the grossest election frauds that had
ever been attempted in San Francisco ; had
kept honest and quiet people from voting, and
had secured Casey's election to the post of Su-
pervisor, by stuffed ballots. The Committee had
sentenced him to transportation, from the country, but his overwhelming sense of guilt and extreme moral cowardice impelled him to suicide,
as a means of escaping hanging, which he was

* Its trials were carefully and justly conducted ; evidence
on both sides sought, and faithfully taken, and the verdict
of guilty had finally to be passed upon by the Executive Committee of twenty-nine, and by still another body consisting
of three delegates from each of the sixty-six companies
comprising the Committee.

persuaded would be his fate from the Committee.

Up to this time, there had been no grave official interposition between the Committee and its purposes. But, on the second of June, a writ of *habeas corpus* was issued, by one David Terry, Judge of the Supreme Court, for the rescue of one Mulligan, a member of the fraternity to which Sullivan had belonged. Mulligan was a prisoner in the Committee's Rooms, undergoing trial at the time, and that laborious body paid no heed to the writ. On the next day, the third of June, the Governor issued a proclamation, declaring the county of San Francisco to be in a state of insurrection, as follows :

EXECUTIVE DEPARTMENT,
Sacramento City, June 3, 1856.

WHEREAS, satisfactory information has been received by me that combinations to resist the execution of legal process by force exist in the county of San Francisco, in this state, and that an unlawful organization, styling themselves the Vigilance Committee, have resisted by force the execution of criminal process, and that the power of said county has been exhausted, and has not been sufficient to enable the Sheriff of said county to execute such process : Now, therefore, I, J. NEELY JOHNSON, Governor of the state of California, by virtue of the power vested in me by the constitution and the laws thereof, do hereby declare said county of

San Francisco in a state of insurrection, and I hereby order and direct all of the volunteer militia companies of the county of San Francisco, also, all persons subject to military duty within said county, to report themselves for duty immediately to Major Gen. Wm. T. Sherman, commanding Second Division California Militia, to serve for such term in the performance of military duty, under the command of said Sherman, until disbanded from service by his orders. Also, that all volunteer military companies now organized, or which may be organized within the Third, Fourth and Fifth Military Divisions of this state; also, all persons subject to military duty in said Military Divisions, do hold themselves in readiness to respond to, and obey, the orders of the Governor of this state, or said Sherman, for the performance of military duty in such manner, and at such time and place, as may be directed by the Governor of this state.   I furthermore order and direct that all associations, combinations or organizations whatsoever, existing in said county of San Francisco, or elsewhere in this state, in opposition to, or in violation of, the laws thereof, more particularly an association known as the Vigilance Committee of San Francisco, do disband, and each and every individual thereof yield obedience to the constitution and laws of the state, the writs and processes of the courts, and all legal orders of the officers of this state, and of the county of San Francisco.

(Signed)   J. NEELY JOHNSON.

Up to this date the whole affair had been tragical, and purely earnest; but tragedy and farce are separated by a single line, and even that was obliterated now. People smiled at first, and laughed broadly, when it was ascertained that at the recruiting quarters, for what was now sometimes styled the Law and Order, and sometimes the Law and Murder party, there were to be found only a few men, the same that might have been picked up at any time for months before, by anybody who would offer them board and quarters for nominal service.   It is understood that, upon this failure, Gen. Wool was applied to by the Governor, but he declined taking any part, and an application was then sent to the President, to furnish troops to the " true and peaceable" citizens of the state for their relief.   While this application was pending, the Committee was quietly proceeding with its Herculean labors. Every steamer bore from the state some of the banished.   Others were sent to Australia and the Pacific Islands.   They had their own police, and made their arrests generally independent of the city police.   Their proceedings in these, and in all other respects, were marked by a fairness, energy, and skill, that would command admiration anywhere.

On the 9th of June they issued the following address :

Bulletin, June 9th.

CASE OF THE PEOPLE.

The Vigilance Committee of San Francisco have just issued the following important and ably-written document :

TO THE PEOPLE OF CALIFORNIA.

The Committee of Vigilance, placed in the position they now occupy by the voice and countenance of the vast majority of their fellow-citizens, as executors of their will, desire to define the necessity which has forced this people into their present organization.

Great public emergencies demand prompt and vigorous remedies. The People—long suffering under an organized despotism which has invaded their liberties—squandered their property—usurped their offices of trust and emolument—endangered their lives—prevented the expression of their will, through the ballot-box—and corrupted the channels of justice—have now arisen in virtue of their inherent right and power. All political, religious, and sectional differences and issues have given way to the paramount necessity of a thorough and fundamental reform and purification of the social and political body. The voice of a whole people has demanded union and organization, as the only means of making our laws effective, and regaining the rights of free speech, free vote, and public safety.

For years they have patiently waited and striven, in a peaceable manner, and in accordance with the forms of law, to reform the abuses which have made our city a by-word ; but fraud and violence have foiled every effort, and the laws to which the people looked for protection, while distorted and rendered effete in practice, so as to shield the vile, have been used as a powerful engine to fasten upon us tyranny and misrule.

As republicans, we looked to the ballot-box as our safeguard and sure remedy. But so effectually and so long was its voice smothered, the votes deposited in it by freemen so entirely outnumbered by ballots thrust in through fraud at midnight, or nullified by the false counts of judges and inspectors of elections at noonday, that many doubted whether the majority of the people were not utterly corrupt.

Organized gangs of bad men, of all political parties, or who assumed any particular creed from mercenary and corrupt motives, have parcelled out our offices among themselves, or sold them to the highest bidders.

Have provided themselves with convenient tools to obey their nod, as clerks, inspectors, and judges of elections.

Have employed bullies and professional fighters to destroy tally-lists by force, and prevent peaceable citizens from ascertaining, in a lawful manner, the true number of votes polled at our elections.

And have used cunningly contrived ballot-boxes, with false sides and bottoms, so prepared that, by means of a spring or slide, spurious tickets, concealed there, previous to the election, could be mingled with genuine votes.

Of all this we have the most irrefragable proofs. Felons from other lands and states, and unconvicted criminals, equally as bad, have thus controlled public funds and property, and have often amassed sudden fortunes, without having done an honest day's work with head or hands. Thus the fair inheritance of our city has been embezzled and squandered, our streets and wharves are in ruins, and the miserable entailment of an enormous debt will bequeath sorrow and poverty to another generation.

The jury-box has been tampered with, and our jury trials have been made to shield the hundreds of murderers whose red hands have cemented this tyranny, and silenced with the bowie-knife and the pistol, not only the free voice of an indignant press, but the shuddering rebuke of the outraged citizen.

To our shame be it said, that the inhabitants of distant lands already know, that corrupt men in office, as well as gamblers and shoulder-strikers, and other vile tools of unscrupulous leaders, beat, maim, and shoot down with impunity, as well peaceable and unoffending citizens, as those earnest reformers who, at the known hazard of their lives, and with singleness of heart, have sought, in a lawful manner, to thwart the schemes of public plunder, or to awaken investigation.

Embodied in the principles of republican governments are the truths that the majority should rule, and when corrupt officials, who have fraudulently seized the reins of authority, designedly thwart the execution of the laws, and avert punishment from the notoriously guilty, the power they usurp reverts back to the people, from whom it was wrested. Realizing these truths, and confident that they were carrying out the will of the vast majority of the citizens of this county, the Committee of Vigilance, under a solemn sense of the responsibility that rested upon them, have calmly and dispassionately weighed the evidence before them, and decreed the death of some and the banishment of others, who, by their crimes and villainies, had stained our fair land. With those that were banished, this comparatively modern punishment was chosen, not because ignominious death was not deserved, but that the error, if any, might surely be upon the side of mercy to the criminal. There are others, scarcely less guilty, against whom the same punishment has been decreed, but they have been allowed further time to arrange for their final departure, and with the hope that permission to depart voluntarily might induce repentance, and repentance amendment, they have been suffered to choose, within limits, their own time and method of going.

Thus far, and throughout their arduous duties, they have been, and will be guided by the most conscientious convictions of imperative duty; and they earnestly hope that, in endeavoring to mete out merciful justice to the guilty, their counsels may be so guided by that Power before whose tribunal we shall all stand, that, in the vicissitudes of after life, amid the calm reflections of old age, and in the clear view of dying conscience, there may be found nothing we would regret or wish to change.

We have no friends to reward, no enemies to punish, no private ends to accomplish.

Our single, heart-felt aim is the public good; the purging from our community of those abandoned characters whose actions have been evil continually, and have finally forced upon us the efforts we are now making. We have no favoritism as a body, nor shall there be evinced in any of our acts either partiality for, or prejudice against, race, sect, or party.

While thus far we have not discovered on the part of our constituents any indications of lack of confidence, and have no reason to doubt that the great majority of the inhabitants of the county endorse our acts and desire us to continue the work of weeding out the irreclaimable characters from the community, we have, with deep regret, seen that some of the state authorities have felt it their duty to organize a force to resist us. It is not impossible for us to realize, that not only those who have sought place with a view to public plunder, but also those gentlemen who, in accepting offices to which they were honestly elected, have sworn to uphold the laws of the state of California, find it difficult to reconcile their supposed duties with acquiescence in the acts of the Committee of Vigilance, since they do not reflect that, perhaps, more than three-fourths of the people of the entire state sympathize with and endorse our efforts, and as all law emanates from the people, so when the laws, thus enacted, are not executed, the power returns to the people, and is theirs whenever they may choose to exercise it. These gentlemen would not have hesitated to acknowledge the self-evident truth had the people chosen to make their present movement a complete revolution, recalled all the power they had delegated, and reissued it to new agents under new forms.

Now, because the people have not seen fit to resume *all* the powers they have confided to executive or legislative officers, it certainly does not follow that they can not, in the exercise of their inherent sovereign power, withdraw from corrupt and unfaithful servants the authority they have used to thwart the ends of justice.

Those officers whose unmistaken sense of duty leads them to array themselves against the determined action of the people, whose servants they have become, may be respected, while their error may be regretted; but none can envy the future reflections of the man who, whether in the heat of malignant passion, or with the vain hope of preserving by violence a position obtained through fraud and bribery, seeks under the color of law to enlist the outcasts of society as a hireling soldiery in the service of the state, or urges criminals, by hopes of plunder, to continue, at the cost of civil war, the reign of ballot-box stuffers, suborners of witnesses, and tamperers with the jury-box.

The Committee of Vigilance believe that the people have entrusted to them the duty of gathering evidence, and, after due trial, expelling from the community those ruffians and assassins who have so long outraged the peace and good order of society, violated the ballot-box, overridden law, and thwarted justice. Beyond the duties incident to this, we do not desire to interfere with the details of government.

We have spared and shall spare no effort to avoid bloodshed or civil war; but, undeterred by threats or opposing organizations, shall continue, peaceably if we can, forcibly if we must, this work of reform, to which we have pledged our lives, our fortunes, and our sacred honor.

Our labors have been arduous, our deliberations have been cautious, our determinations firm, our counsels prudent,

our motives pure, and while regretting the imperious necessity which called us into action, we are anxious that this
necessity should exist no longer ; and when our labors shall
have been accomplished; when the community shall be freed
from the evils it has so long endured ; when we have insured
to our citizens an honest and vigorous protection of their
rights, then the Committee of Vigilance will find great pleasure in resigning their power into the hands of the people,
from whom it was received.

Published by order of the Committee.

[Seal.]   No. 33, Secretary.

Up to the 20th of June, they had disposed
of twenty-six persons, of whom three were
dead, and the remainder banished.*   On Satur-

---

* The style of these notices to leave, was in substance as
follows :

EXECUTIVE COMMITTEE CHAMBERS, }
San Francisco, June 6, 1856. }

W——— H———. Sir : The Committee of Vigilance,
after full investigation and deliberation, declare you guilty
of being a notoriously bad character and dangerous person,
a disturber of the peace, a violator of the purity and integrity of the ballot-box, and have accordingly adjudged the
following sentence :

That you, W——— H———, leave the state of California, on or before the 20th day of June, 1856, never to return under the severest penalties.

In witness whereof, the seal of the Committee of Vigilance is hereunto attached. By order of the Committee :

[Seal.]   33, Secretary.

The seal of the Committee was an eye, which reminded
the recipient of 33's favors that he would not be lost sight
of, if he disregarded the notice.

day, the 21st of June, the Committee sent a force to take possession of some arms that were in transit from Benicia to San Francisco, marked with Gov. Johnson's name. It was a duty which they owed to themselves and the community, to keep out of the hands of the few irresponsible persons who had gathered themselves together here and there, under the appellation of Law and Order men, all means of making themselves dangerous to the public peace and safety, which, as yet, they had not been able to disturb. The captured arms were taken to the Committee rooms about noon, and at a later hour in the day, one of its police, a Mr. Hopkins, was sent out with an order to arrest one Mr. Maloney, who had been of the party in charge of the prize they had taken. Mr. Maloney was found in one of the armories of his little faction, in company with Judge Terry, before named, and several other persons, known to be violently opposed to the Committee. The arrest was of course opposed by his friends, when Hopkins retired to get assistance. He was joined by four or five persons belonging to the Committee, and they followed the other party, which had, in the mean time, retreated, well armed, to another of their quarters, on the corner of Dupont and Jackson streets. They met in Jackson street, and in the affray which ensued, Mr. Hopkins was stabbed by Judge Terry, so as greatly to endanger his life.

A messenger was dispatched instantly to the Committee Rooms, and, in a very short space of time, the large new bell, which they had mounted a few days before, sent forth, for the first time, its three warning peals over the city. The people gathered as swiftly and almost as silently as if by magic. In a few minutes between three and four thousand men were under arms and marching through the streets to their various places of duty. The first movement was to surround the buildings where it was known that the Law and Order arms were deposited. (For the credit of the man, it should have been stated that Gen. Sherman had resigned his post as commander of that valiant body and been succeeded by Mr. Volney E. Howard.) This admirable step, in all probability, saved bloodshed and open collision on that day. The Redoubtables, who were within, were of course safe, and those who were without were equally so ; for they had no means of attack, and needed none of defense.

The excitement of this day's work was increased by the dignity of Judge Terry's position, which, though it had not restrained him from participating in an affair to which he was in no wise a party, and which would, doubtless, have been better preserved in other company than that wherein he was found, did greatly sharpen the interest of the people in the question, what will the Committee do with him ? They found him and his friends safe within the building, which was fire-proof, with the shutters closed. A parley ensued. The besieged wished an opportunity to communicate with their general, which was indignantly refused. They then desired to see some of the Executive Committee of Twenty-nine. This was granted, and a messenger dispatched to request their presence.

Five members of this body—Messrs. Smiley, Vail, Truett, Tillinghast, and Dempster—im-

mediately presented themselves, and concluded
the business quickly by demanding the surrender of Terry and Maloney, and of all the arms
in the building. The demand was acceded to,
and both the prisoners, with about 300 stand
of arms, were removed at once to the Committee Rooms. Their troops then proceeded to
take the arms deposited in the other buildings
which they had surrounded, and by midnight
had in their rooms about 100 prisoners and
between 600 and 700 stand of arms.

During the whole of this time of excitement
the city was as quiet, save the noise inseparable from the movements of such large bodies
of people, as on almost any other day in the
year. There was no shouting, no wildness nor
passion, such as almost everywhere accompany
such proceedings. There were thousands of
people in sight when Terry left the armory to
enter the Committee's carriage which awaited
him, and they were disposed to express their
great pleasure at seeing him, by a simultane-
ous shout, the first low notes of which were
sounded, but suppressed instantly by the
raised hand of one of the Committee. The

same perfect self-control, on the part of the people, had been before observed with enthu siastic admiration by foreigners who were in the city at the surrender of Casey and Cora at the jail. I believe that only the American people can do such extraordinary acts with such perfect coolness and self-restraint, stopping at the very point where prudence and reason bid them. In London, in Paris, in Vienna, or any other city of the continent, when the people undertake the righting of wrongs, what excitements follow the first step! How impossible to control the popular feeling till it has in some measure sated itself—dulled the edge of its fury by some acts of violence, which reason forbade and conscience vainly mourned over after their commission.

Here is an American city revolutionized in spirit, though not in the outward form, almost without bloodshed; not a random shot fired; not a blow struck in passion; scarcely a single step taken by any man, that has not forwarded, directly or indirectly, the purposes first proposed to be accomplished. The laws of that

city and county are administered by a corps
of officers, many of whom are known to have
no legal or moral right to the positions they
hold ; and the people have ample means to
displace them, as they have displaced one of
their supreme judges ; but there is no thirst
for achievement with the men who are doing
this work. Some steps of purification were
indispensable to the safety of property and
life. Those they have taken, with a courage
and resolution that admit of no question ; but
they have never for one moment lost sight of
the line that separates the necessary from the
unnecessary. There is no great interest jeop-
ardized by bearing peaceably with the fraudulently elected officers a few weeks or months
longer — the less that they are conscious of
being faithfully watched — but nothing could
have been mended in the country till its citizens had protested, in some manner as earnest
as that they have adopted, against the further
rule of villainy, corruption, and falsehood.
That well done, convalescence may be considered as an established fact in the civil and
social condition of that peerless state.

The question is often asked—What is to be the end of all this? for even our own countrymen, at this distance, seem, at times, unable to see clearly that there is no party ambition or feud to be served—that the sole motive of the Committee is the public good; and when that is effectually cared for, that their action will cease naturally and easily. It is no partisan warfare to be kept alive indefinitely by the opposing passions or interests of men. Judge Terry remains a prisoner, and will, doubtless, till the Committee find some way of disposing of him that is entirely consistent with the best good of the state; and I believe they would not shrink from any final treatment of his case which they could believe to be demanded by that.

By the steamer of the 5th of August, we learn that they have executed two more men, who, in depravity and criminality, will lose nothing by comparison with the worst they have dealt with before; that they continue their arrests, receiving, trying, and discharging rogues for other parts as rapidly as may be.

The Committee have an onerous duty. They

are heavily taxed in money and time; their business is dangerously interrupted, and they have every motive for bringing their active proceedings to a close, as soon as they can safely and honorably do so. They will not before. Many of these men have their whole stake in the spot they are defending—property, family, home—with no intention of ever seeking another. There need be no fear that they will abuse the power they have assumed for the time. They have shown themselves equal to the worst emergencies of their enterprise. They have proved themselves faithful to the paramount object. No reasonable or worthy person can doubt that they will acquit themselves finally as becomes true men.*

* The steamer of the 20th of August brings us the welcome news of the finishing up of this peculiar revolution. It has furnished, both in its progress and completion, the grandest and most satisfactory testimony to the capacity of republican Americans for self-government. The Committee has shown, in the time and manner of surrendering its power, all the intelligence, purity of purpose, and moderation, which its friends have claimed for it. It did a noble work, and retired, upon completing it, in a manner altogether worthy of itself. The people who can safely conduct such a movement cannot any more be stigmatized as unworthy or incapable. It possesses a moral power, sufficient, if properly used, to

Among the few good persons who oppose this body by disapproving its proceedings, the often-urged argument is, the precedent—the dangerous precedent. To this it may be replied, that there is little danger in a precedent which the people of one of the republican states of America see fit to establish in their experiments of self-government. With a mob or faction, the case is totally different; but this is an expression, either active or acquiescent, by the *people* of California, of their determination to be no longer wronged and disgraced by the worst men among them. It could, in fairness, be made a precedent only for like proceedings under like circumstances; and if ever the same calamitous combination of facts should exist again in the history of any of our states, which, may a good Providence forbid, this precedent will, I hope, strengthen and confirm the people in their self-purification. I should be proud to see it quoted by

avert such painful emergencies. May a like one never again present itself in the history of California ; but, if it should come, may it find men no less worthy and capable than those of 1856. Judge Terry has been set at liberty.

any community in like circumstances to those which have constrained us in the great state of the Pacific. The will of the majority is the universal American law, expressed under constitutional and statute regulations. But can any constitution, or any statute law, emanate from a free people, which shall bind them to submit to systematized frauds in their elections; to public and private robberies, made outwardly respectable by the false position of the robbers; to open and dreadful corruption, which endangered not only the moral life of the state, but that which the popular mind more readily apprehends and appreciates—its commercial and pecuniary character and life?

The precedent, it is easy to see, endangers no rightly-governed life; restricts no true freedom; fixes no unwholesome limitations, and, therefore, should inspire no dread in people who contemplate no wrong. Those who would alarm us by the bugbear precedent, forget that there were precedents being established every day while this misrule continued, the most dangerous that could be furnished — precedents growing out of the worst deeds of the worst men, and becoming bulwarks of defense to others of the same character. Precedent of noble action, taken by a whole people for just purposes of self-preservation or defense, can never become dangerous to the good and just.

This is the commencement of an era of improvement in California, which will lift her out of some of her many degradations. The state will not again become the paradise it has been for rogues and shameless men. The election of this year, it is hoped and expected, will result in the actual choosing of a set of officers by the people, not only in San Francisco, but throughout the state; for the influence of the Committee is felt in the mountains, as well as in the metropolis; and, though we are not to expect any miraculously certain choice of the best men always, we are entitled to expect that the worst will not, as so often heretofore, be successful. Fraudulent elections prevented, an immense source of evil to the social and civil as well as political life of the country is at once cut off.

Society will rise, because open villainy will no more strut proudly in high places, vaunting

itself over integrity and decency. Self-respect
will return to the people to whom it has been
denied by the last few years' experience; and
those who love the country (as who does
not that has lived under its glorious skies?)
will see her leave her shame and humiliation
behind her, as she has hitherto seemed to have
left her nobleness and honor.

This crisis offers the best hopes and opportunities to those seeking a resting-place, where
life can be fully enjoyed, that any part of our
continent has ever afforded. In saying this, I
assume the superiority of the natural resources
of this state—her unequaled climate, her magnificent scenery, her exhaustless wealth, her
varied productions, her salubrious atmosphere.
These are denied by none. But she has heretofore been excluded the consideration of sober,
unadventurous people, by the odium that has
hung over her.

This will now speedily be dissipated. The
country is redeemed from the worst of all des-
potisms—a despotism of ruffians. It has already
a large population, that will compare favorably
in intelligence and honesty with that of any
22

of the new states ; and its attractions will continue to gather to her shores some of the best people of the growing nations.

The period of wild enthusiasm and insane hopes has passed over California ; but a better is before her. In the proceedings of the last few months, she has proved her claim to the confidence of those who, in thinking of emigration, entertain other considerations than those of the mineral wealth of the country, or the chances it affords to speculators.   Business will become better regulated, and labor more settled, as the population takes on a quieter character.

If the great cause with which Mr. Fremont is identified should happily succeed, this fall, the friends of California will, indeed, have cause of rejoicing. Her great pioneer, and her firm and persistent friend, we may look to his elevation as a means of giving her a right position, by connecting her with the Eastern states, and by preserving from the withering presence of slavery the territories which border upon her. California must, in future years, grow greatly by the prosperity and progress of her sister states—those which adjoin and unite her to older members of the republic. But the growth in them which will aid her, cannot be the result of slave-labor, or slave civilization in any sort. Plant slavery all over the broad plains that stretch between the Mississippi and the Sacramento, and there could be no vital circulation between the commercial, thriving East and that remote free state. Slavery ties the arteries of civilization. No life and vigor can travel eastward or westward through its dark dominion. May its black shadow never come nearer to the soil of California than it is to-day.

But let the "talking-wires" span free soil from the Atlantic to the Pacific, and let free labor, with its enterprise, progress, and intelligence, possess and build up Kansas and Nebraska, through which California will ultimately be connected, by railroad, with the East, and, in a few years, she will be garden of the Union. There is no prosperity to which she cannot attain, with true manhood to control, and true womanhood to preserve her. For each of these there is noble duty within her disordered limits.

Let them not shrink from the performance, if they would enjoy its reward, or transmit it to their children.